Music and the Spiritual

Dear MrAza

in deepest affection

Tony

Composers and Politics in the 20th Century

Other Books by Antony Copley

The Political Career of C Rajagopalachari 1937-54:
A Moralist in Politics
Gandhi's Southern Commander
Gandhi: Against the Tide
Sexual Moralities in France 1780-1980
Religions in Conflict
A Spiritual Bloomsbury

Editions

Gandhi and the Contemporary World
Gurus and their Followers
Hinduism in Public and Private

Music and the Spiritual

Composers and Politics
in the 20th Century

by
Antony Copley

Honorary Senior Research Fellow

Series Editor: Marcus Reichert

ZIGGURAT BOOKS
International

Music and the Spiritual: Composers and Politics in the 20th Century
Copyright © 2012 by Antony Copley

Front cover painting:
Music Room 1995 by Roy Oxlade
Back cover photograph:
Author portrait by Matt Wilson, University of Kent

UK office: 27 St. Quentin House, Fitzhugh Grove,
London SW18 3SE, England
Editorial office: 6 rue Argenterie,
30170 St. Hippolyte du Fort, France
Enquiries: zigguratbooks@orange.fr

Printed in England by Imprint Academic
Seychelles Farm, Upton Pyne, Exeter, Devon EX5 5HY

Distributed by Central Books Ltd.
99 Wallis Road, London E9 5LN, England
Tel UK: 0845 458 9911
Fax UK: 0845 459 9912
Tel International: +44 20 8525 8800
Fax International: +44 20 8525 8879
E-mail: orders@centralbooks.com

First Edition

ISBN 978-0-9566579-8-5

Antony Copley is an Honorary Reader and Honorary Senior Research Fellow in the School of History, University of Kent. He is Academic Adviser to the Gandhi Foundation (UK), and a Fellow of the Royal Historical Society and a Fellow of the Royal Asiatic Society. He is a regular reviewer for the Journal of the Royal Asiatic Society and has published books on sexual morality in France, evangelical missionaries in India, and the Indian politicians, Gandhi and Rajagopalachari. His *A Spiritual Bloomsbury: Hinduism and Homosexuality in the Lives and Writings of Edward Carpenter, E.M Forster and Christopher Isherwood* (Lexington, 2006) has been republished in India by Yoda Press under the title *Gay Writers in Search of the Divine.*

Sergei Prokofiev

Acknowledgements

There are many I have to thank for their help in this project. There are those who recommended or lent books; read sample chapters; undertook internet searches; accompanied me to concerts. In no particular order, Rod Kedward, Roy Oxlade, Ursula King, Antony Wood, James MacAuslan, Neil Cheshire, Philip Boobyer, Sarah Carter, Raymond Venables, Julia Twigg, Terry Wheeler, Mike Smith, Jennifer Young, Michael Vaile, Graham and Judith Meadows, Alan Boniface, Malcolm Dodwell, John Rowley, Peter Gibson, Edward Towne. I made good use of Brian Kember's library, so kindly bequeathed.

I am particularly in debt to Robin Cant who came frequently to my rescue when my computer played up. Jonathan Beer in the History Office patiently assembled the text on his computer and printed out on request. Trish Hatton helped tidy up the manuscript. Once again I am indebted to Angela Faunch and the inter-library loan services of the library of the University of Kent. I thank Paul Edlin for waiving my fee for attending the Conference on Polish Music since 1945. I am grateful to Kenneth Fincham and the School of History at the University of Kent for placing their faith in me as one of their Honorary Senior Research Fellows. Messiaen expert, Michael Chandler, was a wonderful communicator on music in his WEA courses. I owe a special debt to my editor, Marcus Reichert who took an early interest in the project and saw it through to publication.

I owe much in the text to the insight of historians, Orlando Figes and the late Tony Judt, and of musicologist, Richard Taruskin.

The ideas of this project were tried out in talks to the Lentils Seminar, University of Kent, to the London Society for the Study of Religions in the Athenaeum, and to the Canterbury branch of the Historical Association in the Cathedral Library.

I thank William Fortescue and Clare Ungerson for their hospitality in Edinburgh during the Festival, for Robert and Lorraine Tollemache for theirs in Highbury.

This is a chance to say how much I have enjoyed the friendship of Martin Gilbert and Rod Kedward since Oxford days, to express appreciation to Rashid Maxwell for sharing his deep engagement with the spiritual, to Hugh Maddox for sharing his religious faith, to my step-mother, Liz, for all her worldly wisdom, and to Elizabeth Taylor for her constructive listening.

Very sadly my very talented sister, Georgina did not live long enough to see the publication of the book. The book is dedicated to her. It is also dedicated to two wonderful artists. I have known Michael Williams since we joined up together for our National Service in the Navy back in October 1955. It has been one of the rewards of my life to see his development as a painter. I have got to know Roy Oxlade much more recently. Our conversations, sympathetic on politics, often contrarian on art, have done much to shape the ideas of this project. He is a brilliant colourist and I am delighted that one of his paintings forms the cover of the book.

Antony Copley
School of History
University of Kent and Adisham

In memory of my very talented sister

Georgina

And for the artists

Michael Williams

and

Roy Oxlade

Dmitri Shostakovich

Contents

Preface

Krzystof Penderecki

Henryk Górecki

Preface

With the Barbican theatre full for one of its Total Immersion weekends for the deeply spiritual music of Jonathan Harvey this January and plans for the South Bank's Alex Ross festival this year, the hour has surely come both for 20th century music and its spiritual content. On retirement I decided this is where I'd like to break new ground though of course one never really does so. I was in large part furthering my interest in the spiritual from my previous work, *A Spiritual Bloomsbury*, a study of Edward Carpenter, E M Forster and Christopher Isherwood and Indian spirituality, and returning to where my academic career had begun almost 50 years ago, the study of 20th century European history.

I have to emphasis this is a project by a cultural historian and not by a musicologist. I've seen myself in listening to the music as Everyman. No doubt we need to listen to music with an informed sense of its structure but, in the end, what matters is our own personal response. It helps to know that the author sees himself as a poet manqué. It makes no claim to being an encyclopaedic account of 20th century music. There is little or no mention, for example, of Carl Nielsen and Jean Sibelius. The composers have been chosen to illustrate a theme, one of placing music on a spectrum of the spiritual from a this-worldly or humanist to an other-worldly and transcendental.

And here I have been extremely fortunate in the way the composers I have chosen have almost all during the time of working on the project been the subject of festivals and specialist concerts. To expand. Alexander Scriabin is enjoying a revival through Vladimir Jurowski and the London Symphony Orchestra. Valery Gergiev and the LSO gave a performance of the entire cycle of seven Prokofiev symphonies at the Edinburgh Festival 2008 and Jurowski reprised his work in the series *Prokofiev: Man of the People?* at the South Bank, January 2012. Dmitri Shostakovich of course remains one of the most performed of composers. Kzrystof Penderecki was the featured composer of the Sounds New Festival 2009 and both he and Henryk Górecki were discussed at the parallel Conference on Polish Music since 1945 at Canterbury Christ Church University, 28 April-2 May. Arvo Pärt has been featured at the Proms and was the named composer for the Sounds New Festival 2011. Alfred Schnittke was the subject of a specialist festival *Between Two Worlds* at the South Bank, 15 November-1 December 2009. Sofia Gubaidulina was the subject of a Barbican Total Immersion weekend *The Journey of the Soul*, 12-14 January 2007, and also featured in the Proms. There was an extensive exploration of the music of Olivier Messiaen in the festival *From the Canyons to the Stars*, February to October 2008, with music performed at the South Bank, Westminster Abbey, and St Paul's as well as at the Proms. Karlheinz Stockhausen was the subject of a Total Immersion day at the Barbican, 17 January 2009, and of two Proms, 2 August 2009. Hans Werner Henze was also the subject of a Total Immersion day, 16 January 2010, as well as a performance of *Phaedra* 17 January at the Barbican and a revival of his opera *Elegy for Young Lovers* at the Young Vic, April 2010. Only Francis Poulenc has been overlooked. In addition there was a Music and Spirituality Conference at the South Bank, 1-2 February 2008, Jonathan Harvey and James MacMillan present. Talks given, printed programmes, above music listened to, constitute a large part of this project. Unfortunately a few programmes have gone missing.

I.

Parameters

Sofia Gubaidulina

Arvo Pärt

Alfred Schnittke

1. *Exploring the Spiritual*

Few words are used so ubiquitously as 'spiritual,' indicative both of its inherent imprecision and its reflection of a deep human need. It would be entirely against the spirit of this project to propose any hard-edged definition. The concept of the spiritual has in general been chosen in preference to that of spirituality, the better to enhance a sense of its open-endedness. But it will do no harm to have some feel for the parameters of the spiritual in advance, though the intention is to let interpretation of the music of the composers suggest its broad horizons. These are but preliminary thoughts, just that.

An overarching theme is of an expression of the spiritual across a spectrum of a this-worldly and an other-worldly. Jonathan Stedall has explored this approach in his *Where on Earth is Heaven?*, and this project proceeds along a not dissimilar path.[1] His answer is implicit in his title. And there is much to be said in a 20th century secular Europe in seeing a this-worldly spirituality as its most powerful expression. It was a century dominated by politics and this project insists on the paramountcy of the political. Conventionally, however, the spiritual finds its expression through the mystical and it is a matter of surprise in so secular an age that there exists so intense an endeavour to express through music the other-worldly and transcendental. But this raises another persistent enquiry in the text, to what extent are the religious and the spiritual in tandem, or does religion act as a constraint on the expression of the spiritual? Equally one can be indifferent to religion yet spiritual. Quite clearly there are very differing modes of its expression.

Primacy of the Political

Emphasising the political is to challenge claims for the autonomy of a work of art. For Roger Fry and Clement

Greenberg, protagonists of Modernism, the work of art is all. In many ways Modernism was no more than an extension of the not very impressive art movement, Aestheticism. This was a claim for Art for Art's sake. Yet it feels extraordinarily arrogant to assert that the artist and art are somehow above History, that they inhabit an entirely self-referential world. Introducing his documentary film on Górecki's Symphony of Sorrowful Songs, Tony Palmer vigorously claimed that all great art is necessarily political. This project insists on seeing the music in the context of its times.

Various characterisations of 20th century Europe, more specifically the short 20th century that ended in 1989, have been made. It was an Age of Extremes, an Age of Anxiety. But pre-eminently it was an Age of Fear. Stefan Zweig's terrifying novella *Chess* identifies the omnipresence of fear. This is the harrowing account of a victim of Gestapo torture who maintained his sanity by memorising a book of chess moves, only on a sea journey to Brazil, persuaded by fellow passengers to play a Grand-Master, for all the horrors of Gestapo torture to flood back into memory.[2] After the age of the dictators came the Cold War and fear of a nuclear holocaust. In his remarkable film *The Lives of Others* (2006) director Florian Henckel von Donnersmarck conveys how in East Germany under the surveillance of the Stasi there was no let up of fear in the post-war Soviet block. Of course fear need not only be of political tyranny, it can also be of a tyrannical conformity. Were not Shostakovich and Britten drawn together by a shared sense of fear, Shostakovich of a Stalinist state, Britten of prejudice at his sexuality? Maybe the simple explanation for the expression of the spiritual in music in the 20th century is quite simply as compensation for this Age of Barbarism.

Art had to confront Evil. Given those crimes against humanity in the 20th century Europe it is hard not to subscribe to St Augustine's belief in Original Sin. Evil became systemic. Jonathan Glover has written one telling account of this Manichean century, though it is more convincing for its exploration of the role of evil than for any prophylactic for its cure.[3] There still rages a debate as to whether Nazism was uniquely evil or parallels can be drawn with other totalitarian systems. Glover classifies three examples of unspeakable evil under the heading of tribalism. Firstly, the recent example of tribal civil war in Yugoslavia. Secondly, Stalinism, with Maoism and Cambodian Pol Pot likewise incorporated under this heading, a totalitarian system seen as driven by a pathological belief in Utopia, inspired by the Enlightenment. Thirdly, Nazism, defined as a lethal combination of tribalism and Utopian belief. Glover sees in all three a fatal inability to recognise in one's fellow human beings a common identity, a demonising of the other: 'respect for dignity is one of the great barriers against atrocity and cruelty.'[4] He puts his faith for a cure in morality, in the Kantian moral imperative: only 'those who have a strong sense of who they are and of the person they want to be have an extra defence against conditioning in cruelty, obedience or ideology.'[5] Under Stalinism there had been an erosion of the truth, a habit of lying, with a consequent loss of moral identity: 'when mass murder is sufficiently reinterpreted people can support it with an unimpaired sense of moral identity.'[6] Nadia Mandelstam saw this as 'a process of turning into wood.' Nazism, in comparison with Stalinism, Glover argues, was exceptional in the degree and thoroughness of its assault on moral identity. If fear might explain the perversion of morality under Stalinism, in Nazi Germany there was a more willing acceptance of its beliefs: 'it is hard to avoid the impression that the idea of duty to obey and conform was more strongly internalised in Nazi Germany.'[7] Glover sees morality as the answer to evil. Might music and the spiritual be another?

Can we characterise the peculiar nature of Nazi evil? Of many interpreters Gitta Sereny has come closest in her two studies of Franz Stangl[8] and Albert Speer.[9] Any moral commentary on the 20th century inevitably sees the death camps as centre-stage. In her study of Stangl, Sereny generalises: 'to achieve the extermination of these million of men, women and children, the Nazis committed not only physical, but spiritual murder: on those they killed, on those who did the killings, on those who knew the killing was being done, and also, to some extent, for evermore, on all of us, who were alive and thinking beings at the time.'[10] Hers is a fundamental insight that we wrongly judge by 'what a man does than what he is.'[11] Stangl, Commandant of Treblinka, she reads as a dual personality, a man who could both carry out mass murder yet love his wife. Born 26 March 1908, an Austrian, he was to be alienated from a hostile father – 'I was scared to death of him' – though his father was to die of malnutrition when he was but eight. Trained as a weaver he joined the police in 1931. Sereny saw a certain determinism in Stangl's career. He had been honoured for finding a Nazi cache of weapons back in 1934 so, once again, post-Anschluss, the Nazis now in power, his main feeling was of fear. From now on Stangl saw himself in a battle for survival. He had himself surreptitiously put on a list of former Nazi supporters. Then he signed a document formally giving up his Catholic faith: 'a decisive step in the gradual process of corruption.'[12] Stangl reflected, 'I should have killed myself in 1938.' Unwisely arresting a leading Nazi official for poaching in 1939, exposing himself once again to party reprisal, Stangl felt he had no alternative but to accept a job in Berlin in T4, the Nazi Euthanasia Unit. Notoriously, this was a training ground for the death camps. Initially he was assigned to construction work at Sobibor. Could he have opted out? Stangl argued he would himself have been sent to a concentration camp. And what would have happened to his family? Besides, 'by seeing he became implicated.' So to his promotion as Commandant of Treblinka. Some 100, 000 were to be murdered in the first two months of his command. He recalled his first day at the camp as entering Dante's inferno. Yet he took pride in running an efficient camp: 'he deliberately manipulated and repressed his moral scruples.'[13] So corrupted did be become that he saw the inmates as 'human cargo,' no longer as individuals. Yet he contrived to square this with his conscience: 'what I did without or against my free will, for that I need not answer (to God).'[14] Here is a fascinating study of how insidiously any one individual can be corrupted by evil.

But here Sereny sees that split. The same perverted admin-istrator was a happy family man, devoted to his wife and totally dependent on her good opinion. Sereny believes had she confronted him with his evil, at least he might have sought alternative employment. Following the abortive up-rising in the camp in August 1943, he was indeed transferred to anti-partisan duties in Trieste. In his conversations with Sereny he speculated that the Holocaust had been legitimised by its bringing about the birth of Israel. Did he indeed at the very end acknowledge his guilt and 'reach that fleeting mo-ment when he became the man he should have been.'?[15]

Furious rows broke out over Jonathan Littell's novel *The Kindly Ones.*[16] How dare the novelist usurp the role of the historian. He was accused of moral relativism and downplay-ing the role of anti-Semitism.[17] Nazism was seen in the novel as embarked on a larger programme of population reduction and racial purification. Littell's story of Dr Maximilien Aue, an officer in the SD, or Security Police, by the author's ima-gining Nazism from the inside, takes us all the more terrify-ingly into the heart of darkness. It is a version of Stangl writ large. Aue is evidently a moral monster, murderer of his mother and step-father, incestuous lover of his twin sister (and her murderer as well?), lyricist of the passive role in sodomy (though that is fair enough), and murderer of his best friend to obtain papers to allow him to escape at the end of the war. Only at the end do we discover that it is a case of like father, like son, his absent father a fanatical member of the post-war Freikorps. Few writers have quite so graphically described Babi Yar, Stalingrad and the camps. Aue looks on his own story as 'the muddled philosophy of a barely half-repentant fascist.'[18] Anyone in his shoes would have acted in the same way. 'What I did I did with my eyes wide open, be-lieving that it was my duty and that it had to be done, disagreeable and unpleasant as it may have been. That is what total war means.'[19] Like Stangl he falls back on a kind of determinism, with little room for manoeuvring 'because of the weight of fate.'[20] Chance had turned him into a murderer rather than a hero. Here is an even more telling imagined reconstruction of the power of evil.

But the novel raises an even more disturbing perspective in ascribing to Aue a kind of perverted idealism. Exposure to Babi Yar prompts Aue's admission: 'ever since I was a child I have been haunted by a passion for the absolute, for the overcoming of all limits, and now that passion has led me to the edge of the mass graves of the Ukraine.'[21] Given the pointlessness of the Holocaust (and Aue is at least committed to trying to take advantage of a Jewish labour force), 'it can only have one meaning, an irreversible sacrifice, which binds us once and for all, prevents us from ever turning back... It's the *Endsieg* or death.'[22] Echoing Glover's insight, Aue sees the necessity for suspension of the Kantian moral imperative, with blind loyalty to Hitler the means of serving the *volk*: 'there can be no other morality.'[23] Perverted idealism connects very uncomfortably with the concept of the spiritual and may be the explanation for the role of the occult in some modern music.

But a more conventional morality does surface. Aue recognises that the sadism of the SS in the camps was a way of blotting out a sense of a shared humanity. A sulphurous Sadism in fact pervades the novel, just as tangible as in Pasolini's extraordinary film *Salo*. And Aue, in the same way as Stangl, gives way to doubt, no longer able to grasp 'the sense of profound necessity in the system.'[24] Can the claim that the SD did not in fact hate anyone, that all they did was objectively pursue their enemies, that 'the choice we made are rational ones,' stand up to scrutiny?[25]

But to revert to that fiercely debated comparative question, was Nazism uniquely evil as a totalitarian system? Here it is intriguing to set along side two conversations between representatives of Nazi and Soviet officialdom, one from Vasily Grossman's novel *Life and Fate*, the other from Littell's.

Their conversations are reversed. In Grossman's the old Bolshevik, Mikhail Mostovskoy, captured at Stalingrad and a POW in a concentration camp, is summoned to meet SS officer Liss. Here it is the German who proposes that the two totalitarian systems are but mirror images of one another, both driven by their will, and if the Soviets hate the Nazis it is as a projection of themselves. Was not Socialism in One Country a nationalism in just the same way as the Nazi? Had not the Nazi purge of Roehm and the SA been the model for Stalin's purge of 1937-8? And, briefly, the Old Bolshevik does experience 'vile filthy doubts' that this might be true, to do so would be to see Stalinism for what it is and to raise the possibility that its rejection was the way to freedom. But, in the end, strength of party loyalty gets the better of him and he scorns all this as vile blatherings.[26] In Littell's novel, Aue is invited to interrogate a Soviet political Commissar, likewise captured at Stalingrad, and it is the Russian who makes the comparison between the two systems, arguing it was the Nazis who took everything from the Soviets, if only to caricature it, Nazism deemed a heresy of Communism, with the Nazis substituting race for class, though both were equally determinist. Aue's riposte is to see Communism as but skin-deep and that in the end old Russian chauvinism and anti-Semitism will prevail.

Stalinism and the Soviet regime of course lasted so much longer than the 12 years of Nazi rule and, in terms of the loss of life through the gulag and man-made famine, it was far more lethal. But one can pose the imponderable question, was the gulag comparable to the genocidal death camps? Was there some glimmer of redemption through the slave labour of the camps becoming an essential part of the Soviet economy? Does the greater rationalism of the Soviet system mitigate its evil? But we must register Orlando Figes's judgement: 'no other totalitarian system had such a profound impact on the private lives of its subjects.'[27] The humanism we will find in 20th century music was in many ways a cry against both systems.

Confronting evil is one inescapable challenge to human creativity in the 20th century. In his novel *Doctor Faustus* Thomas Mann explored the Faustian pact the creative artist made with evil. Moral relativism and ambiguity indeed pervade the century's culture. If SS officers could enjoy music whilst manning the camps, then George Steiner finds himself askng, is there is some inherent flaw in the music itself? Alternatively, he looks to science as gaurantee of civilised values.[28] Are we in danger of making too high a claim for the spiritual in music?

Religion and the Spiritual

Not all will see a tension between religion and spirituality. Certainly in some of the highest expression of art, such as Romanesque sculpture or the music of J S Bach, they entirely overlap. But conventional faith has always distrusted its mystics. Only by listening to the music can one answer the question, does conformity to a religious faith obstruct the expression of the spiritual? Some composers, of course, have no truck with religion and this can, it will be argued, open up the space for the expression of a this-worldly humanist spirituality.

Point of departure for this distinction between religion and spirituality was the research into the beliefs of the citizens of Kendal by two Lancaster University academics, Paul Heelas and Linda Woodhead.[29] It caused quite a stir at the time. They wrote of a tectonic shift in the sacred landscape, those wedded to traditional modes of belief now outnumbered by those wedded to various forms of New Age spirituality. Theirs is a theory of 'subjectivisation.' There is a turning away from life lived in terms of duties and obligations and a turn towards living one's life in terms of one's own subjective experience. Interestingly, they differentiate this from individualisation. If one might question Kendal bearing the burden of such generalisation, and that they are only commenting on small minorities, 5% or so in both cases, they have raised an intriguing distinction. However, theirs is a lop-sided focussing on New Age Spirituality, by no means representative of a longer and richer tradition of the spiritual.

But a dialectical approach, their interaction, may be more illuminating. What if, alternatively, it is conceded that all religions are rooted in mysticism? David Tacey[30] argues that spirituality 'is by no means incompatible with religion but it is existential rather than creedal.'[31] The spiritual is strongly indebted to religion: 'religion offers the spirit a complex language, a sense of tradition and a cultural memory.'[32] But he then provides a pretty devastating account of how religion with its dogmatism fails the human spirit: 'it does not offer a psychology or pathway by which the individual can be transformed'; 'it does not allow for the true radicality of the spirit which is at odds with worldliness.'[33] And he meets the charge that there is a flakiness in New Age spirituality head-on: 'I believe the intelligentsia has grotesquely over-used the term New Age as a defence mechanism against the spiritual and as an excuse for not taking student interests seriously.'[34] His is a powerful statement that religion needs to change: 'I am only interested in a faith that has passed through the fire of atheism, the blaze of modernity, and the critical scrutiny of psycho-analysis and survives. What survives after all else has been burned away or what rises up phoenix-like after conventional forms have been burnt away is the faith that I am interested in. It is the only kind of faith that resonates with the spiritual needs of our time.'[35] This comes very close to the way this project sees the role of the spiritual in music.

Someone who interviewed a number of composers surmised: 'as always there are musicians who find religion too entrapping, too reminiscent of what they've been running away from all their lives. But many others want to find out more about spirituality, whether within a particular tradition or not.'[36] He goes on: 'Spirituality among contemporary musicians includes everything from traditional Christianity to just deeply wanting to know the meaning of life – what Buddhists call the Great Doubt.' Both Philip Glass and Alan

Ginsberg, for example, turned to Buddhism. Indicatively, Peter Maxwell Davies in a radio interview dismissed all religious belief but admitted to a belief in forms of magic. The inspiration for his music came from the seascape of the Orkneys, here was his noumenon.

Can religion protect itself from usurpation by the spiritual? Can theologians reassert its claims? And can it be seen as the source of creativity?

One definition of religion is provided rather surprisingly by Derrida: 'the letter re at the beginning of religion ensures that this peculiar phenomenon of human nature will re-turn, re-vive and re-cur ... Religion is what succeeds in returning.'[37] In other words, we are stuck with it. Even a member of the Dawkins clan concedes that we are hard-wired for religion.[38] But there is a twist to the whole debate. If we are exploring the tension between religion and the spiritual, are we clear as to what constitutes, in the widest possible sense, a religion? Nietzsche wrote of the return of the repressed and it now seems self-evident that the repression of religion by various forms of secularist and materialist ideologies merely sired surrogate religions; in the 19th century, positivism, republicanism, nationalism; in the 20th, the totalitarian movements of Fascism, Nazism and Communism.[39] As Antonio Gramsci with great insight explained: 'the old is dead but the new has yet to be born: in this interregnum there arises a great many morbid symptoms.'[40] It follows that composers in conflict with those totalitarian systems are also embattled with forms, however perverted, of religion.

Can Theology, handmaiden to Religion, shape a more positive relationship between religion and the arts? One who tried to do so was Paul Tillich, a Protestant pastor and the fashionable theologian of the 50's and 60's: 'of all theologians in our century he alone set the agenda for the role of the arts in theological work.'[41] The trouble with John Dillenger's claim is that Tillich is in many ways on the side of spirituality rather than religion. He has two definitions of religion. One, in a narrower sense, is defined by symbols of gods or god, 'with intellectual and practical activities following out of this belief .'[42] He saw such a religion as idolatry. These were churches likely to subscribe to 'the petty bourgeoisie resistance against modern art and existentialism generally.'[43] Throughout his life he was embattled with all forms of heteronomy, demonic claims, as he saw them, to a unique grasp of the truth at any one time. He preferred a definition of religion as 'being grasped unconditionally and inescapably by that which is the sustaining ground and consuming abyss of our existence.'[44] Intriguingly, he saw a convergence between Existentialism and Protestantism, the former of 'man in his estrangement, his finitude, in his feeling of guilt and meaninglessness,' an 'outcry' he saw as universal in the 20th century, [45] and the latter, with its stress on the infinite distance between man and God, of 'man's finitude, his subjection to death, but above all his estrangement from his true being and his bondage to demonic forces – forces of self-destruction.'[46] Tillich is more relevant as an interpreter of art than music, though his advocacy of Expressionism in painting as the vehicle for the spiritual bears a striking resemblance to like claims for Maximalism in music. His significance lies in just the way he did reach out to the spiritual in modern art but did so still in terms of a faith system. His was a quest for ultimacy.

A contemporary theologian who likewise tries to square the circle between religion and spirituality is Karen Armstrong in yet another of her long ruminative journeys through the history of the world's religions.[47] She puts her faith in the apothatic tradition, apothasis literally the breakdown of speech, a wordless spirituality. This is a religious tradition which insists on 'the value of unknowing,' on 'the importance of recognising the limits of our knowledge, of silence, reticence and awe.'[48] Armstrong shows how by the mediaeval period it had become engrained in Western Christian consciousness. But Counter-Reformation Theology, seen as fashioned by an intolerant modernist Church, made the huge mistake of trying to align Theology with the scientific revolution, firstly through Cartesianism, later Deism, with God no longer transcendent but marginalised as no more than an intelligent Designer. Hubristically, scientific rationalism could all too easily undermine these proofs of a natural theology. But science itself by the 20th century in quantum physics came to recognise the limits of knowledge. In a way it itself turned apothatic. Einstein is quoted as recognising that 'the most beautiful emotion we can experience is the mystical.'[49] Even Dawkins conceded he was a pantheist.[50] Armstrong writes: 'the desire to cultivate a sense of the transcendent may be *the* defining human characteristic.'[51] She insists that only the most disciplined ascesis or religious practice, often through ritual, can hope to attain a sense of the divine, though here there does seem to be a paradox, for the divine is seen to be unknowable. Probably it was the lack of any such discipline in New Age spirituality that leads her to berate it as 'often wild, self-indulgent and unbalanced.'[52] Hers is a plea for a modern theology 'that looks unflinchingly into the heart of a great darkness and be prepared, perhaps, to enter into a cloud of unknowing.'[53]

Armstrong's text is doubly germane to this project for it insists on the way music and the apothatic tradition come together. 'Music,' she writes, 'has always been inseparable from religious expression, because, like religion, at its best, music marks the "limit" of reason.' 'Music goes beyond the reach of words: it is not about anything.'[54]

Another text that lies on the borderline between religion and the spiritual is George Steiner's *Real Presences: Is there anything in what we say?* Its value lies in its contextualising a study of music and the spiritual in a broader study of the arts, above all of Modernism. In many ways it is a side-swipe at Modernism. Steiner sees a fault-line in culture between the 1870's and 1930's – he writes of ontological nihilism, deconstruction and fragmentation – and in consequence, art for future generations will be radically different. Up against contemporary radical scepticism he anticipated that his book would attract hostile reviews. For, against the relativist culture of Modernism, he makes the claim: 'pervasively, however, major art in our vexed modernity has been, like all great shaping before it, touched by the fire and ice of God.'[55] 'This essay,' he asserts, 'argues a wager on transcendence.' However difficult it be to put it into words: 'I have argued (for) the irreducible autonomy of presence, of "otherness", in art and text which denies either adequate paraphrase or unanimity of finding.'[56] He takes from Tillich a quest for ultimacy.

And few texts make higher claims for music. It is seen as at the centre of his argument. How inconsolably dreary life would be without music: 'it has long been, it continues to be, the unwritten theology of those who lack or reject any formal creed.'[57] 'The energy that is music is in felt relation to the energy that is life: it puts us in a relation of experienced immediacy with the abstractly and verbally inexpressible but wholly palpable, primary fact of being.'[58] This is what he means by real presence. Oddly, in a way, he never uses the word spiritual: he sticks to theological. He is impossible to paraphrase. Where on a spectrum of a this-worldly and other-worldly spirituality does the following sentence leave us? In seeking the meaning of music, 'we do seem to harbour at the threshold of the unconscious, at depths unrecapturable by speech and the logic of speech, intimations, incisions in the synapses of sensibility, a close kinship between the beginnings of music and those of humanly-enacted meaning itself.'?[59] Clearly he is at one with the apothatic tradition. Yet Steiner seemingly no longer has the same faith in music.

So are we any closer to setting some boundaries in any definition of the spiritual?

Its point of departure is the spirit. In the Greek tradition spirit is opposed to body. In the Hebrew they converge – spirit is the breath. But it is not the same as emotion. Rather it is a need to engage with the very breath of life.

Spirituality need not relate to religion or God. And here I am following an account by Peter Bannister in a seminar on Music and Spirituality at the South Bank. It is an existential awareness of a link with the sacred. It provides meaning. But a distinction has to be drawn between a referential and an absolute, the former linked to society, the second trans-cendental.[60]

Tacey makes some amusing attempts at a definition. One, 'we are overpowered by a force that is greater than we are. This can be miraculous but also can be dreadful and humiliating to the ego. As such spirituality is a kind of alien abduction: we are seized, taken over and coordinated by an outside force.'[61] Another try, spirituality is 'a veritable baggy monster ... it is an inclusive term, covering all pathways that lead to meaning and purpose.'[62]

Into the vacuum opened up by Darwinism and a consequent loss of faith flooded all kinds on new forms of spirituality. The lowest common denominator was the practice of Spiritualism, a positive craze in Belle Époque Europe, especially popular in aristocratic circles in Silver Age Russia. It has been taken seriously by historians[63] as an expression of popular culture, but hardly impinges on serious spirituality. Much more intellectually ambitious attempts to meet the Victorian crisis of faith were Theosophy and its splinter movement Anthroposophy. Both did much to influence the arts in the early 20th century.

And then comes the towering figure of Carl Jung whose depth psychology did more than anything to shape what we might mean by contemporary spirituality. In brief, Jung sensed that traditional religious faith was over. Whilst valuing the role ritual provided as a form of psychological mooring, he sensed modern scepticism has made such faith impossible. The best it could hope for was some continuing presence through the role of metaphor. As Jungian David Tacey puts it, the God of religion was dead, but he would have to be resurrected from below, 'from the ground of the unconscious mind.'[64] Jung was sympathetic towards all attempts to discover alternative forms of spiritual consolation and was surprisingly attentive to spiritualism. If he insisted on describing it in psychological and subjective terms, he never entirely ruled out the objective possibility of spirits.[65] Jung was keenly aware of the danger from a secular age repressing religion. This threatens serious damage to our psychic health, for human beings naturally seek out the transcendent. Worse, terrifying forces have been unleashed through the collapse of faith and our exposure to the forces of the collective unconscious. Jung's was a warning of the danger in this new spirituality. Tacey sees Jung's as a search for a cosmological system that can contain such opposites. He sought to guide us through an entirely new world of dreams and symbols, of myths and archetypes.

The creative artist has a particular role in exploring this new world. In contrast to Freud, Jung does not see art as a product of neurosis. He refused to see the work of art in such reductionist ways. But he does see the work of art as, in his words, an autonomous process. Artists are in a sense driven by forces from the collective unconscious. They are exposed to its dark side, its destructiveness: theirs is a visionary quality, 'something strange that drives its existence from the hinterland of man's mind, as if it had emerged from the abyss of pre-human ages, of a superhuman world of contrasting light and darkness, glamorous, daemonic, grotesque ... a terrifying tangle of eternal chaos.'[66] An artist loses his individual personality: 'he is nothing but his work and not a human being.' He is 'collective man,' 'a vehicle and moulder of the unconscious psychic life of mankind.' And clearly the artist pays a high price 'for the divine gift of creative fire.'[67] The artist explores the same fragmented and grotesque world as the schizophrenic but somehow has the power to harness it: 'far from his work being an expression of the destruction of his personality, the modern artist finds the unity of his artistic personality in destructiveness,'[68] 'a backside of art that art that makes no attempt at ingratiating.'[69] All this hints at that Faustian pact Thomas Mann explored in his novel and there is a disturbing sense that artists do draw on the occult and the demonic, a debt I have become uncomfortably aware of in some modern composers such as Stockhausen and Xenakis. Is it a kind of apologia to say that the artist is but expressing the collective unconscious of his times?

Jung has inspired a considerable literature on the role of myth. Myths are the means by which we make sense of our lives. There are serious spiritual dangers in allowing, as modern western culture has done, Logos to usurp Mythos. This is a theme explored by Karen Armstrong in her *A Short History of Myth*. Picking up on Jung's awareness of the ambiguity of the collective unconscious she recognises that the 20th century has generated very destructive myths and 'that fearful and destructive unreason has always been part of the human experience and it still is.'[70] Even so, she is optimistic on the role of myth: 'if professional religious leaders cannot instruct us in mythical lore, our artists and creative writers can step into this priestly role and bring fresh insight to our lost and damaged world.'[71] As Tacey puts it, archetypes are to become an 'ennabling fiction.'[72]

Is music after all just emotion? Is it an expression of love for the divine? Tagore made much of the role of bhakti (worship) in music. The routine of religious ritual, he believed, cramps the spirit of devotion. Tagore discovered his ideal in the songs of the Bauls, the tribal musicians of Bengal. For Tagore, union with the divine is experienced in the silence, but this must resolve itself in song: 'silence is the culmination, yet even silence is but an aspect of song, hence calls for liberation in song.'[73] But the conclusion of this kind of engagement is passive and surely to be resisted: 'submission is the secret of realization – and the secret of music.'[74]

One of the most astute commentaries on the possibility of a transcendental approach to music was Anthony Storr's.[75] He brilliantly played off the ideas of Schopenhauer and Nietzsche. Schopenhauer may well have been right in seeing Music as the art form which alone communicated direct with the Divine, in his language, the Will. Schopenauer was an atheist but much influenced by Buddhism. And his enjoyment of music was by way of negating desire, an experience of Nirvana. All this was intolerable to Nietzsche who saw music in affirmative ways, encouraging an embrace of life, essentially a Dionysiac experience. It was essential to life. He recognized, though, that the concert hall had replaced the church, that here was a place where the divine could be encountered.

Finally, one further variant in the search for the spiritual is agnosticism. In Mark Vernon's analysis, if agnosticism is seen as one and the same as honest doubt, it is not a version that turns towards scepticism and a kind of religious indifference, 'rather it is a way of life driven by a desire for ultimate things.'[76] He follows Karen Armstrong in turning towards the apothatic tradition, but whereas for her God exists, for Vernon 'God is kept as a radical question.'[77] There is a cultivated sense of uncertainty. Modern science is seen as arriving at just this same outlook. Vernon endorses mere wonderment, a sense of the mystery of things. And the same agnosticism has to be brought to music. Music does indeed open up the soul to what lies beyond. But, 'a degree of agnosticism in religion to the value of religious yearning would seem to be necessary to be open to the music that speaks of divinity.'[78] Beyond all possible enquiry into the existence of God lies the silence: 'religious silence might be said to be like the silence following the performance of a great piece of music.'[79] Many will favour this agnostic stance.

So how does music connect with the spiritual? Firstly, we have to address another conceptual enquiry, how do we interpret music?

Notes

[1] Jonathan Stedall, *Where on Earth is Heaven?*, Stroud: Hawthorn Press, 2009.

[2] Stefan Zweig, *Chess*, translated by Anthea Bell, London: Penguin Books, 2006. For a lament on the passing of civilised values in Europe see his autobiography, *The World of Yesterday*, translated by Anthea Bell, London: Pushkin Press, 2009.

[3] Jonathan Glover, *Humanity: A Moral History of the Twentieth Century*, London: Jonathan Cape, 1999.

[4] Glover, *Humanity*, p.50.

[5] Glover, *Humanity*, p.402.

[6] Glover, *Humanity*, p.282.

[7] Glover, *Humanity*, p.329.

[8] Gitta Sereny, *Into That Darkness*, London: André Deutch, pb edition, 1991.

[9] Gitta Sereny, *Albert Speer: His Battle with Truth,* London and Basingstoke: Macmillan, 1995.

[10] Sereny, *Into That Darkness*, p.101.

[11] Sereny, *Into That Darkness*, p.124.

[12] Sereny, *Into That Darkness*, p.37.

[13] Sereny, *Into That Darkness*, p.160.

[14] Sereny, *Into That Darkness*, p.233.

[15] Sereny, *Into That Darkness*, p.366.

[16] Jonathan Littell, *The Kindly Ones*, London: Chatto and Windus, 2009. (First published 2006.)

[17] Jean Solchany, 'Les Bienveillantes ou l'histoire à l'épreuve de la fiction,' *Revue d'Histoire Moderne et Contemporaine* (2007) Vol.3.

[18] Littell, *The Kindly Ones*, p.17.

[19] Littell, *The Kindly Ones*, p.18.

[20] Littell, *The Kindly Ones*, p.783.

[21] Littell, *The Kindly Ones*, p.96.

[22] Littell, *The Kindly Ones*, p.142.

[23] Littell, *The Kindly Ones*, p.591.

[24] Littell, *The Kindly Ones*, p.761.

[25] Littell, *The Kindly Ones*, p.874.

[26] Vasily Grossman, *Life and Fate* , London: Vintage edn, 2011, pp.377-87.

[27] Orlando Figes, *The Whisperers: Private Life in Stalin's Russia*, London: Penguin edn, 2007, p.xxxii.

[28] This was at a talk to the Edinburgh Book Festival.

[29] Paul Heelas and Linda Woodhead, *The Spiritual Revolution: Why Religion is giving way to Spirituality*, Oxford: Blackwell, 2005.

[30] David Tacey, *The Spirituality Revolution: The Emergence of Contemporary Spirituality*, London and New York: Routledge, 2004.

[31] Tacey, *Spirituality Revolution*, p.8.

[32] Tacey, *Spirituality Revolution*, p.77.

[33] Tacey, *Spirituality Revolution*, pp.36-7.

[34] Tacey, *Spirituality Revolution*, p.64.

[35] Tacey, *Spirituality Revolution*, p.157.

[36] Dimitri Ehrlich, *Inside The Music: Conversations with Contemporary Musicians about Spirituality, Creativity and Conscience*, Boston and London: Shembala, 1997, pp.xi-xii.

[37] As paraphrased by Tacey, *Spirituality Revolution*, p.131.

[38] Nicholas Humphrey, 'The Human Factor,' *The Guardian*, 29 July 2006.

[39] A process explored by Michael Burleigh in his *Earthly Powers*, London: Harper Collins, 2005, and *Sacred Causes*, London: Harper Collins, 2006.

[40] Quoted Tacey, *Spirituality Revolution*, p.134.

[41] John Dillenger, *Paul Tillich on Art and Architecture*, New York: Crossroads, 1987, p.xxvi.

[42] Dillenger, *Paul Tillich*, p.92.

[43] Dillenger, *Paul Tillich*, p.101.

[44] Dillenger, *Paul Tillich*, p.76.

[45] Dillenger, *Paul Tillich*, p.91.

[46] Dillenger, *Paul Tillich*, p.119.

[47] Karen Armstrong, *The Case for God: What Religion Really Means*, London: Vintage, 2010.

[48] Armstrong, *The Case for God*, pp .9-10.

[49] Quoted Armstrong, p.257.

[50] Richard Dawkins, *The God Delusion*, London: Transworld Publications, 2006, pp.39-41.

[51] Armstrong, *The Case for God*, p.19.

[52] Armstrong, *The Case for God*, p.279.

[53] Armstrong, *The Case for God*, p.267.

[54] Armstrong, *The Case for God*, pp.5-6.

[55] George Steiner, *Real Presences: Is there anything in what we say?* London: Faber and Faber, 1989, p.223.

[56] Steiner, *Real Presences*, p.214.

[57] Steiner, *Real Presences*, p.218.

[58] Steiner, *Real Presences*, p.196.

[59] Steiner, *Real Presences*, p.196.

[60] These were the thoughts of Peter Bannister in his talk 'The Necessity of Grace,' in a Seminar in the Southbank Centre, *Contemporary Music and Spirituality*, 1-2 February 2008.

[61] Tacey, *Spirituality Revolution*, p.143.

[62] Tacey, *Spirituality Revolution*, p.38.

[63] For example Janet Oppenheim, *The Other World: Spiritualism and Psychical Research in England 1850-1914*, Cambridge: Cambridge University Press, 1985.

[64] David Tacey, *How to Read Jung*, London: Granta Books, 2006, p.36.

[65] C G Jung, *Psychology and the Occult*, London and New York: Routledge, 1982.

[66] Jung, *The Spirit in Man, Art and Literature*, New York: Routledge, 2001, pp.105-6.

[67] Jung, *The Spirit in Man*, pp.119-20.

[68] Jung, *The Spirit in Man*, pp.137-8.

[69] Jung, *The Spirit in Man*, p.119.

[70] Karen Armstrong, *A Short History of Myth*, London: Canongate, 2005, p.135.

[71] Armstrong, *The Case for God*, p.155.

[72] Tacey, *How to Read Jung*, p.18.

[73] Serena Thielemann, *The Spirituality of Music*, New Delhi: APH Publishing Corporation, 2001, p.158.

[74] Thielemann, *The Spirituality of Music*, p.203.

[75] Anthony Storr, *Music and the Mind*, London: Harper Collins, pb edition, 1997.

[76] Mark Vernon, *After Atheism: Science, Religion and the Meaning of Life*, Basingstoke: Palgrave MacMillan, 2007.

[77] Vernon, *After Atheism*, p.121.

[78] Vernon, *After Atheism*, pp.96-7.
[79] Vernon, *After Atheism*, p.116.

2. *Interpreting the Music*

Writing about music can be a fool's errand. Surely the point is to listen. But this has proved no disincentive and a great deal of ink has been spilt. Music has always been seen as the art form closest to spirituality. How in musical terms to explore that connection?

There are many ways to write about music. Anyone buying a programme at a concert is encouraged to learn something about the cultural context of a piece of music, rather more about its musical structure. These are the two parameters of musical criticism. The authors of major studies of 20th century music which have here been consulted gravitate between these two approaches, Alex Ross prioritising the cultural context, Roger Scruton musical form and Richard Taruskin achieving a balance between the two.[1] All first rate writers on music have to undertake both approaches. I suspect, however, most readers of concert programmes warm to the cultural context but glaze over, if not wholly ignore, any exposition of musical form. Most are simply not equipped to follow this approach. No doubt, many prefer to let the music stir their own imagination, much as Forster suggested in *Howard's End*, where Beethoven's 5th is visualised in terms of goblins and dancing elephants. Music teacher and novelist, Clare Morall is right to tell us that this will no longer do, and that we should at the least try to imagine the shape of the music. Trained as a historian my own natural bias is toward cultural context. But any reading of the spiritual in music has to make some sense of musical form. Morall tartly reminds us that criticism without the technical details 'can sink into the kind of carelessness you often find in films portraying musicians.'[2]

Alex Ross

Alex Ross concludes his hugely engaging volume *The Rest is Noise*: 'the debate over the merit of engagement and withdrawal has gone on for centuries.'[3] This is another way of describing a difference between music which is descriptive and absolute music. This project will argue that the music of engagement can be as equally spiritual as the music of withdrawal. Ross starts out with Strauss's *Salome* and the Austro-German tradition. Alternatively, this project starts out with Russia, for here the spiritual was more deeply embedded in its culture than elsewhere and where it was to be exposed to its most brutal suppression by the Stalinist state. Ross validates a way into discussing music entirely at one with the concerns of the cultural historian, both a biographical approach and a recognition that music inevitably plays off the circumstances of its time, a need to describe its social and political context.

It is worth looking at how reviewers responded to Ross's book. We learn that he was a keen teenage musician and himself a composer. He got his local radio station whilst at Harvard to give whole days over to 'orgies' of Shostakovich, Ligeti and Nielsen. For Alan Rusbridger, Ross is challenging the view of art as a pure art form: 'the history and politics of the century are crucial to an understanding of the music. He wants us to hear the turbulence of our time. He wants us to sit up and make the link.' Here is the book, he continues, that all lovers of 20th century music have been waiting for: 'a subject that has always seemed tantalisingly fragmented and elusive is beautifully explained, crystallised and illuminated.'[4] Another critic puts the big question well: 'is a composer a person who stands a colossus-like – outside the times, tuned in to the eternal spheres – or someone messily implicated in history as it happens?' Ross's is a wonderful interdisciplinary synthesis of history and music. He is especially praised for his skill in describing music. In the end, though, the book is seen to be 'a grand search, unconcluded, for answers to the riddle of what composition really is.'[5]

Peter Conrad takes up the theme of noise: 'the last century was probably the most murderous instalment of human history so far: it was also the loudest, brutally percussive and mechanically brazen.' He also is impressed by Ross's powers of description: 'his rare talent for translating sounds into words. His metaphors leap across the abyss between the two arts.' But then Conrad is wistfully aware 'that print is silent, which is why the task of writing about music is so difficult.' Conrad picks up on Thomas Mann's *Doctor Faustus* and the theme of 'unholy noise' as 'a protest against the fiction of heavenly harmony' as well as Olivier Messiaen's view of the music of Modernism as 'black masterpieces': 'the noise-makers know that in God's absence every kind of sonic outrage is possible.'[6] But then Conrad is *parti pris* against the mystical and the task of this text is to show where in this noise lies the spiritual.[7]

Roger Scruton

Scruton seemingly takes the interpretation in a wholly different direction, one that emphasises the musicological, though does so in an oddly contradictory way, so much so that it is not inherently at odds with Ross's. His ambiguous approach is apparent at the outset:

> The sound world is inherently other and other in an interesting way: it is not just that we do not belong to it; it is that we could not belong to it; it is meta-physically apart from us. And yet we have a complete view of it and discover in it through music, the very life that is out there. There lies the mystery or part of it.[8]

But he can be far more hostile to a hermeneutics of the cultural historian:

> We must be able to hear an order containing no information about the physical world, which stands

apart from the ordinary workings of cause and effect, in what is irreducible to any physical organisation.[9]

For a start, he has no truck with a biographical approach. To prove his point, he claims that Mozart was deeply unhappy at the time he wrote the joyous Jupiter Symphony: 'Mozart disappears behind the work as every artist must disappear when the work is judged aesthetically.'[10]

And this hostile approach proceeds along the following lines. Music cannot be representational. Would we be able, he doubts, to read any content into so-called programme music but for the title? Admittedly, listening inspires extra-musical thoughts (Forster's goblins?) but he immediately queries their being representational: such thoughts are beyond the verbal; 'there is "a peculiar reference without predication" that touches the heart but numbs the tongue.' If we tap into a 'subliminal' narrative, there is nothing akin to a representational painting.[11] Scruton makes much of the distinction, drawn by Croce and his disciple Collingwood, between representation and expression. And this was equally, as we have seen, the viewpoint of Paul Tillich. In expression Scruton finds his source of aesthetic meaning. But if this seemingly opens up a simple proposition that the point of music lies in our emotional response Scruton draws a radical distinction between any emotional response and the emotion expressed within the music. Just how do we hear emotion in music?

Scruton insists on the interiority of music. The emotion we hear is always at one remove. 'The expression penetrates the musical structure,' he explains, 'and is worked through it. In hearing expression in music, we are hearing a distinctively musical process: a kind of musical *interrogation* of human feeling and not the feeling itself.'[12] Only the unusually equipped can read this emotion: 'no wonder that people are tempted to deny that musical meaning exists.'[13] It is cold comfort for the cultural historian to be told that even the expert musicologist can get it wrong. 'It is,' he proceeds, 'surely the capacity to hear music as growing in and through itself, as stating its material, working on it and coming to a conclusion, that is the central experience.'[14] We are ever more distanced. 'Music,' he argues, 'has no secrets, and yet its form and meaning elude our most earnest attempts to describe them.'[15]

Is this but a reformulation of a theory of art for art's sake? Scruton puts this ambiguously. Whilst denying art is instrumental he qualifies: 'we obtain much that is useful to us through the experience of art. But the experience is available only if we forget the use. We must consider the work of art as an end in itself; only then does it become a means for us.'[16] If that suggests some kind of human benefit he quickly scotches such an idea: 'there is it seems to me no future for a theory of aesthetic perception, and no hope of establishing the objectivity of aesthetic judgement by reference to some "commonsense of mankind."'[17] There is an almost existential feel, he posits, to the way we enjoy music. We share in its manner and outlook, join in a particular way of life. Yet he has no time for the subjective permissiveness of response claimed by the post-modernist. On the contrary, we seemingly enter a self-contained world. All this is radically different from the approach of Ross and seemingly leaves a biographical and cultural way into music high and dry.

Yet, as with all good interpretations, there is ambiguity. Music, Scruton recognises, has come out of a society, its worship, dancing, ceremony, even battle. And History has imprinted itself on music: 'a work of music directly acquaints us with a form of human life, and with the style and mannerisms of a period.'[18] 'Listening to music,' he concedes, 'would be a fairly pointless exercise if there was nothing that that we took from what we heard and nothing that we heard in it besides the garlands of a musical Gestalt.'[19] We may not learn new facts from music but 'we come to sense movement and life in another way, to sense its inward meaning and to respond to as in a dance.'[20]

And in obvious ways Scruton himself is a cultural historian. His is a brilliant insight into the origins of atonality as an expression of 'the complex and harrowing emotion that arose with the collapse of spiritual order in Central Europe.'[21] In a critique of the sentimental and banal in contemporary music he asserts: 'such a language could never be used to capture and reflect upon the realities of modern life, or on the unprecedented calamities that inspired *A Survivor for Warsaw* or the *Quator pour le fin du temps.*'[22] And in a language Ross would wholly endorse, he concludes: 'if art ceases to affirm life, then it loses its point: after all life is all that we have.'[23]

Much of Scruton's account flows from his quarrel with Adorno. His is something of a rearguard defence of tonality against atonality. And it is hard today, with the passing of the high modernism of atonality, to accept Adorno's judgement that tonality was a kind of fascist defence of the old order. Scruton's is a fascinating insight that atonality was shot through with anxiety: 'it is a style that reflects the epoch which gave birth to it; nihilistic, yet saturated with romantic longing and *nostalgie de la boue.*'[24] It was driven by the romantic illusion of the artist having access to a 'a new and astonishing truth.' And Adorno did indeed see it as a new religion, one that would purge a bourgeois aesthetic and be the harbinger of revolution. Scruton himself, out of recognition that here was a way of grappling with the need for cultural renewal, cannot help respecting Adorno's critique. Germanely, there were profound correspondences between atonality and spirituality.

Scruton is entirely at one with this project's concern for the spiritual in music. With the decline in religion (though this is to adopt a Eurocentric position) he has a pretty bleak picture of where culture is today: 'in such condition, it is inevitable that people will lose all sense of a sacred community, so as to become locked in the isolation of their own desires.' He begins to share Adorno's sense of the fetishization of culture.[25] But Scruton's is not a religious position: 'words move, music moves, so as to reach out into the silence – so as to claim for our humanity the speechless space surrounding us.'[26] And in possibly the strongest statement of what music be he writes: 'music is heard as though breathed into the ear of the listener from another and higher sphere: it is not here and now, the world of mere contingency that speaks to us through music, but another world, whose order is only dimly reflected in the empirical realm.'[27] If the spiritual has been expressed in the music of a Górecki and Arvo Pärt, it was not in any space carved out by Adorno's dream of revolution, but 'preserved in the catacombs, a secret shrine at which to pour out all the grief and anguish which were the poisoned gift of the revolution.'[28] This is a side-swipe at the totalitarian consequences of revolution, and it will be the aim of this project to show how under totalitarianism we have to listen out for a different and humanist expression of the spiritual. In the recovery of tonality lies, Scruton believes, a spiritual community will be rediscovered, not in the thin music of a Tavener and Górecki but in something much tougher, a musical equivalent of the Four Quartets. Rather surprisingly, Scruton sees Alfred Schnittke as one composer pointing the way.

Richard Taruskin

Richard Taruskin brilliantly squares the circle between the cultural and the musicological. His genius is to show how the insight of the cultural historian can be demonstrated through an analysis of the music itself. He has no hesitation in resorting to the biographical to explore the meaning of the music, as, for example, what lies behind Schoenberg's *Erwartung*, and he is the equal of Ross in exploring the socio-political context. The Great War is seen as radically altering musical expression: 'it cast a retrospective pall over all the seriously spiritual and exalted art the previous century had provided. All rhetoric of hope and glory seemed a lie.'[29] His most unusual, and no doubt controversial claim for his admirers, is to link Stravinsky's neo-classicism to his admiration for the authoritarian politics of Mussolini. Taruskin's is an ex-ceptionally perceptive account of how music encountered totalitarian regimes. This theme will be reprised in the chapter on Poulenc.

Out of the legacy of the Second World War, to follow Taruskin's historical analysis, with its threat of annihilation, came both existentialism – 'man's freedom is a curse from which there can no longer be any refuge in faith'[30] – and the paralysing fear of the Cold War: 'political suspicion, directed not only at the potential enemy, but its fellow citizens, now became a fact of life in East and West alike.'[31] Ever the liberal, Taruskin is always on his guard against a creeping totalitarianism and is equally tough on the regimes of Goebbels and Zhdanov as on the new cult of serialism propagated by Darmstadt and post-war Modernism. The Cold War politicised and commercialised what was inherently apolitical and non-commercial. He takes Adorno to task, and clearly has an issue with Modernism. Taruskin sees as an unprecedented crisis in the 20th century, a fatal clash between the claims of high art and the needs of society, Greenberg's essay *Avant-garde Kitch* the catalyst for this divide. The rift between this self-conscious elite and society was, however, more a phenomenon of western capitalism than under the Soviet regime. With the fall of the Berlin Wall we enter a new phase, 'no longer shadowed by the spectre of totalitarianism, "accessibility" gained a measure of respectability.' Somewhat sarcastically he adds: 'seeing social solidarity rather than social alienation as the most progressive political force is fatal to modernism.'[32]

Through his talent for seeing the cultural expressed through the music he probably surpasses Scruton as musicologist and, indeed, he has no greater admirer than Scruton. In reviewing Volumes Two and Three Scruton judges: 'the result is one of the great cultural monuments of our day, the product of a mind as humane and morally focussed as it is technically assured.'[33] If Taruskin differs from Scruton is not seeing 20th century-music as a battle between tonality and atonality, they probably agree in refusing to see the triumph of atonality by mid-century.

Manna from heaven for this project is Taruskin's recognising the significant role of the spiritual in 20th century music. His leading concept is Maximalism, an emotional intensity in music that spilled over from Romanticism. Some idea of where this project on the spiritual in 20th century music is going can be sensed from Taruskin's survey of Maximalism. Symbolism, the sensory as a way into the spiritual, is one leading component, and Taruskin compares Proust's response to the taste of the madeleine to Debussy's music. Maximalism underlay atonalism. Here Schoenberg, though he used the concept of pantonalism, is crucial: 'one of the most over-determined musical visions at a time of many visionary extremes, Schoenberg's was the most complex and far-reaching maximalism of them all, and by far the most lastingly influential.'[34] Maximalism is pan-European. As the supreme interpreter of Russian music Taruskin gives great weight to Scriabin. But one of his themes is that Maximalism was driven to a point where it could not possibly fulfil its expectations. Scriabin's failure to compose his *Mysterium* is a classic example. Stravinsky is the key figure in a rupture in Maximalism and his 1923 Octet for Winds marks the divide between Stravinsky's own maximalism and neo-classicism: 'the history of twentieth century music as something aesthetically distinct from that of the nineteenth century begins not at the *fin de siècle* but here in the 1920's.'[35] Stravinsky's irony put paid to the spiritual. Mahler was to be forgotten till his revival in the 1960's and Scriabin has yet to be fully revived.

But the spiritual does no go away. Taruskin is wonderfully provocative in reading a revival of Maximalism in the cult of serialism, once again taking music to extremes. And the link here is Messiaen: 'Messiaen, Boulez's teacher, has been a rare keeper of the Maximalist flame through all the reign of irony.'[36] How this is also reflected in electronic music, in Varese and his successors, above all Stockhausen, is likewise explored. And he tracks clearly how a new expression of the spiritual in music is emerging post-war, in the convergence between minimalism and new age spirituality, in the Polish renaissance, and in a Soviet generation of composers who succeeded Shostakovich, in Alfred Schnittke and Sofia Gubaidulina above all. Maximalism staged a come-back: 'Schnittke's post-modernism reengaged with the grandest, most urgent, most timeless – hence potentially most banal – questions of existence, framed the simplest way possible, as primitive opposites.'[37]

And, indeed, the spiritual, in Taruskin's assessment, has become rather worryingly fashionable. He rounds off his survey by reference to a sociological study by David Brooks, *Bobos in Paradise*,[38] which has cleverly shown how a post – Kennedy new American elite tries to justify its new privileged economic status by endorsing the spiritual in art. He ends on a negative note: 'is the new spirituality just another screen behind which high art engages in its traditional business of reinforcing social division by creating elite occasions?'[39]

Modernism and Spirituality

It was almost inevitable with the widespread flow of mysticism into the spiritual vacuum opened by the Darwinian revolution that the history of spirituality and of Modernism should converge. It is a convergence most evident in the years prior to Word War 1 and in the aftermath of World War 11. Pre-1914 Taruskin puts it this way: 'the belief that music in its word-transcending expressivity was the only medium through which eschatological matter – matter of "ultimate reality" – could be adequately contemplated impelled the early modernists on their quest for new horizons.'[40] The emotional intensity of Romanticism spilled over into Modernism. This can be seen in Mahler in his determination to infiltrate oratorio into the symphony, as Taruskin describes it. But Peter Gay suggests that, if in the spiritual maelstrom of the Belle Époque the early modernists sought to promote a new religion of art for art's sake, when this failed to make much impact, chose instead to fall back on the

negative side of this cultural shift, 'working to destroy religion rather than create a new one.'[41] Certainly in the inter-war
years the convergence between the spiritual and Modernism
is far less in evidence.

This became very apparent in the exhibition on Modernism
1918-39 at the Victoria and Albert exhibition. Admittedly,
through Le Corbusier and architecture's endeavour to open
up new living space, and one reliant on as much light as
possible being let in through the use of glass, here was an
aesthetic steeped in mysticism. The chapel at Ronchamp is
one brilliant example. But, on the other hand, there was a
strong wish to imitate in art the character of the machine, the
clean, functional lines of the factory product. Surely this took
art in the direction of a soulless materialism? The way totalitarian regimes took up the ideas of the Futurists, especially
in the propaganda art of a Leni Riefenstahl and a Sergei
Eisenstein, is further evidence of the way Modernism and the
spiritual parted company. So, whatever their overlap in its
founding pioneers, Mahler, Schoenberg, Kandinsky and
Mondrian, this project is not seen as a contribution to the
history of Modernism.

Introducing the Composers

Taruskin has already largely done so. Russia and Scriabin is
the best place to begin, with Scriabin's flirtation with all the
new spirituality movements and his own bizarre egotistical
spiritual quest. It is but speculation to wonder where Russian
spirituality might have taken music but for the repressive
Soviet regime and its vindictive loathing for the spiritual.
There follows an exploration of two composers always
paired, Prokofiev and Shostakovich, though an intriguing
difference is now recognised through Prokofiev's religious
belief in Christian Science and Shostakovich's atheism. Both
were driven in on themselves to discover a humanist spirituality to counter totalitarianism. In the late Shostakovich
there was to be a powerful engagement with death. The post-

Shostakovich generation dug deep to find a new truth. Here we will look at one composer from the oppressed nation-alities of the Soviet system, Arvo Pärt, alongside two com-posers from the end-game of the Soviet system, Alfred Schnittke and Sofia Gubaidulina. In Eastern Europe leading composers of the Polish Renaissance will be considered. Turning to Western Europe, Messiaen, with his passionate Catholic faith, will be contrasted with Poulenc, far more fragile in his belief. And finally, from Germany, through looking at Stockhausen and Henze, we grapple with a spirit-uality which emerges from more extreme forms of experi-mentation.

Notes

[1] Alex Ross, *The Rest is Noise: Listening to the Twentieth Century*, London: Fourth Estate, 2008; Roger Scruton, *The Aesthetics of Music*, Oxford: Oxford University Press, 1997; Richard Taruskin, *The Oxford History of Western Music*, Volume 4, Oxford: Oxford University Press, 2004; Volume 5, Oxford University Press, 2005.
[2] Clare Morall, 'Hitting the right note,' *The Guardian*, 12 April 2008.
[3] Ross, *The Rest is Noise*, p.542.
[4] Alan Rusbridger, 'Sound and Vision,' *The Guardian*, 19 March 2008.
[5] Steven Poole, 'Sound of the Century,' *The Guardian*, 15 March 2008.
[6] Peter Conrad, 'Listen to that siren solo,' *The Observer*, 9 March 2008.
[7] The basic theme of Conrad's monumental *Creation, Artists, Gods and Origins*, London: Thames and Hudson, 2007, is that artists have usurped the role of God and behind this claim lies a passionate advocacy for an atheism and the Darwinian theory of evolution.

[8] Scruton, *Aesthetics*, pp.13-14.

[9] Scruton, *Aesthetics*, p.39.

[10] Scruton, *Aesthetics*, p.115.

[11] Scruton, *Aesthetics*, pp.132-3.

[12] Scruton, *Aesthetics*, p.155.

[13] Scruton, *Aesthetics*, p.161.

[14] Scruton, *Aesthetics*, p.236.

[15] Scruton, *Aesthetics*, p.337.

[16] Scruton, *Aesthetics*, p.375.

[17] Scruton, *Aesthetics*, p.378.

[18] Scruton, *Aesthetics*, p.115.

[19] Scruton, *Aesthetics*, p.231.

[20] Scruton, *Aesthetics*, p.235.

[21] Scruton, *Aesthetics*, p.305.

[22] Scruton, *Aesthetics*, p.488.

[23] Scruton, *Aesthetics*, p.493.

[24] Scruton, *Aesthetics*, p.306.

[25] Scruton, *Aesthetics*, p.506.

[26] Scruton, *Aesthetics*, p.172.

[27] Scruton, *Aesthetics*, p.489.

[28] Scruton, *Aesthetics*, p.472.

[29] Taruskin, *History of Western Music*, Vol.4, p.472.

[30] Taruskin, *History of Western Music*, Vol.4, p.2.

[31] Taruskin, *History of Western Music*, Vol.4, p.7.

[32] Taruskin, *History of Western Music*, Vol.4, p.437.

[33] Roger Scruton, 'Resounding Reason,' *TLS*, 15 July 2005.

[34] Taruskin, *History of Western Music*, Vol.4, p.339.

[35] Taruskin, *History of Western Music*, Vol.4, p.448.

[36] Taruskin, *History of Western Music*, Vol.5, p.37.

[37] Taruskin, *History of Western Music*, Vol.5, p.466.

[38] David Brooks, *Bobos in Paradise: The New Upper Class and How They Got There*, New York: Simon and Schuster Paperbacks, 2000. Bobos is a linking of Bourgeois and Bohemian. It is a wittily satirical study of how a new meritocracy eased their conscience at their success by continuing to endorse the cultural interests of their youth. The Bobos are seen as spiritual pluralists but destined to always be left unfulfilled; 'the accumulatuion of spiritual peak experiences can become like the greedy person's

53

accumulation of money.' (p.237.) And just because it is an unfulfilled journey, the bobos have turned back to religion and a search for order. They have ended up with too 'many compromises and spiritual fudges.' (p.246.) But they certainly want to hold onto their liberated moral code.

[39] Taruskin, *History of Western Music*, Vol.5, p.527.

[40] Taruskin, *History of Western Music*, Vol.4, p.6.

[41] Peter Gay, *Modernism: The Lure of Heresy from Baudelaire to Beckett and Beyond*, London: Vintage Books, 2009, p.29.

II.

Russia and Eastern Europe

Alexander Scriabin

3. *Alexander Scriabin*

As the foremost composer of maximalist music in the early 20th century Scriabin selects himself as point of departure for this project. He brushed up against all the contemporary spirituality movements, read his Madam Blavatsky and joined a Theosophical Lodge in Brussels. But his governing obsession was the Mysterium, an extravagant musical project, visualized as taking place in a seven-day festival in a temple in the Himalayas, the entire world present and culminating in the end of the world and the rebirth of God. A plot of land had been purchased near Darjeeling and Scriabin had kitted himself out with tropical clothing. But Scriabin never got to India and never wrote the music. Yet all his music has to be interpreted in the light of this idée fixe. Here was a highly idiosyncratic spiritual project. One of the most recent interpreters of his music, Hugh Macdonald, drastically contrasts Scriabin the man and his music: 'the horizons of his art never widened. Instead they grew focussed more and more closely on himself and a clearer example of artistic monomania – in his case egomania – is not easy to find in the chronicles of music.'[1] Yet Macdonald and almost all the authorities already cited, certainly both Richard Taruskin and Roger Scruton, all make high claims for his music. But it leaves a nagging question, can such a self-centred man rise to the spiritual? And it has to be emphasised that the enquiry in this project is less to assess the quality of the music, rather its strength as a purveyor of the spiritual. Despite in Scriabin's case a very strong case being made by recent musicologists to focus on the music, for reasons already elaborated on, the only way we can answer that question is by coming to the music through the biographical, the cultural and the philosophical.

Family, Health, Sexuality

What of his family background? His parents exercised little influence. His mother, Lyubov Petrovna, died a few months after his birth. One can only speculate if Scriabin inherited any of his own talent as a pianist from his concert – performing mother. Not until 1913 did he visit her grave at Arco in the Dolomites and the experience was clearly overwhelming. It was even less likely that his father, Nikolai, deemed 'simply Black Hundred' by Faubian Bowers, Scriabin's leading biographer,[2] would be an influence though, at the least, he was unusual within the family in pursuing a diplomatic career over a military and father and son were never to lose contact. Given the time he spent abroad the father entrusted his son to his mother, Elizabeth, her sister, Maria and his sister Lyubov, interestingly sharing Scriabin's mother's name. When Scriabin was three the grandmother handed him over to Aunt Lyubov 'like a precious and delicate toy.' As Bowers puts it, 'Lyubov's attachment to her nephew rapidly reached a state of exaltation.'[3] One need look no further for Scriabin's extreme self-centredness than this all female, utterly loving, upbringing.

Another clue to his makeup lies in his life-long hypochondria. The trigger for this was his almost dying of measles at the age of 14. Then at the age of 20 he suffered a serious injury to his right hand. The pain spread up his arm. His whole career as piano virtuoso was at risk. There had to be long spells to restore his health in the Crimea and eventually Switzerland. At this stage he became a heavy drinker. Between the ages of 20 and 29 Bowers sees him on the verge of a nervous breakdown: 'Scriabin was imprisoned within himself. His only exit was music.'[4] The question has been raised, was he a manic-depressive? Was he even insane? Certainly he exhibited all kinds of obsessive and compulsive disorders. For all his subsequent good health his extreme nervousness at any infection was to be all too gruesomely justified, for it was an infection of the lip, first in evidence in London, March 1914 and to flare up again in Moscow, 4 April 1915 that led to his premature death, 14 April. But out of that early prolonged period of sickness came a very Nietzschean desire to be well: 'a new Scriabin now expressed himself: the Scriabin of victory, the triumphant man who overcomes and conquers.'[5] One dominant cultural characteristic of the Belle Époque was this endeavour to overcome a morbid fear of decadence and entropy through the pursuit of physical health. Scriabin's is a classic case of a search for vitality informing what was, in many ways, an essentially this-worldly spirituality.

Sex was the driving force of this spirituality. There are obvious parallels with the tubercular D H Lawrence, a like obsession with sex and a belief in its powers for transcendence. The parallel is all the closer through their shared emotional bisexuality if biographers are reluctant to see them as practising homosexuals. There is a strong case for seeing the homoerotic as underlying the mystical and so it is important to assess the strength of the homosexual in Scriabin's personality.[6] Of course there was good cause to be secretive, for in Tsarist Russia homosexuality was subject to a ten year term of imprisonment and exile. Was Scriabin's sexuality shaped by his all female upbringing and absence of a father figure? As an artist he was inevitably drawn into a homosexual world, be it, in his case, the homosexual household of his piano teacher, Nicholas Zverev (1833-93) or the homosexual demi-monde he encountered during his visit to Paris in 1896. Scriabin subsequently communicated: 'I drowned myself in pleasures and was put to the test by them. I have known since that the creative act is inextricably linked to the sexual act.'[7]

But what is so intriguing about Scriabin's homoerotic life is his choice of male friends. At Cadet School he was drawn to its leading athlete, Grisha, but this led nowhere. But the diminutive Scriabin was always drawn to physical strength and to a certain grossness. The first of such friendships was with the multi-millionaire music publisher, Mitrofan Belaieff.[8] In 1894 he took Scriabin under his wing, saw to the publication of his scores through his Jurgenson outlet in Leipzig and gave him a monthly stipend of 100 roubles, later raised to 200. He was always generous in his gifts, a concert grand Becker, for example. They met at Glazunov's all-male supper parties and Belaieff was invariably to accompany Scriabin on his European journeys. Belaieff, sixty at the time he befriended the 20 year old Scriabin, was, we learn, 'a rather ugly, coarse featured man, debauched with deep circles under his eyes and surprisingly cruel.' Bowers adds: 'Few men have ever had more adoring friends than Belaieff.'[9] But he was plagued by ill-health – he died 28 December 1903 – and in time Scriabin lost both his monthly stipend and publication from the Belaieff's estate. Scriabin retrospectively wrote of 'his fatherly solicitude.'[10]

In 1900 Scriabin met Alexander Bryanchaninov (1874-1918), of an age, but, as his biographer puts it, 'also one belonging to those startling contrasts with his own person and personality.' He is described as 'coarse, short, thick-set, a very rich gentleman, a big landowner, and square.'[11] In time he became Scriabin's closest male companion, likewise accompanied him on his European trips, and made all the plans for that journey to India that was not to be.

Then there was the fisherman disciple he attracted in Switzerland in 1904, Otto Hauerstein, 'one of those odd relationships where a rough and burly man twice Scriabin's age, was enamoured of him.'[12]

If there is no clear evidence that any of these relationships was sexual, this is surely not the case with cellist Modest Altschuler. Their correspondence certainly suggests physical intimacy: 'how I want to pinch you and squeeze you. Ah you, you, you. Your pussycat.'[13] Interestingly Scriabin displays no class preferences in his friends. Is there some connection between this homoeroticism and Scriabin's straining after some all-powerful spiritual force? And is there in addition the dynamic of guilt for if, for much of his short life Scriabin rejected any such attitudes, as late as 1913 his biographer describes him 'as guilt-ridden still and aware of his sickly excesses'?[14]

Ostensibly Scriabin's cult of sex was heterosexual. There were a few girl friends and two marriages. His first marriage, 27 August 1897, despite Aunt Lyubov's fears for the worst, was to a piano student, the Jewish Vera Ivanovna. Though a marriage blessed with children, Scriabin later wrote: 'I didn't love Vera in the slightest' and conveys an image of Vera on the train en route to their honeymoon in the Crimea that conjures up comparisons with Tchaikovsky's feelings for his wife in Ken Russell's harrowing film *The Music Makers:* 'Is this my wife? I asked myself. Is this my life to be? In that instant I knew I could not love, and worse, never would.'[15] His biographer suggests his 3rd Piano Sonata of 1898 'carries him over the spiritual crisis of his marriage.'[16] His second marriage, though never to be formally registered through Vera's refusal to grant him a divorce, was to Tatyana Schoelzer, and to this he owed his all important friendship with her older brother, Boris, to become Scriabin's leading interpreter and apologist. They had met in fact in 1896 when Boris was but 15 but only got to know each other much better in 1902. There was to be much social awkwardness in this second 'marriage' – for fear of scandal they had had to leave America in a hurry in 1907 – and it was not helped by the ever loyal Vera continuing to be a leading performer of his piano music. Neither wives long outlived Scriabin, Vera dying in 1920, Tatyana, who in the meanwhile had become a mystic, in 1922. To what extent did the nervous spirituality in his music come out of the hothouse of his private life?

Increasingly Scriabin's musical imagination was to focus on the sexual act. The first title for the *Poem of Ecstasy* was 'orgiastic' by which he meant 'orgasmic.' Schloezer acknowledged 'the sexual act was never absent from Scriabin's creative speculation. He saw the sexual act as the prototype of ecstasy.' 'In his imagination the cosmic finale assumed the dimension of a grandiose sexual act.'[17] Even Edward Carpenter, a contemporary writer and poet equally engrossed by Indian philosophy, and whose connection between sex and mysticism in many ways paralleled Scriabin's own, flinched from seeing an exact overlap between orgasm and absorption in the Divine. It is hard to see this slightly built, feminine, Scriabin as sexual athlete and here is a classic case of sex in the head.

The Silver Age

Scriabin was the leading composer of Russia's so called Silver Age. It was an aristocratic culture, alienated from the revolutionary ambition of the intelligentsia, and indeed divided that intellectual class. Orlando Figes brands the post-1905 years as 'the heyday of exotic and pretentious intellectualism.'[18] How such writers as Nikolai Berdyaev and Semyon Frank fit into this flowering of the mystical will be looked at below in the context of the Bolshevik assault on spirituality. Yet it was also a culture all too well aware of decay: 'the notion of full flowering, of fruit decaying, of putrefaction, was central to the sensibility of the Silver Age.'[19] It was open to all the new spirituality movements, Theosophy, Anthroposophy, Buddhism, yoga, vegetarianism, that were likewise to impinge on Scriabin. It was a culture that Diaghilev was to introduce to a wider Europe through the Ballets Russes. Interestingly, the usually polite Scriabin had a violent falling out with Diaghilev in Paris, all over his failure to apologise for the late delivery of tickets for a concert. Its influence only began to wane about 1910 when an altogether more radical, politically-minded, artistic avant-garde took its place.

Scriabin, never close to other composers, was close to the Symbolist poets of the Silver Age. And here was an important source of his spirituality. Symbolism looked beyond the world of appearance to apprehend, as John Bowlt puts it, 'a superior structure beyond the outward flesh of things.'[20] Did not the X-ray prove, it was speculated, 'the real reality beyond the façade of physical objects'?[21] The Symbolist poets were amongst Scriabin's leading disciples, theirs 'a prolonged testament of faith in his genius.'[22] Richard Taruskin sees Vycheslav Ivanov as the most insightful interpreter of his spirituality. They met in 1909 and remained firm friends. Scriabin was also a poet, if not of a high order, his poetry 'best treated as profound or meaningless according to taste,'[23] as one critic waspishly put it. Scriabin, however, saw the poetry and the music as complimentary and, if we are to grasp his intentions, the poetry has to be taken seriously.

The Political

Politically, Scriabin's mind was elsewhere, though not without some attempt at engagement. Maybe it is insufficiently grasped the extent to which a part of the intelligentsia became alienated from the revolutionary movement through its violence. This was in large part a class phenomenon, the liberal nobility turning towards an alternative spiritual culture. And for Scriabin, it was his evident lack of any radical political agenda that did much to discredit him in the eyes of the Soviet regime. His immediate response to the revolution of 1905 was to worry whether a monthly allowance from a new patron, Elizabeth Morozova, would arrive safely. But then, during a stay in Bogliasco on the Italian Riviera, he met amongst the Russian community, George Plekhanov, Russia's leading interpreter of Marxism. In his usual skimpy way of reading Scriabin looked at *Das Kapital* but much more closely at Plekhanov's *On the Question of the Monistic View of History*. Scriabin was a natural Hegelian. To say that he just stopped short of becoming a Marxist, as his biographer suggests, seems an exaggeration. Plekhanov saw him as hopelessly the mystic and Plekhanov's wife, rather revealingly, claimed to notice 'something maniacal in Scriabin.'[24] Boris de Schloezer suggests that Scriabin was attracted to the tightly constructed character of Marxism and 'never questioned the dialectical inevitability of the collapse of capitalist society.' But economic and political upheaval was always secondary to the spiritual.[25]

Even so, Scriabin always saw himself as a revolutionary in music. He was one of many who responded enthusiastically to the outbreak of war in 1914 for here were surely the violent events that would bring about spiritual renewal, the world of his Mysterium. But Scriabin's vision was always a this-worldly one. The death of his daughter by Tatyana, Ariadne, murdered by the Nazis in 1941, is also a reminder that in this most highly politicised of centuries, no-one could hide from politics.

Scriabin's Quest

In a telling way Scriabin connects with that distinction between religion and spirituality. In Orthodox Tsarist Russia Scriabin was inevitably brought up as a conventional believer though his being able to write at the age of sixteen that 'religious feeling is awareness of the divine within one's self' hints at the unorthodoxy to come.[26] The crisis of faith came when he was twenty and has to be connected to the profound trauma of his damaged hand. Initially, he drew a distinction between God the Father and God the Son, seeking out the former, disaffected from the latter. Then he turned Theomachist, one who battles with God. But he emerged an atheist, though always to be steeped in the millenarian and eschatological. And if this suggests a visionary of a catastrophe to come, it helps to be reminded of the original Greek meaning of Apocalypse, a removing of the veil. Scriabin always saw himself as a mystic. Scriabin entered and left the world within the orthodox sacraments, his funeral service in the Church of the Miracle Worker, buried in Novodevinsky cemetery. But the inspiration for his music has to be seen as outside the liturgy of the Russian Orthodox Church.

Now comes the truly challenging part, making sense of Scriabin's philosophy. Many see it as hocus-pocus but Scriabin at the time attracted two committed interpreters of his ideas, Boris de Schloezer and Leonid Sabaneev, and Richard Taruskin also insists on taking the philosophy seriously.

Scriabin was not university trained, and this he regretted, and there was always something amateurish and self-taught about his expression of ideas. He read superficially and tended simply to absorb whatever harmonised with his own instinctive intellectual outlook. He was always more the intuitive than the rationalist. But given the enormous importance he attributed to his expression of spirituality, we have to begin here if we are to make sense of the spiritual in his music.

One of the really critical questions to ask of Scriabin is whether he ever moved beyond an extreme self-centredness, variously described as solipsism and narcissism, for if he was stuck here, it seems unlikely that his music will reach out to the truly transcendental. Narcissistically he declared in his Notebooks for 1904-05: 'I want to engulf everything and absorb everything in my individuality.'[27] Schloezer sees Scriabin under the influence of Nietzsche heading for 'a metaphysical nihilism.'[28] Much hinges on what Scriabin meant by the 'I' and he wrote of the two 'I's. Scriabin read patchily in Hindu philosophy but no commentator suggests that he had stumbled on the Vedantist distinction between the Ego and the Atman, a higher self within, one and the same as Brahma or the Absolute. Can we attribute to Scriabin a sense of the possibility of such self-transcendence?

I see him as closer to the ideas of the 20th century Indian mystic, Aurobindo Ghose, who saw the divine as descending into Man. Aurobindo, the leading theorist of the Extremist party in Indian nationalism in the early century, drew away from politics in 1910 to pursue a life-time yogic quest. But whereas conventional forms of yoga sought a transcendence of the ego toward the divine, Aurobindo sought by his will and through his integral system of yoga to draw the divine or 'supermind,' as he called it, down to the physical. He even imagined the divine taking physical presence in his body.[29] Scriabin evidently also saw himself as becoming God. The problem is whether to give Scriabin the benefit of the doubt and interpret this self-deification as other than extreme narcissism. Schloezer, though his apologist, was always aware of his inability to see outside himself. If he saw himself as a microcosm, and believed this was one and the same as the macrocosm, 'he had not learned to divine the macrocosm through his inner microcosm; he had been unable to ascend to a higher state of being.'[30] Blind to such limitation, Scriabin, via Theomachy and self-deification, worked towards a sense of himself as a 'sacrificing victim': 'through his own death, man resurrects God.'[31] This was to be the climax of the *Mysterium*. Did Scriabin, at the end, as he played the piano become transfigured, as some claimed, a kind of Ramakrishna figure in a state of *Samadhi* (religious trance)? Had he finally escaped self-absorption and touched the divine? Or were all such claims fanciful and no more than a rearticulation of the ideas of Feurbach, what Schloezer named efflorescence, a projection of human consciousness onto God?

Another example of the way in which Scriabin absorbed whatever reflected his own outlook is in his relationship with Theosophy. It was late as 1907, long after his vision of the Mysterium had taken shape, that he read Madame Blavatsky, though here, for once, he was a serious student, reading her *The Secret Doctrine* three times in a French translation. Theosophy altered his cosmology, taking on board the Hindu idea of seven cycles, and Scriabin came to modify his sense of an imminent catastrophe for the entire universe to just that of the age in which we live, though out of impatience for that catastrophe, he drastically advanced the speed at which it would happen. Theosophy wrote of the evolution of the universe going into reverse, a process of involution, and anticipated the idea of a contraction of the universe and a return to the original Big Bang. Scriabin saw such an event as imminent. His closest engagement with the Theosophical movement was in his time in Brussels in 1909 when he joined the Brussels Lodge. Although he never lost his respect for fellow Russian, Madame Blavatsky, he drew away from the next generation of exponents of the doctrine, and by 1913 had all but ceased to be a follower.

Through Theosophy Scriabin was drawn into the Occult and interpreters of his music differ as to whether or not this led him into an expression of the satanic. But interpreters are often unaware of Jung's profound insight that involvement in the occult inevitably carried that risk. Here, Scriabin's two leading interpreters are at variance. Whereas Schloezer saw Scriabin as the master of such dark forces and diabolism as 'completely sterile, lacking creative power,' Sabaneev saw it as the explanation for his music: 'Undoubtedly, the entire spiritual and creative physiognomy of Scriabin's conscious-ness was conditioned by Satanism.'[32] Not that this stopped Sabaneev from being one of the most astute and generous critics of his music. If Scriabin paid the price, he accepted, for an insufficient grasp of religion and philosophy, 'his was the perturbed and inquiring soul of the typically Russian thinker, such as Dostoyevsky and Vladimir Soloviev, who states his problem with childish fearlessness and dares to gaze into the abyss.' 'To my mind,' he continues, 'all these peregrinations may be summed up as the wanderings of Parsifal, the pure in heart, guided by intuition and true instinct.' But it came at a cost: 'he escaped from the clutches of the Nietzschean creed to fall captive to the occult doctrine and perhaps its most vulgar reaction': 'his religiosity is deficient in majesty and profundity and is magical rather than mystical.'[33]

It might be questioned, given the temptation to compare Scriabin with Indian thought and his indebtedness to Theo-sophy, if Scriabin in fact tapped into a specifically Russian tradition of spirituality.

Interpreting the Music

Connecting the poetry and philosophy to the music is the most difficult bit. All the critics cited agree that Scriabin's music is extraordinary. Even Roger Scruton is enthusiastic, though I suspect through his belief that Scriabin deliberately fell short of his bête-noire, atonalism: 'Scriabin's music illustrates the way in which tonality can be reconstructed from its own ruins.' He sees Scriabin's music as a kind of 'orphaned tonality': 'the daring of Scriabin's "mystical harmonies",' he argues, 'lies in the fact that they impose large and barely tolerable harmonic and melodic obligations.'[34] His is, of course, special pleading, for the thrust of modern musicological scholarship on Scriabin, what Richard Taruskin labels as 'techno-essentialist historiography,' is to jettison the poetry and the philosophy, the better to argue that Scriabin is indeed a progenitor of atonality.

But is this not to try and annexe Scriabin to a doctrine of art for art's sake? This is clearly wrong-headed for Scriabin always saw the music as secondary to his mystical vision and as a means for realising the kingdom of God on earth. Richard Taruskin makes the strongest possible case for taking the poetry and philosophy seriously and, above all, trying to see how they were expressed through the music. But there is a built–in predicament in reading Scriabin's music. The grand project, to which all his compositions were somehow directed, the Mysterium, was never written. For all the enormity of his vision Scriabin wrote comparatively little and we fall back on his symphonies and piano sonatas.

We have to say something of a first phase in Scriabin's composition. His piano concerto, marked by a crisp lyricism, had been decidedly Chopinesque: Macdonald writes of its 'uncharacteristic self-effacement.'[35] Although Scriabin acquired a reputation as a cosmopolitan, Macdonald doubts if he ever absorbed any foreign culture and sees a far stronger case for him as Russian composer. Taruskin agrees and following Schloezer – and indeed I suspect Schloezer is his source for the very concept of Maximalism – sees him as the supreme Russian romantic composer. The first phase also includes the first two symphonies. Macdonald tartly writes of the First, 'it aspires more than once to grandeur and attains only grandiloquence.'[36] Bowers, more charitably, hears a 'foretaste of the mystically mature author,'[37] and this is the more accurate. It ends with a choral setting of Scriabin's poem, a Nietzschean paean of praise to the triumph of art.[38] But Macdonald is kinder towards the Second: it 'closes Scriabin's productive first period in a worthy manner.'[39]

Then Scriabin turned to an Opera, its composition never seriously undertaken, its plot steeped in all the Wagnerian and Nietzschean ideas he had absorbed, the story of a kind of proto-fascist superman. He would lead the uneducated masses to some state of blessedness, offering himself through his suicide as a sacrifice, aided and abetted by the king's daughter, herself a symbol of their passivity. She likewise kills herself. There are odd premonitions here of Stravinsky's theme of sacrifice in *The Rite of Spring*. But Scriabin set this aside for the even grander project of the Mysterium.

This was the project that underpinned all the compositions of his second phase and what some see as the beginnings of a new and third phase in 1914. His biographer makes a claim that the 3rd Piano Sonata, first performed in Paris 10 July 1900, as the beginning of this new phase in his composing: 'Scriabin now closed and locked the door on his early compositions. Aromas of Chopin, Schumann and Liszt dissipate themselves in thin air. He dispels his heritage as the adult relinquishes his dependence on family.'[40] The first idea for the Mysterium came to Scriabin in 1901. As Schloezer puts it: 'the evaluation, not only aesthetic but philosophical of Scriabin's entire career, depends on the status of the Mysterium.'[41]

What triggered it? Was it the crisis in his marriage? The central idea of the Mysterium was simple: Scriabin saw himself as the messiah of some cataclysmic event, an experience of ecstasy in death, 'the ancient dream,' as Schloezer expresses it, 'of a universal reunion of humanity with divinity.'[42] At the very least this was less elitist and more democratic than the Opera, for collective humanity would itself be actively involved in this final transfiguration. This original vision was not to be greatly altered over time though there were to be accretions, especially from Theosophy. Nor, for all its extravagance, was it particularly original, for the idea that man has lost his innocence through consciousness and could only recover it through some apocalyptic experience was common coinage at the time. The obsessive way in which Scriabin worked on his plan for a great festival in which this event would occur – the Himalayas the preferred venue, though so delighted was by his reception in London in 1914 he saw London as an alternative venue – anticipates the way the College in Hermann Hesse's 1946 novel *The Glass Bead Game* planned spiritual festivals. But built into the maximalist outlook, as Taruskin points out, is a recognition that such extravagant visions can never be realised and Scriabin had to fall back on his *Prefatory Act,* and even this only appeared as a poem. Enough musical fragments, however, were there for Alexander Nemtin to reconstruct how these two final pieces might have sounded.

The first serious venture of the second phase was his 3rd Symphony, *The Divine Poem,* his longest work. Taruskin picks up on the symbolist poet Ivanov's summary of Scriabin's philosophy, the petty 'I' being transformed by some violent means into a new and collective humanity, a transcended 'I.' This is the one completed work of Scriabin which is programme music. In the first movement we allegedly hear the way the transcendence of the petty 'I' is imperfectly realised. The music seemingly inhabits a dark and frightening space. I assume the so called Nietzschean trumpet heralds despair, for the music then slides away, almost haunted, expressing hopes unfulfilled and something post-coital. The second movement is a story, in a way, of the prodigal son, of his losing the petty 'I' in sexual indulgence, that very Gidean quest for self-annihilation through orgasm. The music is exceptionally erotic and languorous. In the Third movement Scriabin draws on the Hindu notion of the world as play, Krishna's delight in sporting with the gopis (female cowherds), and at last Scriabin, ever the optimist, breaks through into an expression of joy, 'the breathlessness of happiness.'[43] Interestingly, in the piece is to be heard the sound of bird-song, a foretaste of Messiaen, Scriabin's obvious successor as composer of the spiritual.

The young 8 year old Pasternak heard this music in 1903 whilst staying at his father's dasha outside Moscow, Scriabin their neighbour. 'For what music it was,' he recollected. 'The symphony was continually crumbling and tumbling like a city under artillery fire and was all the time being built up out of debris and wreckage to the point that was indistinguishable from frenzy and at the same time as new as the forest, breathing life and freshness.' 'In general' Pasternak continued, 'he cultivated various forms of inspired lightness and unencumbered motion on the borderline of flight.'[44] He fell so hopelessly under Scriabin's spell that he mistakenly believed he definitely was to be a composer rather than a poet. Perceptively, Pasternak recognised that Scriabin's belief in the Superman was 'a characteristically Russian craving for the extraordinary' and it took his own insight as a poet to recognise 'those inner correspondences, accessible to music, with the surrounding world, with the way in which people of those days lived, thought and dressed.'[45] Scriabin was entirely at one with the Symbolist poetry of the Silver Age.

Scriabin turned more overtly mystical in his 4th Symphony, *The Poem of Ecstasy,* three years in the writing and first performed in America 10 December 1908 and Russia 19 January 1909. Bowers saw it as a manifesto of sex. The Guardian critic wrote of 'its onanistic throbs' in a promenade performance 21 July 2008 and he may have a point: masturbatory sex permits the most sustained controlled flights of fantasy.[46] It is filled with Scriabin's characteristic recourse to repeated climaxes. Swan saw the theme of the world at play as once again explored, 'its unrestricted activity,' but here the autobiographical content of the 2nd and 3rd 'gives way before a cosmic conception of unheard of dimensions, reincarnated in music as baffling as it is unconvincing.'[47] If Macdonald turns the poetry against the music and sees Scriabin as 'burdened by own creative gift,' he still sees the

work as 'of great strength, vitality and originality': 'the supreme musicianship generated absurd and strictly speaking
redundant fantasies in words.'[48] It is now Taruskin begins to
make exceptional claims for the spiritual in the music. In the
Poem of Ecstasy we hear, he believes, an absolute music,
'capable of directly incorporating and transmitting all the
ineffable – which is to say non-paraphrasable – expressive
and metaphysical content at which the nature-imitating arts
could only hint.'[49] Through 'the dawn of satiety and quies-
cence,' Scriabin has passed from the phenomenal to the
noumenal.

Even more euphoric language describes his final orchestral
piece, the 5th Symphony, *Prometheus, the Poem of Fire*. The
Brussels Theosophical lodge that he joined, Sons of the
Flame of Wisdom, worshipped Prometheus. Scriabin linked
him with Lucifer and Satan. Incidentally, this was also
Marx's favourite myth. And now another of Scriabin's
distinctive interests appears. He shared Rimsky-Korsakov's
synaesthesia, and clearly believed coloured light would
enhance the music. Macdonald, however, sees nothing exceptional here; synaesthesia was a commonplace among
artists of the day. But even he goes along with the spiritual
endeavour of the work: Scriabin has moved beyond the
'ecstatic sensual experience' of the *Poem of Ecstasy* to an
'ecstatic creative experience,' one portraying the birth of
time. In seeking to move beyond time Scriabin's mature
music 'gets as close to the quasi-religious ideal as the
limitations of a merely human art-form allowed.'[50]

Now we hear the famous Promethean chord, the chord of the
pleroma as Scriabin saw it, signalling, quoting Taruskin, 'the
all encompassing hierarchy of the divine realm, located
entirely outside the physical universe, at immeasurable
distance from man's terrestrial abode, totally alien and
essentially "other" to the phenomenal world and whatever
belongs to it.'[51] Here is a music that 'creates no desire,'
offers no ego identification.[52] And this is true, for if there is
that familiar stabbing trumpet sound, both the piano and

violin solos are as if from a distance, there is nothing triumphalist here, though in the final choral moment there is an absolutely blazing visionary sound.

Scriabin fell out with Koussevitsky over payment for the two Russian performances. In February 1913 Henry Wood gave it an acclaimed performance in London though quite a few of the audience did not have the stomach to listen to it the second time round.

Was there to be a third phase, a late Scriabin? The answer lies with his late music for piano. Macdonald goes so far as to compare the late sonatas to Beethoven's last quartets. Two stand out. The 7th, the so called White Mass and a favourite of Scriabin, is almost tinsel light in tone: it as if the fingers are gingerly touching some sacred object. It turns more impassioned before ending once again on an inward note; light and dark compete but the light prevails. In contrast, the 9th, the Black Mass, one Scriabin feared to play, is seen as evil incarnate: in Swan's exaggerated response, 'a diabolic nightmare, a deed of black sacred magic, the most perfidious piece of music ever conceived.' 'A veritable picture of Dorian Gray.'[53] Certainly it strikes a sinister note, as if some intruder had entered the house, and is fiendishly difficult to play, but hardly satanic. Far more revelatory than the late sonatas are Five Short Preludes, and certainly here a new Scriabin is apparent, and, in Macdonald's appreciation, he had at last outreached the poetry: 'Beethoven, who Scriabin despised, could match the density of the music, but few others, not even Schoenberg in his own short pieces of a few years later.'[54] Is this how the Mysterium might have sounded?

So how to assess Scriabin? Macdonald's is the most teasing conclusion. He saw him as the unreconstructed narcissist: 'he lived in a mirrored gallery of tiny dimensions where his own image seemed to him to stretch far in every direction. He lacked common humanity as a man and universality as a musician. He was a monarch of all he surveyed, deluded into believing what he surveyed was the universe itself.' If this is both a snub to the man and to his claim to the spiritual Macdonald comes up with a curious back-handed compliment: 'if however we seize the advantage that music more than any other art possesses, of allowing our imagination and sensitivity to act in place of his (a powerfully self-seeking personality), the music will proclaim its own unquenchable life, independent and sturdy, outliving its creator and aspiring to that immortality to which he imagined he alone held the key.'[55] Taruskin is more generous and wholy persuaded of the music's spirituality: 'we seem to experience an eschatological revelation, a gnosis that only music can impart: the full collapse of time and space in the dissolution of the ego.'[56]

Notes

[1] Hugh Macdonald, *Skryabin*, London: Oxford University Press, 1978, p.7.

[2] Faubion Bowers, *Scriabin: A Biography* (2nd Revised Edition), Mineola, New York: Dover Publications, 1996, p.117. The Black Hundreds were gangs who carried out anti-semitic pogroms.

[3] Bowers, *Scriabin*, Vol.1, pp.109-10.

[4] Bowers, *Scriabin*, Vol.1, p.149.

[5] Bowers, *Scriabin*, Vol.1, p.187.

[6] The strongest case for this is made by Jeffrey J Kripal in his brilliant study of Ramakrishna, *Kali's Child: The Mystical and the Erotic in the Life and Teachings of Ramakrishna*, Chicago: University of Chicago press, 1995. Whilst refusing to see any essentialist connection between homosexuality and mysticism I explore their links in my own study of three English homosexual writers and Indian mysticism, *A Spiritual Bloomsbury: Hinduism and Homosexuality in the Lives and Writing of Edward Carpenter, E.M. Forster and*

Christopher Isherwood, Lanham etc: Lexington Books, 2006.

[7] Quoted Bowers, *Scriabin*, Vol.1, p.226.

[8] His Russian name is spelt Belyayev but he named his publishing firm Belaieff. This is the spelling Bowers uses and is preferred here.

[9] Bowers, *Scriabin*, Vol.1, p.190.

[10] Bowers, *Scriabin*, Vol.1, p.329.

[11] Bowers, *Scriabin*, Vol.1, p.279.

[12] Bowers, *Scriabin*, Vol.2, p.50.

[13] In a letter Scriabin wrote May 1907 from New York, quoted Bowers, *Scriabin*, Vol.2, p.167.

[14] Bowers, *Scriabin*, Vol.2, p.247.

[15] Bowers, *Scriabin*, Vol.2, p.88.

[16] Bowers, *Scriabin*, Vol.1, p.255.

[17] Boris de Schloezer, *Scriabin: Artist and Mystic*, translated by Nicolas Slonimsky, Berkeley and Los Angeles: University of California Press, 1987, p.212.

[18] Orlando Figes, *A People's Tragedy: The Russian Revolution 1891-1924*, London: Pimlico, Random House, 1996, p.208.

[19] John E Bowlt, *Moscow and St Petersburg 1900-1920: Art, Life and Culture in the Russian Silver Age*, New York: The Vendome Press, 2008, p.202.

[20] Bowlt, *Moscow and St Petersburg*, p.92.

[21] Bowlt, *Moscow and St Petersburg*, p.114.

[22] Bowers, *Scriabin*, Vol.2, p.240.

[23] Macdonald, *Skryabin*, p.9.

[24] Bowers, *Scriabin*, Vol.2, p.118.

[25] Schloezer, *Scriabin*, p.66.

[26] Bowers, *Scriabin*, Vol.1, p.138.

[27] Quoted Schloezer, *Scriabin*, p.122.

[28] Schloezer, *Scriabin*, p.141.

[29] For a very scholarly recent study of Aurobindo see Peter Heehs, *The Lives of Sri Aurobindo*, New York: Columbia University Press, 2008.

[30] Schloezer, *Scriabin*, p.174.

[31] Schloezer, *Scriabin*, p.233.

[32] Schloezer, *Scriabin*, p.138.

[33] Leonid Sabaneev, 'Scriabin and the Idea of Religious Art,' *The Musical Times*, 1 September 1931, pp.789-90.

[34] Scruton, *Aesthetics*, pp.277-8.

[35] Macdonald, *Skryabin*, p.28.

[36] Macdonald, *Skryabin*, p.29.

[37] Bowers, *Scriabin*, Vol.1, p.270.

[38] One critic writes of 'this hymn to the greater glory of art' it 'has the effect of pouring a vat of warm treacle over everything that precedes it.' Andrew Clements, *The Guardian*, 18 August 2010. A review of Gergiev's performance at a prom.

[39] Macdonald, *Skryabin*, p.31.

[40] Bowers, *Scriabin*, Vol.1, p.253.

[41] Schloezer, *Scriabin*, p.160.

[42] Schloezer, *Scriabin*, p.180.

[43] Bowers, *Scriabin*, Vol.1, pp.340-41.

[44] Boris Pasternak, *I Remember. Sketch for an Autobiography*, Translated by David Magershack, New York: Pantheon, 1959, pp.36-7.

[45] Pasternak, *I Remember*, pp.42-3.

[46] Tim Ashley, 'A Promenade Performance,' *The Guardian*, 21 July 2008.

[47] Alfred J. Swan, *Scriabin*, London: John Lane, Bodley Head, 1923, p.94.

[48] Macdonald, *Skryabin*, pp.45, 51.

[49] Richard Taruskin, *Defining Russia Musically: Historical and Hermeneutical Essays*, Princeton, New Jersey: Princeton University Press, 1997, p.321.

[50] Macdonald, *Skryabin*, p.54.

[51] Taruskin, *Defining Russia*, p.341.

[52] Taruskin, *Defining Russia*, p.349.

[53] Macdonald, *Skryabin*, pp.105-6.

[54] Macdonald, *Skryabin*, p.67.

[55] Macdonald, *Skryabin*, p.68.

[56] Taruskin, *Defining Russia*, p.349.

4. *Under Soviet Rule*

How were composers to respond to the Revolution and the new Soviet state? If this cannot become a full political history, we have to have some overall idea of how the new regime regarded the intelligentsia and the nature of its drive against spirituality and religion if we are to have any insight into the reaction of Prokofiev and Shostakovich and their successors to their political situation.

Might the composers see virtue in the Revolution? Many interpreters of the Revolution feel that an opportunity to modernise along constitutional and democratic lines was betrayed by the Bolsheviks. Is this fair? Orlando Figes, in his magisterial study *A People's Tragedy,* suggests that under the last two Tsars, Alexander 111 and Nicholas 11, Tsarism set itself against any reformist programme in the name of ancient Byzantine and Muscovite traditions of absolutism. If there were the beginnings of a civil society in the wake of the famine of 1891 it was mortally weakened in the reaction to the Revolution of 1905 and the only serious alternative by 1917 was Revolution. Even a reforming conservative like Stolypin was responsible for the death or exile of some 6000 opponents of the regime and the Tsarist State is seen as unleashing a war of terror against its own people. But the caveat is whether the possibility of a democratic Russia lay in the Constituent Assembly of 1917.

A more serious charge against the Bolsheviks is their failure to build a democracy on the popular base of the Soviets after their seizure of power.

Another very worrying aspect of late Tsarism is the rise of a kind of proto-fascism. Under Alexander 111 in the 1880's and in the aftermath of the 1905 October Manifesto pogroms of the Black Hundreds spread, Jews the special if not only victims, some 3000 murdered in 1905. Then there was the disgraceful Beillis trial in 1913, Russia's Dreyfus affair: the

Tsarist regime had 'committed suicide in the eyes of the civilised world.'[1] During the Civil War the Whites kept up widespread Judeophobia: 'the whole of the White movement was seized by the idea that the persecution of the Jews was somehow justified as a popular means of counter-revolution.'[2] If the record of the Soviet regime on anti-Semitism was itself to become unhealthy, here was good cause to be rid of the Ancien Regime.

The worst legacy of the Tsarist period, and one compounded by the Civil War, was social violence. It was driven by social envy: 'for the vast majority of the Russian people the ending of all social privileges was the basic principle of the revolution.'[3] A loathing of the *burzhoois* was something wider than the middle class, a reference to all internal enemies. It was a social violence rooted in a peasantry often indifferent to human life and, through the migration of the peasantry into the towns, to taint working class militancy: 'a means,' explains Figes, 'of assisting the plebeian crowd and despoiling and destroying symbols of wealth and privilege.'[4] Gorky, the Soviet artist par excellence, had always been aware of 'the exceptional cruelty of the Russian people, and was appalled by peasant violence in 1917 and beyond, with the burning of the manors of the landlords and their libraries. In the cities he witnessed 'pogroms of greed, hatred and vengeance,'[5] though the looting of the wine cellar of the Winter Place was possibly no great crime. And Figes's most telling insight is to see how the violence from below engendered the Terror: 'however hard it may be to admit, there is no doubt that the Terror struck a deep chord in the Russian Civil War mentality and that it had a strange mass appeal.'[6] The new People's Courts were no better than lynch law.

A fatal link was made between this endemic violence and the Bolshevik party. Just possibly Figes is unfair to Lenin but he refuses to see him as the democrat: 'in everything he did Lenin's ultimate purpose was the pursuit of power. Power for him was not a means, it was the end in itself.'[7] Inspired by the hero of Chernychevsky's rebarbative novel *What is to be*

Done, Rachmetev, Lenin made a cult of violence, and the Bolshevik party as a whole acquired a Jacobin syndrome: 'it was as if the cult of violence was central to the Bolshevik self-image, an end in itself rather than a means.'[8] It was acted out in the Revolutionary Tribunals of the Cheka, first version of the Soviet secret police: 'virtually anyone could be arrested and almost anything could be construed as counter-revolutionary behaviour.'[9] Out of Trotsky's war communism, named 'barracks communism' as it was imposed by the Red army, lay the origins of the gulag: 'the mentality of dragooning half-starved peasants into building sites and into factories.'[10] Only a truly threatening rebellion from below by both peasantry and working class against an emergent Bolshevik totalitarian state forced Lenin in 1921 into the respite period of NEP. But no-one could be unaware of its potential menace.

Here was a disturbing new political dispensation for creative artists.

How did the new Soviet state confront the intelligentsia? In fact, as we have seen, this formation divided between the Idealists with their religio-mystical culture during the Silver Age and the Marxist materialists. Could Russian spirituality survive under the new order? The fate of two of its leading lights, Nikolai Berdyaev and Semyon Frank, will illustrate this story.

In Lesley Chamberlain's persuasive analysis,[11] Berdyaev emerges as the leading exponent of this spirituality. He was a fascinatingly ambiguous figure. With 'his long hair and hard, bright visionary eyes,' 'a disturbed adult who with the addition of further psychic ingredients, could be possessed,' he seems a character out of a Dostoyevsky novel. He came from a military noble family in Kiev. He drew his inspiration from the great spiritual thinker of the 19th century, Vladimir Solovyov. Otherwise his mysticism grew out of Plato, Plotinus, the Greek Church Fathers, Nicholas of Cusa and Jacob Boehme. He was wedded to the idea of Russia possessing a unique Truth; were it to abandon its Christian mysticism it would lose its humanity. But he shared the vision of the radical intelligentsia that Russia had to undergo a spiritual renewal. He never looked back and saw it as his life's work to spiritualise the new revolutionary society. It looked as if he might be given that opportunity for, post the revolution and during the Civil War, he opened in Moscow his Religio-Philosophical Academy, became Professor of Philosophy at the University of Moscow and President of the Union of Writers.

Semyon Frank came from a middle class background, Jewish on his father's side, and was altogether a more sober character. He was a conventional philosopher but a theocrat, a committed defendant of orthodoxy. He was convinced the new Russia had to be grounded in religious, moral values if it were not to go astray. He stood for the sacredness of private experience. For a while he ran a Historical-Philological faculty in the University of Saratov, but retreated to Berdyaev's Academy in Moscow, and just in time, for two Saratov academics were imprisoned for questioning dialectical materialism and suggesting there might be a God. But there was an altogether more terrifying warning in the so called Tagantsev affair, when a Cheka-inspired trial condemned completely innocent academics and writers in Petrograd of treason. Gumilyvov, one of Russia's leading poets, was.murdered. Anna Akhmatova had been his first wife.

Lenin was almost pathologically hostile to this spirituality. He saw it as a battle to the death between Rationalism and Idealism. Lenin himself was a crude positivist. His opponents saw him as subject to 'the tyranny of vulgarity': 'no-one in the history of philosophy had ever expressed himself so bluntly and with such violence.'[12] Here was a new Jacobin-style cult of Reason. His was an Enlightenment project, 'forcing less-than-rational, unkempt, spontaneous, spiritual Russia into harness.'[13] To talk of an inner world was to talk of phantoms. The private was to be entirely subsumed by the public. For Lenin, Berdyaev was 'the prime symbol of the mystical world the rational Lenin wanted to banish.'[14] When Lenin was felled by the first of his strokes 25 May 1922 Trotsky took up the cudgels. He saw Berdyaev as no better than a member of the Black Hundreds and a fascist and believed Frank was capable of encouraging counter-revolution in the name of the Orthodox Church. Interestingly, Trotsky was the first to recognize the phenomenon of 'inner migration,' the way out for those intellectuals who might have endorsed the original revolution but then came to despise the new regime. Was that indeed a definition of Shostakovich? He intriguingly had been playmates of a son of the Losskys, amongst those to be exiled. On 28 September 1922 Berdyaev and Frank, along with a generation of fellow Idealists, were banished. Both kept alive the traditions of Russian mysticism and the faith till their deaths, Berdyaev in Paris in 1948, Frank in Hendon, Britain, 1950.

But how on earth was a creative artist to deal with such an assault on the spiritual?

Spirituality came under for more vindictive assault than religion under the Soviet system. But no totalitarian regime could tolerate a separate sphere of religious belief and inevitably it too came under ruthless attack. At the outset the Bolsheviks were too preoccupied with mere survival to give full attention to dealing with the rivalry of the Russian Orthodox Church. They began by seizing all church lands and proceeded 23 January 1918 to separate Church and State. Tragically, this was to be no Cavourian solution of a free church in a free state. The Russian Orthodox Church was to be given little opportunity for reform as progressives had sought under Tsarism. The Bolsheviks quickly set about humiliating the church by prizing open the tombs of saints to expose the decomposition of their bodies. But the new Patriarch, Tikhon, like the spiritualist philosophers, was initially set to one side. The ideological retreat of NEP in the economic sphere compelled Lenin to step up in the cultural. Dechristianisation began in earnest.

By way of seeking a scapegoat for the terrible famine of 1921 all church valuables were seized. To meet the oppostion, especially fierce at Shuya, some one hundred miles north east of Moscow, the new Metropolitan of Petrograd, Veniamin was arrested and executed, and between 1922-3 some 7, 100 clergy and 3, 500 nuns were murdered. Patriarch Tikhon was also arrested though international protest facilitated his release, if only after he had pleaded guilty. He died 1925. The Bolsheviks seemed to recognise the enormity of their programme for they fell back on a policy of divide and rule, favouring the pro-Bolshevik reformist Renovationist church and privileging the sects, granting them, for example, the right to set up their own agricultural communes. Debates between believers and atheists, set up by Lunacharsky, proved counter-productive and were withdrawn. And it has been argued that the Bolsheviks were always driven more by considerations of power than ideological concerns. They made a connection between religion and the threat from the non-Russian nationalities. Their primary aim was to contain counter-revolution.

Even so, there was an ideological campaign.[15] A special Anti-Religious Commission was set up under Yaroslavksy, one of Stalin's protégés and a great survivor. For Stalin, the former seminarian, 'giving up the Orthodox faith and Georgian nationality symbolized something mystical to him. Turning to socialism was an initiation into a new godless international brotherhood.'[16] There was a new newspaper, *Bezbozhnik*, The Godless, and its atheist propaganda was to be spread by the League of the Militant Godless, set up in 1925. Initially the League under Yaroslavsky's Presidency stuck by his preference for propaganda over Kostelovskaia's for a more aggressive interventionist campaign.

Soviet dechristianisation was always part of a far greater project of social engineering. Their greatest fear of counter-revolution, and seemingly the greatest barrier to the Soviet vision of a new proletarian and industrial society, lay with the peasantry. In 1929 Stalin through collectivisation launched the most revolutionary programme to date. By playing off imaginary strata of poor and middle peasants against the so-called rich peasants, the Kulak, cast as a class villain – and it is important to recognise that the same mentality as branded Jews sub-human in Nazi propaganda was used in Soviet propaganda against the Kulak – Stalin sought to browbeat the whole peasant community into collectivist agriculture. One way to intimidate the peasantry was to step up the attack on religion, with the church being the focal point of village life. There was some resistance to the closure of churches but the peasantry was often passive in the face of such outrageous force.

The radical interventionists now saw that their hour had come. Although the League expanded to a membership of 5.5 million by 1932 its intellectual calibre was always poor. The Komsomol were drawn into this crude assault on religion though, given Figes's telling description of it 'as a social club for bored teenagers,'[17] this may not have greatly altered the outcome. One suspects soldiers and workers drafted in were far more intimidating. Even so, the Komsomol was a breeding ground for anti-religious views, seen by the young as a progressive outlook. Another means had been the setting up of Anti-Religious Universities, 84 by 1931. Increasingly, the League and the Komsomol became but instruments of the Communist party in imposing totalitarian political control. Even so, the damage to the organisational strength of the Russian Orthodox Church was huge and by 1939 it had reached its nadir. In Pskov, for example, 19 out of 23 churched had been closed and most of its clergy arrested.

But a more insidious attack on the church than such vandalism lay in the attempt to fashion an alternative church, a new secular faith. The Bolsheviks simply plagiarised the rituals of Orthodoxy and replaced its baptism, marriage and funeral services by Octobering, Red Weddings and Revolutionary Funerals. The service of Transfiguration was replaced by one of Industrialisation. They tried to introduce a new calendar.

The cult of Lenin became central to the new secular religion. Here a simply massive programme of social engineering was at work and Daniel Peris, historian of this process, conceded that 'the contemporary sincerity of the effort to forge a new Homo Sovieticus cannot be denied.'[18]

But the state was up against deeper loyalties than to the rituals of the church. The peasantry clung to more ancient pagan loyalties. 'Transforming rural religion,' states Peris, 'would require that popular culture be comprehensively re-created.'[19] You could insist that the peasants replace their icons in the icon corners of their homes by a portrait of Lenin and turn them into godless corners, but would this work? The evidence suggests that the old ways continued on into the 1930's. The State had no option but to turn a blind eye to such expression of the faith outside the churches. Soviet propagandists acknowledged the failure of its programme, 'not offering atheism per se as a substitute faith but promoting instead vague ever changing "scientific materialism", a philosophical world view of any proper Marxist-Leninist.'[20] And, of course, the party was itself driven increasingly by other than ideological concerns: 'material advantages – privileged access to housing and health care and a superior education for their children – were what motivated the nomenclatura.'[21]

But none of this describes the sinister way the Soviet system tried to control the mind. As Figes puts it: 'any distinction between private and public life was explicitly rejected by the Bolsheviks.'[22] The very word for 'conscience' all but disappears and is replaced by one implying the idea of consciousness. Cleverly the Soviet system exploited a Russian Orthodox tradition for public confession, and the role of denunciation infiltrated society. If the secret police had an army of informers by the mid-1930's it was less through the secret police themselves and more by a system of self-policing that the surveillance society worked: 'the idea of mutual surveillance was fundamental to the Soviet system.'[23]

Each individual became defined by a relationship to the State. Is anything left of the autonomous personality?

In his remarkable novel *Life and Fate* Vasily Grossman did not give up on the individual. He posed the question that is at the heart of the Soviet story and the creative artist: 'does human nature undergo a true change in the cauldron of totalitarian violence? Does man lose his yearning for freedom? The fate of both man and the totalitarian State depends on the answer to this question. If human nature does change, then the eternal and world-wide triumph of the dictatorial state is assured; if his yearning for freedom remains constant, then the totalitarian state is doomed.' Grossman was an optimist and believed that the individual's yearning for freedom never went away. To quote again: 'his yearning was suppressed but it continued to exist. Man's fate may make him a slave but his human nature remains unchanged. Man's innate yearning for freedom can be suppressed but never destroyed.' 'Human groupings have one main purpose,' one character in the novel asserts, 'to answer everyone's right to be different, to be special, to think, feel and live in his or her way.'[24] If the very pressures of totalitarianism forced on all but the exceptionally brave a double life, it had necessarily to be through a kind of subterfuge that the creative artist sought to express that sense of individuality. This is the source under the Soviet system of the expression of the spiritual.

The composers under review reacted differently to the challenge to religion but all were affected by the greater Soviet threat to spirituality. If Shostakovich as an atheist may have been less concerned by the persecution of Orthodoxy than Prokofiev, a convert to Christian Science, the later generation of Alfred Schnittke and Sofia Gubaidulina, as believers, were clearly distressed, as were the Catholic composers of the Polish Renaissance and Protestant Arvo Pärt. The Soviet brand of totalitarianism was more dirigiste than the Nazi in trying to shape the creative life of its artists. As the film director Aleksandr Sokurov pithily puts it: 'the totalitarian state doesn't have the objective of destroying artists but of making them submit to its influence.'[25] So firstly to Prokofiev, though he is inevitably paired with Shostakovich.

Notes

[1] Figes, *A People's Tragedy*, p.244.
[2] Figes, *A People's Tragedy*, p.676.
[3] Figes, *A People's Tragedy*, p.521.
[4] Figes, *A People's Tragedy*, p.188.
[5] Figes, *A People's Tragedy*, p.495.
[6] Figes, *A People's Tragedy*, p.525.
[7] Figes, *A People's Tragedy*, p.504.
[8] Figes, *A People's Tragedy*, p.505.
[9] Figes, *A People's Tragedy*, p.535.
[10] Figes, *A People's Tragedy*, p.723.
[11] Lesley Chamberlain, *The Philosophy Steamer: Lenin and the Exile of the Intelligentsia*, London: Atlantic Books, 2006. References here to the paperback edition, 2007.
[12] Chamberlain, *The Philosophy Steamer*, p.28.
[13] Chamberlain, *The Philosophy Steamer*, p.270.
[14] Chamberlain, *The Philosophy Steamer*, p.31.
[15] Two good sources for this dechristianisation campaign are Arto Luukanen, *The Party of Unbelief: The Religious Policy of the Bolshevik Party 1917-1929*, Helsinki: Studia Historica, 1994; Daniel Peris, *Storming the Heavens The Soviet League of the Militant Godless*, Cornell University Press, 1998.
[16] Luukanen, *The Party of Unbelief*, p.45.
[17] Figes, *A People's Tragedy*, p.790.
[18] Peris, *Storming the Heavens*, p.71.
[19] Peris, *Storming the Heavens*, p.21.
[20] Peris, *Storming the Heavens*, p.93.
[21] John Gray, 'Tyrannies of Old,' *New Statesman*, 31August 2009.
[22] Figes, *The Whisperers*, p.37.

[23] Figes, *The Whisperers*, p.180.
[24] Grossman, *Life and Fate*, pp.199-200, 214.
[25] Steve Rose, 'Delusions and grandeur,' *The Guardian*, 15 November 2011.

5. *Sergei Prokofiev*

Prokofiev and Shostakovich belonged almost to two different generations. Prokofiev, born 15 April 1891, old calendar, 27 April new, grew up in Russia's Silver Age, Shostakovich, born 25 September 1906, was always far more the composer of the Soviet period. One indication of their difference lies in their response to Scriabin, Prokofiev playing his music right through to concerts in America in the 1920's, Shostakovich branding him 'our bitterest musical enemy.'[1] Prokofiev was always far more the traveller, with a prolonged period of exile, 1918 to 1936: Shostakovich, heavily restricted in his freedom to travel, tied to Russia. Temperamentally they were far apart, the breezy, arrogant Prokofiev compared to the introverted, conflicted Shostakovich. Or is this unfair to Prokofiev? If David Nice writes of 'his usual tactless petulance, '[2] Simon Morrison,[3] on the evidence of unpublished private diaries Prokofiev kept in the 1930's, sees a less abrasive and more generous personality. But of course one overwhelming fact drew them together, how to survive as creative artists under Soviet totalitarianism. Not that they sought each other out to meet the challenge: Prokofiev was invariably rather patronising towards Shostakovich, and Shostakovich was, as ever, morbidly shy. One has a sense of Prokofiev in his early life as the prima donna, trying to live up to his reputation as an enfant terrible, but forced by the exceptional pressure of events, following his return to Russia, finally to grow up and to come to terms with the full horror of the human struggle, whereas Shostakovich was always embattled. The question here is, does their struggle for self-expression partake of the spiritual?

Prokofiev's biographer sees him as a 'confident, self-renewing personality.' Maybe more can be made of his being a gifted chess player, who could challenge and beat Capablanca: 'Capablanca's self-confidence in the virtues of precision and simplicity were essentially his own.'[4] He was un-Russian: 'no composer on the face of it is less representative than Prokofiev of the Dostoyevskyan chaos, contradictor-iness and darkness the westerner expects from a Russian creative artist.'[5] He lacked the anguish of Shostakovich. Yet the way Russia drew him back from exile and how this supremely self-confident man entered into a struggle, almost literally to the death, with Stalinist Russia and, in the process, discovered his own spiritual humanism is an exceptional story of self-discovery.[6]

Family

His was a happy childhood in the Ukraine. His father, an agronomist and estate manager, is seen as essentially a typical liberal of the 1860's. His early death at 64, 23 July 1910 left Prokofiev in search of father figures. Morrison makes the point that Prokofiev was peculiarly dependent on mentors: 'he channelled his creative energies through the visions of others.' Diaghilev, Meyerhold and Eisenstein cited as examples. But then adds in a brilliant insight: 'official artistic doctrine became his muse.'[7] But the stronger influence on him was his mother, serf by background, quick to see and nurture his musical talent. She was to join him in exile. She died 13 December 1924. His Aunt Katya, until her death in 1929, was the last of his mother figures.

There is little of Scriabin's melodrama in Prokofiev's personal life. There were romantic friendships with men in his youth, the best known with the homosexual pianist, Maximilian Schmidthof, who pestered him to play his concertos. Just how disturbed was Prokofiev by his suicide in 1913? Schmidthof's sister, Katya was still asking for financial help on his first return from exile in 1927. Prokofiev writes of her asking for help 'in the same sweet unceremonious manner her brother would affect when touching me for money.'[8] He transferred moneys to her and showered her with gifts on his departure. Prokofiev never wholly shook off the rumour that he was bi-sexual but that is hardly surprising for someone part of the Diaghilev circle. In 29 September 1923 there was a civil wedding with the Spanish singer – she was already expecting a child – Lina Lodina, a happy marriage, blessed with two sons. But it was to break down on his return. His first meeting with the Jewish Mira Abramovna Mandelson was in the Caucasus resort of Kislovodsk. Lina resorted to Christian Science beliefs to win him back. She accused Mira of seducing him, and threatened she 'would rob his life of spiritual purpose, earthly desire stood in the way of the divine.'[9] But 15 March 1941 Prokofiev left Lina and the children to live with Mira. Not until 13 January 1948 did they marry but then the regime closed in with a vengeance. Lina, always at risk as a foreigner, was arrested 20 February 1948 for espionage and sentenced to twenty years in the gulag, only to be released 30 January 1956. Thereafter the two wives battled over the composer's inheritance. Mira died 6 June 1960, Lina, at 91, 3 January 1989. All this had profoundly disturbed Prokofiev and Morrison states from 1948 his career 'went into free fall.'[10]

Christian Science

Was Prokofiev religious, let alone spiritual? Soviet historian, Sheila Fitzpatrick rather dramatically begins her review of Simon Morrison's book: 'now comes the shocker from Simon Morrison, Princeton musicologist: Prokofiev *wanted* to write simple, life-affirming music because he was a Christian Scientist.'[11] There was some attachment to Orthodoxy from childhood. His father was an atheist but his mother, if her faith wavered through the death of two daughters, brought her son up with some respect for Orthodox rituals and certainly they attended church at Easter. When visiting a church in the Kremlin on his return in 1927, 'I was embarrassed at entering a church in a hat and decided to take mine off,' only to be told that churches were now seen as museums.[12] Nor was Prokofiev entirely impervious to the spirituality of the Silver age, for he shared in its neo-paganism and a cult of the sun: here he was at one with Scriabin's 'reaching out to the divine self.'[13] But Nice's summary maybe the best we have to date: 'no dabbler in Ouija boards or visitor to fortune tellers Prokofiev drew the spiritual line at an attachment to Christian Science which begins in the early 1920's but even this was to try and give meaning to his ambition and achievements.'[14]

Quite why he and his wife converted is never fully explained. Christian science, founded by Mrs Mary Baker Eddy (1821-1910), its first church opened in 1879, was one of several new faiths Protestant America and Canada engendered at the time; 'an observer might almost conclude if there was some ecological niche unfulfilled, some discernible human need unmet, this environment would find someone who could reveal a new redemptive pattern.'[15] In her *Science and Health* (1875) Mrs Eddy claimed mind prevailed over body and that health could always be restored by right thinking. Prokofiev clearly believed 'that sickness was an illusion that stemmed from a loss of harmony with the godhead.'[16] Was all this brought about by recovery from a life-threatening illness in March 1919 from scarlet fever and diphtheria and a throat abscess?: 'I had slowed down a little before my illness but the fever seemed to have cleansed me and I returned to work with renewed vigour.'[17]

He responded to other faiths: he was much moved by the singing of the Benedictine monks at Ettal in the Bavarian Alps in 1923 and enjoyed long conversations with Father Isodore. Was he also affected by attending nearby the Passion play at Oberammergau?

And this should put us on our guard at overemphasizing the political in explaining Prokofiev. Morrison puts this case very strongly: 'committed to sustaining a positive outlook that denied any finality or legitimacy to evil, he could not have imagined that his future career would be immortalized – and trivialised – in history textbooks as a parable about the traumatic upheavals of twentieth-century life.' His faith was a vital form of self-protection: 'in the 1930's and 1940's he succeeded in tailoring his religious sentiments in a creative context that was relentlessly hostile to them.'[18] In all kinds of ways his Christian Science beliefs were to influence his music: 'Christian Science is helping me enormously in my music. To put it more exactly, I do not see any more of my music outside of Science.'[19] This can be exemplified in many ways; his insistence on a happy ending for the ballet *Romeo and Juliet*;[20] seeing in Fortinbras's speech at the end of *Hamlet* 'a paean to the human spirit, the manifestation of the divine.'[21] It seems Soviet theatre may have ruled out the religious but not the transcendent.

Could Prokofiev square his faith with Soviet ideology? 'In his wartime and post-wartime statements,' Morrison claims, 'Prokofiev fashioned the discourse of Christian Science to accord with the discourse of Socialist Realism.'[22] But it proved an impossible synthesis. The failure of his socialist realist opera *A Story of a Real Man* brought this home to him: 'he could not artistically overcome what could not be defined.'[23] Transcendence had in the end proved impossible. Yet Morrison's conclusion is upbeat: 'here one confronts, in all its oddness, the twist of fate that brought a Christian Scientist home to Stalin's Russia. Much as Christian Science urged its believers to look towards the light, so did the positive – or to invoke a Soviet cliché, "life-affirming" – sentiments of Prokofiev's music privilege exhilarated listener engagement. Even as his career turned tragic, his works celebrated on their own terms, a state of happiness.'[24]

But there was a more obviously spiritual dimension to Prokofiev's outlook. In 1917 he undertook a serious reading of Kant and Schopenhauer. Here was evidence of his seeking a hidden meaning beyond the phenomenal world, Schopenhauer's belief that in music we can know the *Ding an sich* (thing in itself). He even named some piano pieces *Chose en soi*. It may not be much to go on but it suggests Prokofiev in his music sought the noumenal.[25]

Return of the Exile

Prokofiev is a telling case of the impossibility of escaping the political in the 20th century. The paradox is the political being the forcing house of his spirituality. Under Tsarism he had been curiously privileged. His talent was soon recognised. Diaghilev, for one, refused to be put off by his arrogance and recognised his genius. As a widow's only son he was exempted from military service. How much attention did he pay to the revolutionary events of 1905 and 1917? In 1905 he signed a student letter of protest threatening to leave the Conservatoire. He claimed to have welcomed February 1917 'with open arms. I was in the streets of Petrograd while the fighting was going on, hiding behind corners when the shooting came too close.'[26]

Admittedly he had great trouble getting his works performed 1916-18 and Nice sees these years just as taxing as the later Soviet years. Whereas so many artists were caught up in the new Soviet regime Prokofiev kept his distance: 'he had little to fear from Lenin's regime; his contacts with it were small but select.'[27] He later admitted: 'I had not the slightest idea of the scope and significance of the October Revolution. It never occurred to me that like any other citizen I might be of use to it,' but equally, 'had been subconsciously affected by the revolutionary events that had shaken Russia to it foundations' and wished to write 'something huge, something cosmic.' This was his cantata, *Seven, They are Seven.*[28] Gorky this time had him spared conscription.

Above all he was protected by his relationship with Anatol Lunacharsky, First Soviet Commissar for Education and the Arts. Chamberlain sees this failed playwright as 'a weak character, something of an actor.'[29] Did Prokofiev know of his strange experiment pre-revolution, together with Gorky, the VPERED (Forward) group, to shape a new working class culture, a forerunner of the Proletkult?: 'Marxism was to be seen as a form of religion, only with humanity as the Divine Being and collectivism as the Holy Spirit.'[30] And

Lunacharsky was to be so upset by the false rumour of the destruction of St Basil's cathedral that he resigned. In fact he revelled in his new post and soon withdrew his resignation. Here was a Bolshevik 'as "soft God-seeker", with a philosophical curiosity that verged on the mystical.'[31] This was the man who protected Prokofiev's interests till his fall in 1929. He let him leave in 1918: 'you are a revolutionary in music as we are in life – we should work together. But if you want to go to America I will not stand in your way.'[32] At the time a friend warned him: 'you are running away from history and history will never forgive you: when you return you will not be understood.'[33] When he met up again with Lunarchasky in 1927 Prokofiev found him a 'bit flabby compared with how he was in 1918.' He was not quite sure what to make of his compliments of *Love of Three Oranges*: 'as if he were paying a compliment to a young lady, so sweetly I couldn't think what to reply.'[34] But possibly he should have paid more attention to Lunacharsky's telling him 'on balance he would like to leave the Ministry of Enlightenment, at the same time trying to suppress a giggle.'[35] Lunacharsky's days were numbered. And Prokofiev, despite interesting Meyerhold in the case, got nowhere in securing the release of his cousin, Shurik, from prison.

In many ways Prokofiev's dicing over his return remains enigmatic. Admittedly under NEP music in the Soviet regime was every bit as modernistic, or, to use the Soviet word formalistic, as in the West. Did Prokofiev hope when he first returned from 19 January to 23 March 1927 to profit from this permissiveness? But all this dramatically changed through the cultural revolution and the ultra-leftism of RAPM, the Russian Association of Proletarian Musicians. Did he pay no attention to the fact that three who did return, Mayakovsky, Marina Tsvetaeva, Esenin, all committed suicide? He was certainly close to Mayakovsky. And on his return in 1927 was present when the poet read out a poem querying why Gorky stayed in exile. Almost certainly Gorky's return was the telling example. But we now know from his unpublished diaries that during all those four visits,

1929-34, including his final return in June 1936 that he had no intention of settling for good. Nice argues he saw it as relocation rather than repatriation. Had he been fooled, as so many were, by the replacement of RAPM by the Union of Composers: 'the long term implications of centralized control did not occur to most creative artists, relief at being freed from the strictures of the Jacobin fringe group overshadowed all considerations.'[36] And Donald Sassoon[37] has shown that, for all the dirigisme of the regime, Soviet composers were in all sorts of ways materially benefited. Prokofiev was assured of a good flat, educational benefits for his children and good health care.

Most importantly, he was convinced that his works would be performed in Russia. Had he not done enough to ingratiate himself with the regime through his ballet *Pas d'Acier,* ostensibly all about a Soviet factory, and his highly popular film music for *Lieutenant Kije*? Besides, the new ideology of socialist realism laid down in 1932 was so indeterminate when it came to music, surely, he felt, his New Simplicity, his way of characterising his new style, would meet its requirements of accessibility and happiness? 'And he really did want to evoke 'the heroic aspects of socialist construction. The new man. The struggle to overcome obstacles.'[38] 'All I missed was the bigger picture and that it seemed,' Prokofiev felt, 'only the Soviet regime could provide.'[39] The Soviet authorities certainly saw him a major catch. But Russia was already in the grip of Terror. Prokofiev had been deceived by his extraordinary self-confidence. He had entered a trap.

Terror moved in waves and Prokofiev returned between those of 1934-5 and 1937-8. It is tempting to see Stalin as but a latterday Caligula, exercising merely arbitrary power. He was bent on setting up untramelled personal rule. But it was more than mere megalomania. In the early 1930's Terror was a means of controlling a society subject to violent change through collectivisation. And Stalin recognised that Russia had to industrialise to meet the threat from Nazism. In Orlando Figes's interpretation the Yezhov terror of 1937-8 was a means of stifling any form of opposition in the event of a German invasion, for had not the revolution itself been a product of war? But the search for imagined traitors took on a monstrous paranoid dimension.

Yet behind this horror a new kind of Communist party was emerging, an elite of industrial and technical intelligenstia, together with the military and the police. Could Prokofiev adjust to this new society?

Religion and Spirituality in Prokofiev's Music

Is there a divide between the music of exile and of return? An underlying lyricism, what indeed Prokofiev highlighted in his concept of New Simplicity, connects all his work. One contemporary critic felt the earlier work had the edge: 'all the same, the exorcising of the old *diablerie* leaves an impression of insipidity. The lyrical Prokofiev is delicious as a foil; it is not quite good enough to stand on its own; it is egg without the salt.'[40] But Gerald Abrahams was writing before the late symphonies. There is of course another teasing question. At what point did Prokofiev become a truly serious artist? He was always something of an 18th century court composer, ready to please any patron. Distinctively, the music of exile has religious themes. Obviously in atheist Russia this was all but banned and following his return Prokofiev, forced to mature as a human being and undertake an altogether tougher self-exploration, discovers an entirely new music of spirituality. The focus will be on the symphonies. I was fortunate enough to hear a performance of the entire cycle by the London Symphony orchestra, under Valery Gergiev, at the Edinburgh festival 2008.

3rd Symphony

He was always a great recycler and his 3rd Symphony largely flowed from his opera *The Fiery Angel*. The libretto was based on the Russian Symbolist Valery Bryusov's novel, published in 1910 in the journal *Very* (The Scales). Set in the 16th century Italian Renaissance, a time of alchemy and magic, it is a story of sexual and religious obsession, of a hysteric, Renata, driven to a frenzy of love though the Devil's deluding her into believing that the godlike, blond Count Heinrich was Madiell, the Fiery Angel. The story is narrated through the memory of Ruprecht, landknecht, sailor and gold-digger, a self-taught individualist. Prokofiev came across the novel in America in 1920, immediately set about writing a score, though he took quite some liberties with the plot. Ruprecht becomes just a gullible knight, recruited by Renata in her visionary quest for Heinrich. Renata enters a convent and proceeds to infect the nuns with her hysteria. Interestingly, Prokofiev was staying near Ettal monastery in Bavaria at the time of writing the score. If Prokofiev clung to the role of magic in the opera, it is seen as a dead-end. He had not been seduced by the occult. Completed in 1925, plans for a production in America in 1926 fell through, likewise under Bruno Walter in Berlin in 1927 and Prokofiev had to settle for but a concert performance of the 2nd act in Paris in 1928. Indeed, a full concert performance had to wait till 1954 in Paris. Later, he recalled: 'I wrote a great deal of music for it, but I never had any luck with it.'[41] So Prokofiev compromised by turning it into a symphony, first perform-ed under Pierre Monteux in Paris, 17 May 1929. David Fanning[42] sees the First movement as anticipating Alfred Schnittke's First Symphony, beyond anything in the Polish Renaissance of the 50's and 60's, and certainly beyond any-thing of the neo-Stravinskyian community at the time. In fact, even Stravinsky, always sniffy of Prokofiev's music, praised its first movement.

My own response to hearing Gergiev's highly intelligent reading of the Symphony was of its being so much more coherent than the Second, of Prokofiev exploring the false spirituality of Renata, and of his anticipating the collective mania of Huxley's *Devils of Loudun* and Arthur Miller's *The Crucible*. He saw it as 'one of my best compositions' and, indeed, it moved beyond being a Fiery Angel Symphony into being 'a pure symphony.'[43]

4th Symphony

The 4th Symphony was likewise recycled, this time from the Ballet, *The Prodigal Son*. This had been Diaghilev's brain child – by 1929 biblical themes had become fashionable – and it was to be the last production of the Ballets Russes during his life-time. He died 19 August 1929. The biblical story was modified, sisters were added, the riotous living of the prodigal son became orgies. It was all to Prokofiev's liking: 'It is seldom,' he wrote to his Christian Science friend, Warren Klein, 'that I have worked with such pleasure as I did on the piece.'[44] Did he, as an exile, identify with the story of the prodigal son?

He would have known of Rembrandt's painting in the Hermitage though on his visit 10 February 1927 his official guide chose to privilege the jewelry. Does he convey, to quote Simon Schama in his study of Rembrandt, a son 'broken by the journey from transgression to atonement' or a father whose gesture of forgiveness is also 'an act of resurrection, a transformation of death into life.'?[45] Possibly, for Prokofiev vividly describes how the prodigal son in the final scene of the ballet 'crawled across the whole stage on his knees, staff in hand, the upper part of his body moving with remarkable plasticity.'[46]

Would he have shared the Dutch theologian, Henri Nouwen's reading of the painting as an invitation to identify with both the prodigal and elder son before, as we mature, with the forgiving father?[47]

The ballet was in fact successfully performed in both Paris and London so its transformation into a symphony was not this time the rescue of a neglected work. Koussevitsky commissioned it for the 50th anniversary of the Boston Symphony orchestra in 1930. The music, in fact, considerably varied from that of the ballet and Prokofiev was subsequently in 1947 to revise it heavily, to bring it into line with Soviet expectations of the positive. Morrison interprets this as amending 'the tale of an uncertain, questing liberal filtered through a heroic paradigm.'[48]

As I heard the work in Edinburgh, Prokofiev clearly revelled in describing the scenes of corruption and the orgies in the First Movement, whilst portraying the father's forgiving in the Second in gentler, more lyrical tones. The Third describes seduction by the Siren, the Fourth returns to the orgiastic theme of the first.

Concerto for Cello and Orchestra

So to the Soviet years and his extraordinarily painful process of self-discovery. He deceived himself that he was free to write as he liked. In an interview in 1937 with the Russian emigré in America, Vernon Duke, he claimed: 'here is how I feel about it. I care nothing for politics – I'm a composer first and last.' As long as the authorities left him free to compose and perform his work he was happy with his life in Russia.[49] His new kind of Simplicity would meet the requirements of socialist realism. But he deceived himself. Sheila Fitzpatrick has the brilliant insight 'that Soviet-flavoured simplicity, coming from a sophisticated European like Prokofiev could look like sarcasm or parody.'[50] Prokofiev himself saw that in his desire to avoid falling back on the old formulas of the old simplicity the new 'with its novel forms and chiefly new tonal structures was not understood.'[51] Critical response to his Concerto for Cello and Orchestra, begun in 1935 but only completed on his return and performed in 1938, proves her point. The critic, A Ostretsov damned it: 'it re-echoes with moods of the disillusioned and weary art of the urbanized lyricist of the contemporary west.' He continued: 'we do not share the composer's humanistic sympathy with these persons. ... To mirror aright the anaemic "superfluous man" of the contemporary west, one must go some distance away from him – the distance of the Soviet witness watching the downfall of a dying class.' 'We hear it as a symphonic monologue for the few, as a sad story of the overblown culture of individualism.'[52]

In fact when I heard this piece I was disappointed – it seemed to me rather grounded and that Prokofiev's imagination had failed to take flight. Subsequently, through the genius of Rostropovitch's playing, it was redeemed and performed as his Cello Concerto No 2 in 1952.

And if we see this as a work of unrepentant individualism, there were to be a horrible warning. He was due to work with Meyerhold in a production of *Hamlet* but 20 June 1939 the theatre producer was arrested, charged, amongst other errors, with privileging abstraction and experiment at the expense of the Russian people in a production of *Boris Gudonov*. His wife was murdered 16 July 1939, and he was executed 1 February 1940. In a lecture wisely never published, Prokofiev demurred: 'the official directive concerning the struggle against Formalism has been carried out too zealously.'[53] He could not even win with a Cantata to Stalin. Morrison suggests setting Stalin's words to music was not intrinsically different to Beethoven Schiller's. And there were to be many other examples of this pathetic attempt by Prokofiev to sell his soul to the system. Did he betray his underlying integrity?: the cantata 'upheld beliefs in transcendence and transformation, beliefs formed in political as well as religious faith.'[54]

And did he really believe he was immune to the Terror?: 'Prokofiev maintained the air – the external semblance of indifference,'[55] but friends abroad found him 'introverted and intemperate.'[56] Following his last visit abroad 16 April 1938 he had to exchange his external passport for an internal and never got it back. His children anyway had always been held as hostages. Yet this imprisoning climate was to be the context for the discovery of an entirely new spirituality in his music. Here we will overlook much of his late music, the opera *War and Peace*, the film music for *Alexander Nevsky* and *Ivan the Terrible,* in favour of his final three symphonies.

5th Symphony

Necessarily there had to be a let up in terror if the Russian people were to be drawn into a war of patriotic defence. Already in 1940 many prisoners, though not the political, were released from the gulag. Following the German invasion of Russia in June 1941 the regime saw the wisdom of a cultural thaw. To survive, the regime needed every measure of public support. Some freedom was granted to the Orthodox Church and many churches reopened: 'public displays of religious patriotism were permitted, though not exactly encouraged.'[57] In fact there was to be a dramatic revival of religious life 1943-8. Some saw 'a sort of spiritual purification, a violent purging of "the inhuman power of the lie."'[58] And, indeed, for many there was liberation from fear, a kind of 'spontaneous' de-stalinization. Artists felt somewhat freer.

In the years 1943-8 Prokofiev wrote his finest music. The paradox for Prokofiev is that in his 5th Symphony, his darkest commentary on Stalinism, seemingly he came into line with the expectations of the doctrines of socialist realism. He saw it as 'the triumph of the human spirit.'[59] In the first movement David Fanning[60] hears a sense of heroic inspiration, akin to the patriotic music of *Ivan the Terrible*, indeed just that lyricism the Composers Union had been looking for. I experienced the movement rather differently, a sense of a dying fall, the fluttering descent of a stricken bird, echoing the doomed love of Romeo and Juliet from his ballet suite. In the second movement, again with reference to the ballet, Fanning sees the opening up of 'a chamber of horrors.' The third is 'drawn inexorably towards fatalism,' 'at one point going into an overt funeral march.' But then comes that extraordinary lyrical final movement, ostensibly about the war, but surely to be heard as a defiance of Stalinism and a triumphant reassertion of the human spirit. Prokofiev had in fact betrayed socialist realism through this very passionate expression of his own individuality. It was first performed in Moscow, 11 January 1945, Prokofiev making his last appearance as conductor. Shortly afterwards he fell down the stairs, a fall from which he was never to recover.

6th Symphony

Three years later came the 6th Symphony, today seen as his finest, premiered 11 October 1947. Fanning sees it as the most autonomous of his symphonies, the least dependent on earlier music. It is also, he comments, 'his darkest and most intense symphony.' Morrison sees it as incorporating the introversion of his Violin Sonata and 9th Piano Sonata. Prokofiev saw it as coming out of all those emotions that surround the end of war: 'now we are rejoicing in a great victory, but each of us has wounds that cannot be healed. One has lost those dear to him, another has lost his health. This must not be forgotten.'[61] Again it is his humanism that shines through: 'if earlier in his career he had emphasised divine inspiration, now he stressed human potential.'[62]

The first two movements struck me as painfully self-exploratory. But the work was disastrously mistimed. As Fanning expresses it, 'Prokofiev was unveiling his most tragic, most emotionally and structurally complex symphony at a time when Stalinist policies, administered in the Arts by Andrei Zhdanov, demanded pretty much the exact opposite.' As an outcome of victory Russian nationalism had never been higher. But for the Soviet state this was matched by its paranoid distrust of the west. Any exposure to the west, be it both through the huge number of Russians who had been POW's or the army in its war of liberation through Eastern Europe all the way to Berlin, was seen as potentially subversive. Might not such contact generate just the same kind of opposition that had led to the Decembrist revolt of 1825? On

5 November 1947 Prokofiev had been crowned for his patriotic music the People's Artist. But with the 6th all but disgrace ensued. 'The end of 1947,' Morrison argues, 'marked the end of Prokofiev's tenure at the forefront of Soviet music, a position he had struggled to achieve for over a decade at the expense of his marriage, his health and elements of his technique.'[63]

7th Symphony

The final years were humiliating. His health deteriorated. Shostakovich pleaded with Molotov to let him enter the Kremlin hospital February and March 1950. Official ostracism lasted longer than it did for Shostakovich. For the first time in 1948 Prokofiev 'became afraid.'[64] He had the resilience to undertake further gestures of ingratiation, his opera *Story of a Real Man*. Faced by its failure Prokofiev's response was 'I just don't understand.' A like fate befell the folklore ballet *The Storm Flower*. Belatedly the regime responded to his financial needs in March 1952. Could he win favour with his 7th Symphony, embarked on in 1952?

This was to be his 'Youth' Symphony. It is a surprisingly genial work, with a dance-like almost Viennese feel to it. All the morbid anguish of the two previous symphonies had been washed out. Is it a work of nostalgia? David Fanning hears 'the presence of a sad and wise adulthood contemplating the out-of-reach quality of youth.'[65] If so, it's a remarkable statement from a man seriously ill and in sight of death. It was to be premiered 11 October 1951. He died 5 March 1953, the same day as Stalin. There were to be no roses left for his funeral.

Prokofiev's was a deeply troubled journey of self-discovery. His natural inclination was to accommodate and he always believed he had the flexibility to please his masters. His self-confidence buckled under Stalinism. He hid his religious beliefs, anathema to an atheist state. But under the duress of the Stalinist state he discovered inner resources and fought his way to an expression of a deeply humanist spirituality. The prima donna came of age.

With no consolation of any religious belief, Shostakovich struggled through to a similar mode of survival, with an ever greater inwardness in his music.

Notes

[1] Taruskin, *History of Western Music*, Vol.4, p.227.

[2] David Nice, *Prokofiev: From Russia to the West 1891-1935*, New Haven and London: Yale University Press, 2003, p.274.

[3] Simon Morrison, *The People's Artist: Prokofiev's Soviet Years*, Oxford: Oxford University Press, 2009.

[4] Nice, *Prokofiev*, p.100.

[5] Nice, *Prokofiev*, p.xi.

[6] I am also drawing on two autobiographical pieces see Sergei Prokofiev, *Soviet Diary 1927 and Other Writings*, translated by Oleg Prokofiev, London: Faber and Faber, 1991. His short *Autobiography*, written in 1941, falls short at 1937. It was first published in Russia in 1956.

[7] Morrison, *The People's Artist*, p.283.

[8] Prokofiev, *Soviet Diary 1927*, p.97.

[9] Morrison, *The People's Artist*, p.161.

[10] Morrison, *The People's Artist*, p.311.

[11] Sheila Fitzpatrick, 'Many Promises,' *London Review of Books*, 14 May 2009, p.27.

[12] Prokofiev, *Soviet Diary 1927*, p.148.

[13] Nice, *Prokofiev*, p.90.

[14] Nice, *Prokofiev*, p.xi.

[15] John McManners (ed.), *The Oxford Illustrated History of Christianity*, Oxford and New York: Oxford University Press, 1992, p.390.

[16] Morrison, *The People's Artist*, p.27.

[17] Prokofiev, *Autobiography*, p.266.

[18] Morrison, *The People's Artist*, p.4.

[19] In a letter 31 July 1931, quoted Morrison.

[20] In fact he settled for the agreed Shakespearean ending when told that 'strictly speaking your music does not express any real joy at the end.' Prokofiev, *Autobiography*, p.299.

[21] Morrison, *The People's Artist*, p.84.

[22] Morrison, *The People's Artist*, p.250.

[23] Morrison, *The People's Artist*, p.330-31.

[24] Morrison, *The People's Artist*, p.392.

[25] Nice discusses this, pp.256-7.

[26] Prokofiev, *Autobiography*, p.258.

[27] Nice, *Prokofiev*, p.139.

[28] Prokofiev, *Autobiography*, pp.259-61.

[29] Chamberlain, *The Philosophy Steamer*, p.52.

[30] Figes, *A People's Tragedy*, p.735.

[31] Nice, *Prokofiev*, p.140.

[32] Quoted by Nice from Prokofiev's own memoir, p.142.

[33] Prokofiev, *Autobiography*, p.262 .

[34] Prokofiev, *A Soviet Diary*, p.103.

[35] Prokofiev, *A Soviet Diary 1927*, p.92.

[36] Nice, *Prokofiev*, p.303.

[37] Donald Sassoon, *The Culture of the Europeans: From 1800 to the Present*, London: Harper Collins, 2006. See the section 'Communism and the Regulation of Culture,' pp.882-901.

[38] Prokofiev, *Autobiography*, p.295.

[39] Nice, *Prokofiev*, p.319.

[40] Gerald Abrahams, *Eight Soviet Composers from 1800 to the Present*, Westport Connecticut: Greenwood Press, 1943, p.37.

[41] Prokofiev, *Autobiography*, p.267.

[42] See his programme notes, *Prokofiev The 7 Symphonies 15 August 2008*.

[43] Prokofiev, *Autobiography*, p.285.

[44] Nice, *Prokofiev*, p.260.

[45] How Simon Schama describes the painting in *Rembrandt's Eyes*, London: Penguin Books, 1999, p.685.

[46] Prokofiev, *Autobiography*, p.286.

[47] Henri J M Nouwen, *The Return of the Prodigal Son: A Story of Homecoming*, New York etc: Image Books Doubleday, 1994.

[48] Morrison, *The People's Artist*, p.284.

[49] Morrison, *The People's Artist*, p.53.

[50] London Review of Books, 14 May 2009.

[51] Prokofiev, *Autobiography* , p.294.

[52] Quoted Abrahams, *Eight Soviet Composers*, pp.33-4.

[53] Morrison, *The People's Artist*, p.111.

[54] Morrison, *The People's Artist*, p.66.

[55] Morrison, *The People's Artist*, p.69.

[56] Morrison, *The People's Artist*, p.73.

[57] Peris, *Storming the Heavens*, p.221

[58] Orlando Figes, *The Whisperers*, p.440.

[59] Morrison, *The People's Artist*, p.250.

[60] Edinburgh International Festival Programme, 16 August 2008.

[61] Quoted Edinburgh International Festival programme, 17 August 2008.

[62] Morrison, *The People's Artist*, p.251.

[63] Morrison, *The People's Artist*, p.294.

[64] Morrison, *The People's Artist*, p.305.

[65] Edinburgh International Festival Programme, 17 August 2008.

6. *Dmitri Shostakovich*

Making sense of Shostakovich is much like making sense of the 20th century. Its appalling history became his own. No interpretation can avoid a marriage of the personal and the political. But does he rightly belong to a project on the spiritual in music? If he more than matches Prokofiev in the ultimate if battered triumph of the human spirit, and this is one expression of the spiritual, in late Shostakovich, in his last three symphonies and late quartets, as he struggled with ill health and faced the prospect of a premature death, there is a new, far more inward and quietist tone to his music and a far more harrowing expression of the spiritual. Seeing Shostakovich's deteriorating physical appearance over time is rather like exposure to the portrait of Dorian Gray, the dreadful demands of the times in which he lived, no more so than the experience of the Terror in 1937, leaving terrible traces on his appearance and his inner self. He was driven evermore inward to survive and it is that inwardness that led to a new kind of music. But there is a deeper constituent. Shostakovich was responding to that vindictive suppression of Russian spirituality by the early Bolsheviks. His music, especially at the end, was a lament for its loss.

The Personal

None of this troubled self was evidenced in his family background. One has a sense of a lively if somewhat reserved personality, that might have developed in an entirely different way but for the constraints of the Soviet system. His younger sister Zoya observed: 'he was full of mischief and good spirits in the first years of his life and indeed he remained so until they started beating the fun out of him.'[1] It is oddly similar to the life of Benjamin Britten, another composer whose early expressiveness was to be hemmed in, in his case through social prejudice against his homosexuality, and it was entirely appropriate that these two composers became so close. Little in his background forecast the later conflicted adult.

His was a happy childhood. His parents married 2 February 1903. He was born 12 September 1906, the middle child of three, Marya an elder sister, Zoya a younger. Was it just a little ominous in terms of the future role of the gulag in his life that both his parents had Siberian origins, his father's family through exile to Siberia following involvement in the Polish uprising of 1863, his mother's through her father managing a gold mine? His father, Dmitri Boleslavovich, (1875-1922), civil servant, farm manager, commercial manager of an armaments factory, is seen as a jolly man who spoilt his son, and whose early death in 1922 from tuberculosis, brought on by the privations of life following the revolution, was a mortal blow for his son.

Yet here was a dependency which fatally failed to equip him with the means of coping with authority. There is a revealing account of his relationship with Asafiev, 22 years his senior, to become one of the leading Soviet musicologists and one of Shostakovich's more malign critics: 'Shostakovich admitted that the hardest thing in life for him was to ask anything for himself.' When he submitted his 1st Symphony to Asafiev he stated: 'I am afraid of rejection. Terribly afraid. And I always fear people with status.'[2] He had a terror of officials.

His relationship with his mother, Sofiya Kokaoulina (1878-1955), was closer but emotionally cramping. It was she who spotted his talents as a pianist and composer. But securing his entry to the St Petersburg Conservatoire at the age of 13 effectively ended his childhood. Brilliant hostess she may have been, and she has been described as 'an aristocratic lady from a typical gentry family,'[3] but she was hopelessly ill-equipped to run the family on her husband's death – she failed as a shop cashier – so it was left to Shostakovich to be the bread-winner as a pianist in the Picadilly cinema. He became a kind of busker. She became wholly dependent on him and hence highly possessive: 'he was the centre of her world and she paid far more attention to him than to his sisters ... this close identification with his professional life also created a lot of pressure on him.'[4] She lived with him till her death. Do her demands on his emotional life do something to explain the somewhat strangled tone of much of his music? He was to burn all his letters to her on her death.

It certainly helps to explain his ineptitude with women. At 16, recovering from TB in the Crimea, he fell in love with Tatyana Glivenko, a love, she claims, that lasted their entire lives. But through his indecisiveness which she in part attributes to his mother she married someone else in February 1929. The pianist Elmira Nazirova – we now know she did much to inspire the 10th Symphony – provides a telling portrait of his clumsiness: 'it was completely perplexing. He couldn't talk to one quietly even for a moment. He would be constantly lighting cigarettes, getting up to open the window, sitting down again, and then getting up again to walk about. After a few minutes, his complex personality would start to make me feel quite strange.'[5] His mother opposed his first marriage to the physicist Nina Varvar, and his still holding onto the hope that Tatyana instead would join him no doubt explains his failure to turn up at the first wedding ceremony, and, in the end, they were married in secret at a civil ceremony 13 May 1932. Shostakovich believed in free love and an open marriage but affairs led to their divorce in 1935. However, they quickly remarried and there can be no doubt Nina did much to shield him from his life's traumas – she has been described as 'spiritually a person of great beauty'[6] – and provided a strong family environment for their two children. She died suddenly 9 November 1954. Then came his mother's death 9 November 1955.

There followed a disastrous second marriage to Komsomol activist, Margarita Kainova – did she physically resemble Nina? – that ended three years later. But his third marriage to Irina Supinshaya – the musicologist Lev Lebinsky, through Shostakovich's ineptitude, had had to act as go between – worked wonderfully well. But Shostakovich agonised over

their differences of age – he was 56 to her 27. Galina Vish-
nevskaya writes: 'it was with her Dmitri Dmitriyevich finally
came to know domestic peace.'[7] They married November
1962. Significantly, shortly after the marriage, Shostakovich orchestrated Mussorgsky's *Songs of Dance and Death*.
Crucially Irina helped him through his long illness and her
presence does much to explain the stoicism yet serenity of
his late music.

Yet in many ways his attitude to women was conflicted. He
had planned a Wagnerian trilogy of operas on women in the
1930's, but the fate of *Lady Macbeth of Mtsensk* put paid to
that ambition. All of this suggests he was sympathetic to women. Yet there is a revealing moment when later, discovering
the contest over Prokofiev's estate between his two wives, he
stated: 'in general women are disgusting, most terribly disgusting.'[8] Was he in fact a misogynist? This is relevant to
discussing his spirituality as, it can be argued, all such conflict blocks its expression.

Can we ever grasp the extraordinary pain that drove Shostakovich ever more inward? Change in appearance is one
indicator. Here is life-time friend Isaak Glikman's description in the 1930's: 'the refinement of his face, its individuality, its noble aspect, with his wonderful grey eyes flashing
from behind his spectacles, with their wise expression,
penetrating, thoughtful and splintering with laughter.' He
continues: 'of decent height, slender, yet supple and strong.
His clothes always suited him and he looked irresistible in
tails or dinner jacket. His head was covered with a wonderful
dark copper-coloured hair, which was carefully combed, or
else fell in poetic disorder with that dashing unruly lock of
hair falling forward onto his forehead.' Here is another description of the young Shostakovich: 'he is very handsome …
the oval of his pale face, the form of his lips, the round
receding chin and his intelligent eyes which seem clouded as
if in some kind of fog – all this recalls the inspired images of
heads of Beethoven and Mozart.'[9] There are many references to his high sense of humour. Yet by 1941 the writer and

another close friend, Mikhail Zoshchenko, whilst recognising him as 'tough, acerbic, extremely intelligent, strong, perhaps, and not all together good-natured,' infers, 'Great contradictions are at play in him. One quality obliterates another. It is conflict of the highest degree ... almost to the point of catastrophe.'[10] By November 1954 one Lev Lebedinsky, another musicologist, could write of 'his strange, almost schizophrenic character.'[11] When Robert Craft met him in October 1962 he recorded: 'he is the shyest and most nervous human being I have ever seen. He chews not only his nails but his fingers, twitches his pouty mouth and chin, chain smokes, wiggles his nose in constant adjustment of his spectacles, looks querulous one moment and ready to cry the next ... There is no betrayal of his thoughts behind those frightened, very intelligent eyes.'[12] The film director, Grigori Kozintsev, wrote of 'his modesty and utter truthfulness' but continued, 'his inner life runs like an incessantly working motor, an ever-open wound. It is impossible to define this part of his life in words.'[13] Out of that suffering though, came the extraordinary emotion of the music.

In the end what seems the strongest aspect is his ever increasing loneliness. His most intimate friendship was with the musicologist Ivan Sollertinsky, whom he first met whilst preparing to take an examination on Marxism-Leninism in 1927 and this larger-than-life character became his closest friend. Sollertinsky's first wife observed: 'they were simply in love – didn't conceal their delight in each other. Sollertinsky never tired of repeating: Shostakovich is a genius.'[14] Here were two friends who revelled in each other's humour; 'they were each quite indiscriminate when it came to being humorous, and if they were too young to be bitter they could still come mercilessly close to being malicious.'[15] Laurel Fay sees him as the one person Shostakovich ever deferred to as junior to senior: 'he could confess and ask absolution.'[16] No-one replaced him following his early death at 41, 11 February 1944.[17]

What is striking about Shostakovich is that loss of his early exuberant sense of humour. Even so, assisted by a large glass of vodka he could still be the life and soul of a party. Ed Vulliamy has suggested he never lost a sense of existential irony.

The Political

As with Prokofiev the catalyst for the spiritual was the political. But Shostakovich engaged in a radically different way with the Soviet project. In terms of forebears, his revolutionary credentials were impeccable. Far from reading into his life a prolonged battle with the system as Volkov's *Testimony*[18] has encouraged, Shostakovich is best seen as one increasingly disillusioned by the betrayal of the humanitarian ideals of the Revolution. Various myths have attached to him. Did he but 13 in 1917 witness the death of a child during the February days? Was he present at Lenin's return to the Finland Station? It feels a little odd that also at his school were the sons of Trotsky and Kamenev, but then there was always to be his uncanny closeness with the Soviet political elite. It was not so exceptional that he received phone-calls from Stalin. But he was also friendly as a schoolboy with the young Nikolayevich Lossky, son of the Losskys, amongst those exiled on Lenin's Philosophy Steamer, and maybe Lossky's assessment of Shostakovich's early political sympathies should be taken seriously: 'during the spring of 1918 during Trotsky's rise to power Mitya never so much as hinted at any kind of sympathy with the existing regime and I can vouch that was the case until 1922.'[19] In terms of any political entanglement the young Shostakovich led a seemingly charmed life throughout NEP and the cultural revolution of 1929 to 1931. Wisely he kept his distance from such radical organisations as RAPM (Russian Association of Proletarian Composers) though still dedicated his 2nd and 3rd Symphonies to Soviet causes. But then in March 1936 came the trauma of the decree, Muddle instead of Music and the fiasco of his opera *Lady Macbeth of Mtsensk*.

This is of course a very familiar story though still mysterious. For a start the opera had initially been a huge popular success and seemingly exemplary in its Socialist Realism. Shostakovich had sought to portray Katerina Ismailovna in a Soviet way, as victim of a petty merchant background. His ballet *The Limpid Stream* equally fell foul of the system despite its being all about life on a collective farm. Rather weirdly the 4th Symphony, which had to be withdrawn, was written as a memorial to Kirov, murdered 1 December 1934. Shostakovich wrote of it: 'it is a particularly onerous and difficult task. But responding to the social demands of our remarkable era with works that meets its requirements and acting as its trumpets is a matter of honour for each Soviet composer.'[20] At some level this was his genuine intention.

Ever afterwards Shostakovich lived with fear. A character in Vasily Grossman's novel *Life and Fate* says of Shostakovich: 'he admits his errors, writes letters of repentance – and then returns to work. It's like water off a ducks' back.'[21] This suggests an almost playful relationship between Shostakovich and the Stalinist State. If it were ever like this, and surely it never was, it was absolutely untrue during the Yezhov purges of 1937-8. The pianist Elmira Nazirova describes this well: 'he remembered 1937 with such horror that I think what went on then had an even greater effect on his life than the war and all the tragedies that followed.'[22] He literally went in fear of his life. Already he had seen the risk. Dedicatee of his 1st Symphony, Mikhail Kvadri, had been shot in 1929. There was to be the terrifying investigation over his friendship with his patron, Marshal Tukachevsky, and the Marshal's murder in the summer of 1937. As luck would have it his investigator himself fell victim to the terror. His brother-in-law, the physicist Vsevolod Fredericks, husband of his elder sister, Mariya, was arrested and died soon after his release on the eve of war. His wife's mother was also arrested though she survived the gulag. As his sister recalled: 'Danger hung over Mitya; he feared arrest and was terrified that he would be unable to resist torture and would admit to anything under interrogation.'[23] Later he admitted: 'I'd sign anything even if they hand it to me upside down. All I want is to be left alone.'[24] He had discovered that there could be no intermediary patron between himself and the State. His actual answer to 1937 was his 5th Symphony.

Why did the regime of the Terror persecute Shostakovich? Was this humiliation of its most distinguished composer its perverse way of demonstrating its totalitarian control of the arts?

Shostakovich had to experience the same trauma all over gain with the Zhdanov decree of 1948. With the renewed post-war paranoia about western influence, Shostakovich, whose music enjoyed ever more popularity through the Leningrad Symphony in the West, was hugely at risk. One forgets that Zhdanov was the second most powerful political figure of the Soviet Union at the time. (He died of a heart attack in 1948.) This time Shostakovich had to stand before the Plenum of the Union of Composers, and be publicly humiliated. He was branded an enemy of the people. In fact he read out someone else's prepared speech. Did he fall victim to other composers, jealous of his international success? One such was Tikhon Khrennikov, First Secretary of the Union of Composers, writer of patriotic music otherwise deemed facile and comically derivative, Zhdanov's instrument in enforcing state control of music from the cradle to the grave.[25] Any favourable recognition in the West could, of course, in the emergent Cold War prove fatal. And once again it was an oddly personal encounter with Stalin, whom he had met for the first time in 1943 during his abortive attempt to win the prize for a new national anthem, that came into play. Initially after the war Stalin had granted his request for better living conditions. Now, out of a job, ostracised by his fellow composers, it was at this point Stalin phoned to enquire after his health, expressed surprise that his music was banned, but insisted that he attend the Cultural and Scientific Congress of World Peace to be held in New York, 25-28 March 1949. Once again, in a wholly different context, Shostakovich found himself publicly humiliated through the craven speech he had to give. The not very likeable pro-American Russian emigré composer, Nicholas Nabokov, saw this as 'part of the punishment, part of a ritual redemption he had to go through before he could be pardoned again.'[26] Once again Shostakovich sought political redemption through a new symphony, his 10th.

And then came Khruschev's thaw. Angrily Shostakovich rejected any mere correction to the Zhdanov's decree: 'No nothing should be corrected, the only thing is to revoke the decree, revoke it.'[27] If in fact only a correction indeed was made, he was no longer black-listed. But there was an appalling price to pay. Khruschev insisted on overt support for the party by all Soviet artists. In retrospect, it is surprising that Shostakovich had avoided joining the party down till 1960. The emergent dissident movement was appalled by his surrender and saw his joining as an act of betrayal. Did he join out of fear? Or just to get the party off his back? Was he even drunk at the time of signing the request to join the party? Admittedly he contrived to be absent from the meeting itself. Lev Lebedinsky recalls an extraordinary comment at the time: 'I am scared to death of them. From childhood I have been doing things that I wanted not to do. I'm a wretched alcoholic.'[28] Do we hear here the guilt complex of a survivor? Or does a merely bureaucratic explanation do, he had to join the party to become Chairman of the RSFR Composers Union? It is generally agreed that the Dresden Quartet (1960) is an autobiographical statement of anguish at his decision. Yet he became a model party member, turned against Solzhenitsyn, signed a letter against Sakhorov. Later he took his role as Deputy for Villages in the Supreme Soviet very seriously. He remained part of the official establishment till his death.

But he has his apologists. Fyodor Druzhinin, member of the Beethoven Quartet, has a different take. Shostakovich was in fact burdened by public recognition. Under the aegis of the watchful party eye of the Union of Composers, Shostakovich underwent the most anguished period of his life and art.

He was painfully torn between a sincere desire to repay all unsolicited honours through his work, and his real artist's view of what was going on in the country. He continues: 'It seemed to me that Shostakovich's already battered and morbid psyche would buckle and shatter under this collective onslaught of "progressive forces". And he was also beset by illness and old age, thoughts of death and the pointless waste of time entailed by his official duties.'[29] Elizabeth Wilson herself is even more generous: 'it is blatantly obvious he disassociated himself inwardly from the official statements he was expected to sign and parrot in public.'[30]

Volkov has the theory that all along Shostakovich was playing the role of the *yurodivy*, the Holy Idiot – there was always a subtext to what he said and wrote – but I think this fails to grasp the intolerable burden of fear that he endured. He was all but crippled by the system. Was his only means of survival, of preserving his integrity, through the music? Can the spiritual transcend fear?

Religion and the Spiritual

There was little or no tension in Shostakovich between religion and spirituality. If his birth and death were marked by religious ritual, formal religious practice played little or no role in his life. Maybe his younger sister, Zoya, overstates her claim that religion played little part in his childhood – 'our parents were not church goers,'[31] – for in Boris Lossky's qualification they observed 'at least the most common of the Church customs.'[32] Certainly his father was given a full religious funeral service. Did Shostakovich collapse onto his father's face and hands in the coffin? He kept a crucifix by his bedside all his life.[33] On the other hand, in a letter to his mother 3 August 1923 in protest at the oath taken in the marriage ceremony, he expressed some kind of hostility to organised religion: 'the oath sworn before the altar is one of the worst features of religion, love cannot last that long.'[34] So was he being merely disingenuous when he claimed religious belief was one reason why he could not join the party in 1960?[35] Volkov quotes Shostakovich as claiming 'I was never a crude anti-religionist.'[36] But there is no evidence of any protest at the anti-clericalism of the Soviet state. Can we make much of his puzzlement at the strongly religious nun-like pianist Mariya Yudina, who somehow survived the whole Stalinist era? What did he make of her interpretation of the 14th as 'a prayer kneeling in front of the Holy Mother of God for those in mourning, for joy'?[37] What is missing in his music is the sound of the liturgy of the Orthodox Church: if Shostakovich was influenced by any sacred music it was Jewish.

Did he entertain any Christian belief in an after-life? Speaking of someone who had died after eight heart attacks, he said: 'he is no longer alive … but I know that soon over there we will meet.'[38] It is in his attitude to death that Shostakovich is at his most spiritual. Another response to late Shostakovich by the pianist Evgeni Shendorovich leads us back to the music: 'it seems to me Shostakovich's work is indeed on a par with a tragedy of Sophocles in the profoundly philosophical concept, its universal all-embracing force.'[39]

There are many accounts of Shostakovich as himself spiritual. The conductor Nikolai Malko describes him as 'spiritually strong and self-reliant.'[40] Another conductor, Thomas Sanderling, who met him in 1969, recalled 'the immense power that emanated from him … Anyone who came into contact with Shostakovich could not but be intensely aware of being in the presence of a person of great spiritual purity and moral fibre.'[41] The pianist Mikhail Druskin, recalling the composer in his youth, puts this in a different but telling way: 'it was Shostakovich's vocation to realise the concept of tragedy, for this was how he perceived the world.'[42] Was he above all a moralist? Sanderling sees him as inheriting the predominantly moral tone of the great Russian tradition: 'this morality was the salient feature both of Shostakovich's music and of his everyday conduct.'[43] Possibly Sofia Gubaidulina, a leading composer of the later dissident genera-

118

tion, by way of a comparison with Prokofiev, is the more
perceptive: 'he was able to transform the pain that he so
keenly experienced into something exalted and full of light,
which transforms all worldly suffering. He was able to trans-
figure the material into a spiritual entity.'[44]

Is it even possible to express the spiritual under a totalitarian
system? We have to trace the varying ways in which Shostakovich sought to maintain his personal integrity. How to
read his early music? Was he an avant-gardiste at one with
modernism? Was this somehow, however sarcastic, more
earth-bound and so leading away from any transcendence? If
there remains the paradox that much of his middle period,
from the 5th Symphony onwards, is in some way exemplary
in its socialist realism through its expression of the heroic, it
was through his very embattled relationship with the system,
and forced ever more inwards, that Shostakovich, like Prokofiev, discovered and expressed the triumph of the human
spirit. Even so, there is a sense that Shostakovich is equally
addressing a sense of spiritual exhaustion. But it is in the late
Shostakovich, in his last three symphonies and in his
chamber music that the most truly autobiographical music is
heard, and here, in his absorption with the prospect of death,
that the most genuinely spiritual, if stoical, music can be
heard.

His Early Music

One can but speculate how the young Shostakovich might
have developed. Once again one is struck by a comparison
with the ebullient early Britten. In both composers that
youthfulness was to be mortally damaged. Gerald Abrahams,
writing in 1943, saw his 1st Symphony, a product of NEP,
'the golden age of Soviet music,' as his finest work.[45] Was
he an avant-gardiste? The 1st Symphony was premiered 12
May 1926 but it was only in 1927 that Shostakovich started
to study the scores of Schoenberg, Bartok and Hindemith.
Richard Taruskin writes of the early Shostakovich 'as some-

one out to debunk and discredit the musical status quo from within.'[46] But that is a different position from seeing him as an avant-gardiste. In many ways Shostakovich lived his entire life under the false charge of being a formalist or modernist. There were other reasons why the Soviet authorities feared him. Abrahams emphasises his sense of the sarcastic: 'he is by nature a wit (or a humorist) and wits do not make good hymn writers. He tries to be a Marxist, but fantastic Gogolian humour keeps breaking in.'[47] It was a tone that ran through his early music till the showdown in 1936: 'a severe check was soon to be put to Shostakovich's parody and sarcasm, his vulgarity and his modernism.'[48] Taruskin suggests there was another reason why the Soviet critics feared the opera, it lay in its brutal sexual content: 'totalitarian regimes fear nothing nothing so much as an unleashed libido.'[49] But surely it was the satirical they feared most. Bakhtin has shown that nothing is so corrosive of power as humour. Shostakovich had to be 'corrected' and, tellingly, in his response to 'just criticism,' his 5th Symphony, there is 'the total suppression of the satirical mode.'[50]

But such a fundamental trait could not be exorcised altogether and certainly Shostakovich gave free rein to it in his satirical work, the cantata *Rayon* – it takes its name from those booths at fairs when you can peep through and see a series of pictures on a revolving drum – his bitter response to the Zhdanov decree of 1948. However, it had to await its first performance till January 1989 in New York. There could be no Soviet license for the satirical. The regime recognised, as Plato had done, that music posed a threat: 'if Shostakovich could be summarily silenced and brought low, then nobody was safe. It was demonstration of the omnipotence of Soviet power over the arts in the wake of the 1932 perestroika.'[51]

Was something permanently crushed in the young composer? When the 4th Symphony was finally first performed December 1961, one listener ruminated; 'why do Shostakovich's later works lack this quality – impetuosity, dynamic drive, contrasts of rhythm and colour, tenderness and spikiness?

One involuntarily thinks what a different path he could have taken, how different his life could have been if it were not for the historic Decree which warped the living spirit in him.'[52] Yet the early music was taking him away from the spiritual. Experience of oppression took him in another direction, forced him to draw ever deeper on his inner resources, and to become the supreme commentator on the appalling events of his day.

Public Music

The conflicting claims of the antagonists in the Cold War have always made interpreting Shostakovich's public music contentious. Taruskin opens up the debate well: 'was he toady or victim? Secret voice of conscience or accomplice to deception? Nation's darling or party-propped demagogue? Keeper of the Beethovenian flame or cynical manipulator of clichés?'[53] In contrast to Volkov and his successors, who insist on a hermeneutics of dissidence, Taruskin pleads for a multi-valent approach. And surely he has got it right. 'The meaning of an artwork,' he insists, 'indeed of any communication is never wholly stable but is the product of its history, a history that only begins with its creation.'[54] In a sense his is a post-modernist approach: 'as contexts change, subtexts accumulate. What made Shostakovich's music the secret diary of a nation was not only what he put into it but what it allowed listeners to draw out.'[55]

Shostakovich was notoriously averse to interpreting his own music: he 'insisted on keeping the latent content latent – and keeping it labile.'[56] It means that we are free to read either the Terror or the Nazi invasion into the 7th Symphony. Taruskin also has a profound warning against a too literal interpretation: 'the aspiration to literal truth brings always the possibility, indeed the virtual certainty, of falsehood.'[57]

But there are problems with Shostakovich's public music. Striving after the heroic, no doubt to meet Soviet expectations, Shostakovich always veered towards the verbose. Frustrated as an opera writer Shostakovich resorted to the operatic in his orchestral writing. Taruskin recognises this limitation in describing the 7th as 'the bombastic anachronism, some kind of woolly mammoth out of the Stalinist deep freeze.'[58] Of course Shostakovich bucked the system, eschewing the heroic in his introspective 8th or Haydnesque 9th. Taruskin seeks to square the circle by defining him as a public artist: 'The mature Shostakovich,' he believes, 'was an *intelligent*, heir to a noble tradition of artistic and social thought – one that abhorred injustice and political repression but also one that values social commitment, participation in one's community and solidarity with people.' He proceeds: 'he found a way of maintaining public service and personal integrity under unimaginably hard conditions. In this way he remained in the time-honoured Russian if not exactly the Soviet sense of the word a "civic" artist.'[59] But this in the end feels restrictive. The really interesting insight into his music will seek to separate out the personal from the political. However conscientiously Shostakovich sought to write public music, one suspects his heart was not in it.

Of course, in just the same way as in Prokofiev's late music, a profound humanitarianism is being expressed and this can be read as an expression of the spiritual. Shostakovich provides a vital clue as to what lies beyond the public: he is quoted as saying of the 7th, 'this is music about terror, slavery, spiritual exhaustion.'[60] Shostakovich equally reached out to what had died under Soviet dictatorship, the death of the spiritual. This he sought to recover in the increasingly private music of his last years.

Private Music: The Late Symphonies

During the last seventeen years of his life Shostakovich was beset by serious illness. The first signs of what was motor neurone disease but wrongly diagnosed as polio came in 1958, weakness in his right hand, later the same in his right leg, and in time he was visibly lame. In February 1964 he suffered his first heart attack, in July 1971 his second. Extreme ill-health was not new. In his youth he suffered from severe anaemia and succumbed to tuberculosis of the lymphatic system, necessitating in 1923 an operation on his neck. He became ever more preoccupied with death. Family and friends died, his elder sister, Mariya, Vadim Borisovsky, Viola player in the Beethoven Quartet, David Oistrakh and others. At the end he was going blind.

There is a new tone in the music. Taruskin, admittedly, still hears the public and political: 'as Shostakovich, a world-renowned and much revered figure, reached the stricken and debilitated end of the road, and as the Soviet state stumbled toward its own debilitated end, the composer could afford to lower his guard, if ever so slightly.' More pertinently he argues: 'there is the increasingly resolute denial of optimism, of "self-affirmation", which is to say the denial of the *sine qua non* of Soviet art.'[61] Volkov put it more dramatically: 'the music of the final period expressed fear before death, a numbness, a search for a final sanctuary in the memory of future men: explosion of impotent and heart-breaking anger.'[62] And the 13th Symphony has to be seen as a transitional work. But, paradoxically, by joining the party Shostakovich seemed to shed his preoccupation with the public and be better able to explore the more private and personal.

Once again with the Babi Yar, the 13th, Shostakovich fell victim to bad timing. It was premiered 18 December 1962, the day after Khruschev, in one of those famously philistine speeches, pronounced to an assembly of Moscow intellectuals the end of the Thaw. The authorities tried to put off its performance – its initial conductor, Evgeni Mravinsky, lost his nerve but his replacement, Kiril Kondrashin was made of sterner stuff – but they did not have the nerve to ban it. Oddly it was the setting of Yevtuschenko's poem *Babi Yar* in the first movement that was the given reason rather than the poems directed at society under Stalinism, on the grounds that it privileged the Jews at the expense of Russians and

Ukrainians as victims of the atrocity. In fact, this was just a screen for a policy of official anti-Semitism. Down till 1948 anti-Semitism had been taboo but following the setting up of the state of Israel, with Russian Jews seen as having an alternative loyalty, Russian anti-Semitism resurfaced. From the 8th Quartet, the Dresden, Shostakovich had identified with the plight of the Jewish people and was appalled by the rise of anti-Semitism: 'it is an outrageous thing, and we must fight it. We must shout it from the rooftops.'[63] He identified himself as fellow victim. Volkov's quotation, 'Jews became a symbol for me. All of man's defencelessness was concentrated in them'[64] is surely authentic.

He had set the poem to music even before he approached the poet and then wrote the music around the other four poems in under six weeks. Setting words so brilliantly to music is a reminder of how much was lost through his abandoning opera. Significantly the poem itself is as much about Russian pogroms as Babi Yar itself and universalises anti-semitism by reference to Dreyfus and Anne Frank. When Anne Frank refuses to recognise the fatal 'breaking down the door,' 'no it's the ice breaking,' you can hear it crack in the brass and drums, a horribly fierce, apocalyptic orchestral sound. In the second movement, *Humour*, in music that is Mahlerian and almost jaunty, Shostakovich takes up the theme of the perennial jester, abrasive, acerbic, and surely here he is using laughter to scorn the system. The third movement, *In the Store*, he adopts a darker and more subdued tone, recognition of the pain that Russian women had had to endure. The music for *Fears*, the poem the poet wrote at Shostakovich's request, is surely the most overtly anti-Stalinist music he wrote, again beginning very sombre, with a chilling drumbeat, and a tuba solo as if from a subterranean chamber, the chorus entering with a wraith-like whisper, but the bass solo is aggressive and self-accusatory, for the poem is about how Russians betrayed one another under the Terror. There is a terrible pain in the brass though it ends on an oddly plaintive note, almost light-hearted. The final movement *Career* mocks the opportunism under the Soviet system whilst admiring those who remained true to themselves. In the lyricism at the end, in the violins, a quiet humanism is being reasserted. With the harp and the piano it dies away to a hush. Film and theatre director Grigori Kozintsev reflected on the 13th: 'the essence of Shostakovich's music lies in the conflict between the spirituality of man and the inhuman forces that are hostile to that spirituality. He raises Yevtuschenko's rather facile poetry to a different level; his prison *is* a prison, his humour is fearless and joyful, a victorious life-affirming force.'[65]

In the 14th Symphony Shostakovich moved from the public death of the holocaust to a more private death. It was written during a spell in the Moscow Kremlin hospital – the hospital was quarantined during an influenza outbreak – and it was here he read the poets in translation around which the symphony is set, Lorca, Guillaume Apollinaire, Rainer Maria Rilke and the Decembrist, Wilhelm Kuckelbecker. He feared he would die before it was performed or recorded and hurried on its first performance, a closed concert in the Senate hall of the Conservatoire in Moscow, 21 June 1969 – symbolically, his arch critic Pavel Apostolov died of a heart attack during the performance – and, to meet the prima donna demands of the soprano and bass soloists, two separate performances in Leningrad and Moscow, 29 September and 1 October. Point of departure had been Mussorgsky's *Songs and Dances of Death* but other influences were Mahler, Britten – dedicatee of the Symphony – as well as Lutoslawski and Penderecki. The Symphony is in eleven sections and one critic has read into this the movements of the Requiem Mass and Shostakovich indeed thought of it first as an Oratorio. But the Symphony is without consolation. 'Death is terrifying, there is nothing beyond,' he is quoted as saying, 'I don't believe in a life beyond the grave.'[66] Did he identify with fellow pessimists, Gogol and Chekhov? Sir Duncan Wilson, a friend of Britten's, wrote to him: 'I think we all felt that here was a man who had looked at his eleven aspects of death in the face, and many other mysteries as well.'[67] Elizabeth Wilson herself states: 'In no other work does Shostakovich reveal such total pessimism, untinged by the light of redemption or the comfort of reminiscence.'[68] But Andrew Huth has a subtle caveat: 'but this overwhelming protest is not just against mortality but at premature death, death inflicted on the innocent, at the butchers who spread death in the world.'[69] We move outward from an awareness of Shostakovich's own premature death to those who died under the Terror and in the Gulag. Taruskin still sees him at war with the system: in the 14th, 'a full texted and explicit death affirmation, Shostakovich spat in its face.'[70] Musically Shostakovich is seen as returning to that freedom of expression of the 1920's.

It is difficult not to see the Symphony as about the loss of spiritual freedom. Solzhenitsyn faulted the work for its lacking 'light,' for not sharing in Mahler's redemptive hope. But then Shostakovich was not conventionally religious. Had he indeed betrayed that Russian mystical belief in the eternal life? In fact, of course, this is once again Shostakovich's affirmation of his deep humanism, an acceptance of the all too human. Even so, Kozintsev sees the positive: 'even in the face of extreme horror what one hears is not the victory of darkness and death but the victory of creativity.'[71]

Elizabeth Wilson wrote of the 15th: 'the Symphony has the air of a valedictory statement, here Shostakovich appears to transcend his inner experience, distilling it into musical substance of unique transparency.'[72] As befits a retrospective work the first movement evokes the sardonic humour of his early music. But there is a complete change of mood with the Adagio and a return to that of the 14th. Initially this is mournful and resigned, with low rumbling on the brass – no raging here against the dying of the light – but then comes a trademark explosion of sound though it subsides, the tingling sound of the xylophone. Uninterruptedly into the 3rd movement, scherzo-like, an abrasive cheerfulness and with a break into the 4th, a return to inwardness, almost Wagnerian in tone, out of the depths a quietly lyrical passage in the strings. It is as if we are now in waiting, Shostakovich reluctant to shape his finale, his orchestral farewell. Then another full-blown explosion of sound, falling away, like the felling of a great beast, resignation but with some humour, the occasional dissonance to suggest life remains, before it fade away.

The Late Quartets

In the 1950's, inspired in part by hearing Bartok's quartets in New York, Shostakovich turned to chamber music. Here was a music all the more autobiographical and in that sense dissident: 'it was manifestly an anti-Soviet move of a sort, for, as both the Soviet government and its citizens knew long before it became the trendy slogan in the West, the personal is political.' Taruskin also points out: 'it was also anti-Russian, for there was little tradition of Russian chamber music. Under the Soviets, it was always vaguely suspect as aristocratic or genteel, and in 1948 it was openly denounced.'[73] Taruskin takes Shostakovich to task for being too autobiographical in the 8th: the message, he feels, is too explicit and lacks mystery. Do we indeed hear here Shostakovich's anguish and guilt at joining the party? And Taruskin is averse to too biographical a reading anyway: 'definite reading, especially biographical reading, locks the music in the past. Better let it remain supple, adaptable, ready to serve the future's needs.'[74] And maybe holding back from a too biograpical approach will open the music more generously to a spiritual reading.

Elizabeth Wilson senses this brilliantly: 'the last three quartets are arguably the summit of his achievement, ranging from the dark, death-ridden intensity of the one-movement span of the Thirteenth, and the swing between the tender passion and wistful serenity of the Fourteenth, to the distilled utterance of the six awesome elegiacal Adagio movements of the Fifteenth.'[75]

In the 13th, in the sound of tapping on the violin, Russians would hear 'the sinister sound of the final nailing down of the coffin lid.'[76] In the 14th the Adagio 2nd movement has to be heard as a soliloquy on death. It was the Tanyeev Quartet who first performed the 15th: 'we were shaken to the core by the scale of tragedy in the quartet, and tried to give it every ounce of our soul.'[77] It is almost as if Shostakovich saw the demise of the quartet itself as a form, with the frequent resort to solo playing. This is Shostakovich's respectful and resigned acceptance of his own non-transcendent death. One has to turn to those extraordinary late paintings by Edward Munch of his own terminal illness to find a parallel poignancy.

And then his final work, the Viola sonata, reflecting a mood of 'exalted philosophical resignation ... a fitting requiem to man who had lived through and chronicled the scourges of a cruel age.'[78]

Initial western response to all these late works was a puzzlement, seen as 'gnomic and depressed, faint echoes of the composer of the Fifth Symphony.'[79] But Gerard McBurney follows this up: 'if through illness and isolation the late music is distinguished by a curious poetry of blackness, what first puzzled listeners, but now seems to his admirers to be richly ambiguous and suggestive.'[80,81]

It will be apparent how difficult it is to describe Shostakovich's music though this is not to surrender him to the musicologists. Here was another composer driven by the duress of the Soviet system to discover the full extent of his humanity, an expression of a humanitarian spirituality. It feels even more appropriate to look at the Gulag[82] and Memoirs of its victims[83] when considering Shostakovich rather than Prokofiev. But the non-religious Shostakovich goes beyond the political in the late music and touches on a different spirituality, an exploration of death, if again humanist and stoical, a kind of quietism, but surely also touching on the transcendental.

Was there a more gifted composer at conveying feeling?

Notes

[1] Quoted Elizabeth Wilson, *Shostakovich: A Life Remembered* (New edition), London: Faber and Faber, 2006, p.8. This is not strictly a biography, more an assembly of memories, but it gives us much the greatest insight into Shostakovich's personality.

[2] Quoted in 'Shostakovich, LASM and Asafiev 9 November 1925,' in Rosamund Bartlett and Laurel E Fay (eds.), *Shostakovich in Context*, Oxford: Oxford University Press, 2000, p.56.

[3] Bartlett and Fay (eds.), *Shostakovich in Context*, p.170.

[4] Observation of his first great love, Tatyana Glivenko, in Wilson, *Shostakovich*, p.98.

[5] Quoted Nelly Kravetz, 'New Insights into the Tenth Symphony,' in Bartlett and Fay (eds.), *Shostakovich in Context*, p.171.

[6] Levon Atovmyan, Wilson, *Shostakovich*, p.125.

[7] Wilson, *Shostakovich*, p.399.

[8] Recollection of biologist Flora Litvinova, Wilson, *Shostakovich*, p.352.

[9] Wilson, *Shostakovich*, pp.123-4.

[10] Wilson, *Shostakovich*, p.181.

[11] Wilson, *Shostakovich*, p.307.

[12] Wilson, *Shostakovich*, p.424.

[13] Wilson, *Shostakovich*, p.420.

[14] Wilson, *Shostakovich*, p.74.

[15] Conductor Nikolai Malko's recollection in Wilson, *Shostakovich*, p.75.

[16] Bartlett and Fay (eds.), *Shostakovich in Context*, p.73.

[17] His 4th Quartet was dedicated to him.

[18] Solomon Volkov (ed.), *Testimony: The Memoirs of Dmitri Shostakovich* (First published 1979), London: Faber and Faber, 1989. Unrepentantly Volkov wrote the story all over again but in his own name in *Shostakovich and Stalin*, New York: Little, Brown and Company, 2004. It seems somehow appropriate that so autobiographical a composer should have attracted a false memoir.

[19] Wilson, *Shostakovich*, p.17.

[20] Quoted Bartlett and Fay (eds.), *Shostakovich in Context*, p.83.

[21] Grossman, *Life and Fate*, p.655.

[22] Quoted Bartlett and Fay (eds.), *Shostakovich in Context*, p.170.

[23] Wilson, *Shostakovich*, p.133.

[24] Wilson, *Shostakovich*, p.212.

[25] See his obituary by Gerard McBurney, *The Guardian*, 19 September 2007.

[26] Wilson, *Shostakovich*, p.276.

[27] Quoted Wilson, *Shostakovich*, p.334.

[28] Wilson, *Shostakovich*, p.377.

[29] Wilson, *Shostakovich*, p.438.

[30] Wilson, *Shostakovich*, p.428.

[31] Wilson, *Shostakovich*, p.10.

[32] Wilson, *Shostakovich*, p.33.

[33] Recollection of his son, Maxim. Wilson, *Shostakovich*, p.349.

[34] Wilson, *Shostakovich*, p.94.

[35] Wilson, *Shostakovich*, p.379.

[36] Volkov, *Testimony*, p.39.

[37] Wilson, *Shostakovich*, p.405.

[38] Recollection of the Polish composer Krzysztof Meyer, Wilson, *Shostakovich*, p.526.

[39] Wilson, *Shostakovich*, p.513.

[40] Wilson, *Shostakovich*, p.100.

[41] Wilson, *Shostakovich*, p.475.

[42] Wilson, *Shostakovich*, p.46.

[43] Wilson, *Shostakovich*, p.265.

[44] Wilson, *Shostakovich*, p.348.

[45] Abrahams, *Eight Soviet Composers*, p.9.

[46] Taruskin, *History of Western Music*, Vol.4, p.784.

[47] Abrahams, *Eight Soviet Composers*, p.18.

[48] Abrahams, *Eight Soviet Composers*, p.23.

[49] Taruskin, *History of Western Music*, Vol.4, p.795.

[50] Taruskin, *History of Western Music*, Vol.4, p.791.

[51] Taruskin, *History of Western Music*, Vol.4, p.790.

[52] A quote from Flora Litvinova's diary, Wilson, *Shostakovich*, p.391.

[53] Taruskin, *Defining Russia*, p.484.

[54] Taruskin, *Defining Russia*, p.476.

[55] Taruskin, 'Shostakovich and Us,' in Bartlett and Fay (eds.), *Shostakovich in Context*, p.7.

[56] Taruskin, *Defining Russia*, p.483.

[57] Taruskin, in Bartlett and Fay (eds.), *Shostakovich in Context*, p.15.

[58] Taruskin, *Defining Russia*, p.485.

[59] Taruskin, *Defining Russia*, p.496.

[60] Quoted Taruskin, *Defining Russia*, p.489.

[61] Taruskin, *Defining Russia*, p.491.

[62] Volkov, *Testimony*, p.xxxiv.

[63] Quoted Wilson, *Shostakovich*, p.407.

[64] Volkov, *Testimony*, p.119.

[65] Wilson, *Shostakovich*, p.421.

[66] Wilson, *Shostakovich*, p.471.

[67] In a letter 9 October 1969, Quoted Wilson, *Shostakovich*, p.472.

[68] Wilson, *Shostakovich*, p.465.

[69] Andrew Huth, Programme Chronicle, London Symphony Orchestra, 27 March 2008.

[70] Taruskin, *Defining Russia*, p.491.

[71] Wilson, *Shostakovich*, pp.474-5.

[72] Wilson, *Shostakovich*, p.493.

[73] Taruskin, *Defining Russia*, p.490-1.

[74] Taruskin, *Defining Russia*, p.97.

[75] Wilson, *Shostakovich*, p.497.

[76] Wilson, *Shostakovich*, p.498.

[77] Wilson, *Shostakovich*, pp.503-4.

[78] Wilson, *Shostakovich*, p.528.

[79] David Schiff, 'Fruit of the Poison Tree,' *TLS*, 6 May 2005.

[80] Gerard McBurney, 'In from the Cold,' *Saturday Guardian*, 14 January 2006.

[81] See an important new study of the quartets by Wendy Lesser, *Music for Silenced Voices: Shostakovich and His Fifteen Quartets*, Yale University Press, 2011. In these we find 'true Shostakovich territory ... let's call it death.'

[82] I read Anne Applebaum's, *Gulag: A History*, Penguin Books, 2003.

[83] Nadezhda Mandlestam's, *Hope Against Hope*, London: Harvill Press, 1971, the most remarkable. Surely Shostakovich will have seen a terrible warning in the fate of Osip Mandlestam.

7. *The Polish Renaissance:*
Krzystof Penderecki and Henryk Górecki

This is the story of the dissolution of the Soviet Empire and of the relationship of a select number of composers to that decline. Indisputably here is a new generation of composers who reconnect with both religion and spirituality, though the interesting question lies in the balance between the two. As ever under Soviet rule, the composer could not escape politics and we have to ask in what ways their music reflected the cynicism of the intelligentsia at an oppressive and decadent, though seemingly entrenched system. Did the religion and the spiritual in their music contribute to its unravelling? The music of the satellite states will be explored through the example of Poland, followed by the music of composers within the Soviet Union itself, including its oppressed nationalities. But, first, this account of the composers has to be set in its political context.

Post-War Eastern Europe

Just how crushing of any creativity was the Stalinist Empire in Eastern Europe? It was an entirely unimaginative transfer of the Soviet model, with the same command economy and the same party monopoly of power. It was a kind of colonialism in reverse, with Russia providing the raw materials and the satellite economies turning them into manufactured goods. The ultimate sanction was the Soviet army; in Tony Judt's words, 'the greatest military force Europe has ever seen.'[1] Stalin assumed that the west would accept his setting up a kind of buffer zone against any further invasion of the Soviet Union as a legitimate raison d'état. But the combination of western dissent at the subversion of democracy in Eastern Europe, above all in Czechoslovakia, and the seeming threat in Soviet eyes of western intervention through Marshall Aid, led to the Soviet takeover and the Cold War:

'the second Stalinist ice-age was beginning.'[2] How did this affect the intelligentsia?

The non-communist intellectuals went under first but communist sympathisers were equally targeted. Exactly the same paranoia that drove the Terror in the Soviet Union in the 1930's drove the purges of the Communist parties in the satellite states, together with exactly that same self-punitive acceptance of guilt by the intelligentsia. Judt writes of the monumental scale of state punishment: 'virtually the entire population of eastern Europe fell under Kremlin suspicion in those years.'[3] It led to the eclipse of any form of civil society: 'Eastern Europe was slipping into a coma: a winter of inertia and resignation, punctured by cycles of protest and subjugation, that would last for nearly four decades.'[4]

We have already seen how Prokofiev and Shostakovich faced this challenge. Now it was to be the experience of creative artists under the Stalinist Empire. Peculiarly damaging was the way the Cold War cut off composers from the west. Out of Stalin's paranoia, driven 'by a deep-rooted anxiety about Russian and more generally "Eastern "inferiority",'[5] all western influence was held suspect and had to be avoided. Here was a political system utterly stifling of any creativity.

Into this febrile world came Khrushchev's secret speech exposing Stalinism to the 20th Party Congress of February 1956. Was this but a ploy to blame Stalin the better to save the system? But any hint of de-Stalinisation was toxic in the satellite states. Poland will be looked at separately. On 23 October 1956 Hungary embarked on a rebellion that led to a multi-party democracy, withdrawal from the Warsaw pact and a declaration of neutrality. But there was no question of the Soviet Union tolerating any such rebellion, no possible anticipation of 1989. 'In the mid-fifties Communism was a much more self-confident, ruthless, unyielding force,' observes Dominic Sandbrook, 'than the sclerotic incarnation of the Eighties.'[6] By the 4 November Budapest was encircled, Imre Nagy's appeal to the West, itself locked into its own repressive role at Suez, was doomed, and the rebellion was crushed. Judt sees the Hungarian uprising as 'a brief and shapeless revolt in a small outpost of the Soviet Empire,'[7] but its impact on the intelligentsia was devastating. For many, initially sympathetic to the communist venture, but already disillusioned by the purge trials, now 'communism was forever to be associated with repression not revolution,'[8] and a new generation of dissidents was born in the East. Worse, they discovered the indifference of their peers in the west, still sympathetic to the Soviet project, and, as Judt sees it, they gave way to cynical resignation.

But Khrushchev had taken the measure of resentment at Soviet rule and permitted something of a relaxation, a thaw which gave some license to the creative artists. But such as this was, it was put paid to by the Kremlin coup of October 1964 and Brezhnev's coming to power: 'the Soviet Union was settling in for an indefinite twilight of economic stagnation and moral decay.'[9]

Alfred Schnittke's biographer, the cellist Alexander Ivashkin, branded the Brezhnev years 'an era full of restrictions, bureaucracy and idiocy.'[10] Might the system reform itself? Out of a belief that there was 'a third way,' socialism with a human face, liberals in both Poland and Czechoslovakia entertained the delusion that the one party state could itself introduce a form of democratic socialism. This was the hope behind Dubcek's reforms in the Prague Spring. He believed Brezhnev would wear these changes but Brezhnev thought otherwise: 'you cannot deviate from Marxist-Leninism and the weakening of any of the links in the world system of socialism directly affects the socialist countries, and they cannot look on indifferently upon this.'[11] So to the invasion of Czeckoslovakia by the combined forces of the Warsaw pact, Poland, Hungary, Bulgaria, East Germany and the Soviet Union. Judt is very clear about the consequences: 'never again would it be possible to maintain that Communism rested on popular consent or the legitimacy of a reformed party or even the lessons of history.' Dubcek's

Action programme, far from being a beginning, was an end: 'Communism in Eastern Europe staggered on, sustained by an unlikely alliance of foreign loans and Russian bayonets: the rotting carcass was finally carried away only in 1989. But the soul of communism had died years before in Prague, in August 1968.'[12]

At this point journalists and artists were treated as social pariahs. 'What followed' in Neal Ascherson's account, 'was simply 21 years of wasted life, young people growing middle-aged as they breathed the foul air of a police state.'[13]

Yet, of course, to almost universal amazement the system unravelled. Who takes the credit? Was it Gorbachev or was it its opponents? Judt believes that in such a centralised system only an initiative from the Soviet Union could set change in motion. After the passing of a sick and elderly leadership, Brezhnev in November 1982, Andropov in February 1984, Chernenko in March 1985, the young and fit Gorbachev was elected Secretary General 11 March 1985. Here was a rerun of Dubcek's delusion that the one-party state could itself introduce reform and yet retain control. The very means Gorbachev chose, *perestroika,* the restructuring of its economy, and *glasnost*, or openness, would inevitably subvert the system. Simply by allowing open election to the Congress of People's Deputies, the presence of critical voices, put paid to any idea of a managed pluralism. How would the satellite states respond?

Post-Prague 1968 the idea of reform did not go away but, rather than seek the overthrow of the system, there was a campaign to get it to live up to its constitutional pledges and introduce some form of civil society. One of the great ironies of the Brezhnev years was Russian acceptance of the Helsinki Accords of 1975 which, whilst seemingly guaranteeing the Soviet Union from interference in its domestic affairs, laid down a template of civil rights and this inspired an entirely new form of resistance. The Soviet system would have to recognise the civil rights of its own citizens. The most famous example was the Czechoslovak Charter 77. Judt has high praise for Vaclav Havel: 'no one individual of comparable public standing emerged in any other Communist country.'[14] The role of the intellectuals in corroding the system was considerable in both Poland and Czechoslovakia though less evident in the Soviet Union itself. But when revolution came it did so with exceptional speed.

The opposition knew an entirely new situation opened up when Gorbachev renounced the Brezhnev doctrine of the right to intervene. Before the UN, 7 December 1988, Gorbachev declared: 'Freedom of choice is a universal principle. There could be no exception.'[15] Admittedly, the opposition found this an almost impossible promise to believe: 'they kept an air cocked for the grind of distant tanks.'[16] As Judt observes: 'no other territorial empire in recorded history ever abandoned dominance so rapidly and with such good grace and so little bloodshed.'[17] Above all, it put paid to fear. In Judt's words, 'the fear of being alone – the impossibility of knowing whether your own feelings were shared by others, was dispatched forever';[18] in Ascherson's account, 'it was in 1989 that ordinary people, on an enormous scale, by the millions, lost their fear.'[19]

Maybe perversely the question that has to be addressed of the revolutions of 1989 is, was this a change for the better? Timothy Garton Ash hedges his bets. At one point he commented: 'the year 1989 was one of the best in European history. Indeed I am hard pressed to think a better one.'[20] But a qualification quickly followed: 'In my darker moments 1989 seems to me like the last, late flowering of a very aged rose. This is not the big-hearted Europe of which visionaries like Vaclav Havel dreamed in 1989.'[21] One of the consequences of a non-violent revolution was that the old elites, the *nomenklatura,* far from being violently displaced, simply reinvented themselves in the new democracies and the very process of *perestroika* got terribly out of hand. Seamus Milne, with particular reference to the fall of the Wall and of East Germany sees the passing of a country with full employment, social equality, cheap housing, transport and culture, the best child care system in the world and freedom in the work place. Graphically of Russia, he writes: 'post-communist catastrophe produced the greatest economic collapse in peace-time modern history.'[22] These are sobering observations and qualify any excessive euphoria.

But, of course, supremely it opens up the possibility of freedom of expression. How did the composers relate to the oppressive system and to the dissident movement? Is there a morbid possibility that it was confrontation that made their music and that creativity flagged after liberation?

Polish Composers

For all the outreach of Soviet socialist realism and its anti-formalism to the satellite states Poland was to buck the system and in the late 1950's, through the Warsaw Autumn festivals, there was to be an astonishing expression of modernist music. So much so that the historian of this movement, Bernard Jacobson, queried, 'was there to be a new tyranny of intellectually determined hyper-modernism, Darmstadt usurping Moscow?'[23] In fact, the leading composers in time emerged far more conservative and, their relevance to this text, deeply catholic and evidently spiritual. Four composers dominate this movement, two from an older generation, Andzej Panufnik (1914-91) and Witold Lutoslawski (1913-94) and two from a younger, Krzystof Penderecki, born 23 November 1933 and Henryk Górecki, born 6 December 1933 and to die, after a long illness, 12 November 2010. Once again this has to be set in its political context.

Poland endured a truly horrific war. It was caught between two totalitarian systems and suffered appalling losses. We have already seen how Shostakovich responded to the holocaust and Russian anti-Semitism. Polish composers faced a greater burden. Some three million Polish Jews were murdered, either shot by SS Einsatzgruppen or cremated in the death camps of Treblinka, Belzec and Sobibor, and all this by 1942, prior to Auschwitz. Timothy Snyder has shown how the real killing fields between Germany and Russia stretched from the Baltic States to the Ukraine, cutting through Poland, with Belarus at its epicentre.[24]

But Poland was pincered by the Nazi-Soviet pact and Russia committed yet further atrocities against the Polish people. Quite possibly 1.25 million Poles, mainly women, children and the elderly were deported to labour camps in the Artic or Kazakhstan: two years later but 800,000 were still alive. Notoriously, Stalin set about the elimination of men of active age, Poland's present and future elite, ordering the murder 5 March 1940 of some 14,700 Poles in POW camps, and 11, 000 in prison. The mass murder in Katyn forest is the best known.[25] The lie that this was a German atrocity was sustained by the Communist rulers of Poland and Russia, even Gorbachev reluctant to reveal the whole truth: it was left to Boris Yeltsin to come clean. Again, notoriously, Stalin stood aside during the Warsaw uprising of the Polish Home army in 1944, deeming this 'a handful of power-hungry adventurers and criminals.'[26]

Snyder terrifyingly suggests that both Nazi and Stalinist atrocities had a strand of rationalism to them: 'what is crucial is that the ideology that legitimated mass death was also a vision of economic development.,' though surely truer of the gulag than the Nazi labour camps. No wonder the Poles have a different awareness of the war, its outbreak being a double invasion, 1 September 1 and 17 September 1939, and with no sense of its end in May 1945 through the ongoing occupation by one of the belligerent states.

Even so, Poland, post-war, carved out for itself a form of exceptionalism. Stalin recognised 'that Soviet rule was more obviously resented in Poland than anywhere else'[27] and that, if there was to be a stable buffer zone in Eastern Europe, then he would have to make concessions. If in the rigged elections of 1947 the same old party bureaucratic elite prevailed, nevertheless, the new regime did not impose collectivisation, the Catholic Church remained publicly active, the Universities were left intact. If Gomulka was duly sacked for his opposition to collectivisation, and talk of a 'national' path to socialism and replaced by Bolislav Bierat, he escaped a show trial during the purges, though it came close; before Beria's death the papers had been prepared. In 1956, if Poland echoed some of the Hungarian resistance with demonstrations in Poznan and Gomulka's return to power, it escaped invasion and Gomulka, recognised as a good party man, hung on. Now came the Khruschev thaw and a period of cultural renewal in Poland.

But there followed a long struggle between the state and dissidence. There were the beginnings of a revisionist movement, Leszak Kolakowski its leading theorist. With student unrest in 1968, Adam Michnik a key figure, Gomulka authorised brutal reprisals. Jews especially were targeted. Between 1968-9, of the 30,000 remaining, 20,000 left. Did this cost Gomulka his job? Then in 1970 came a major strike in the Gdansk ship-yard. Intellectuals now looked to Labour. Michnik, in his *A New Evolution,* took up the idea of insisting that the regime live up to its progressive rhetoric and permit the forming of a civil society. KOR, the Committee of the Defence of Workers, was set up September 1976, and the Charter of Workers Rights drafted in 1979.

To what extent was this opposition galvanised by the visit of the recently elected Pope John Paul 11 on 2 June 1979? Judt writes of 'the peculiarly messianic style of Polish Catholicism' and of Pope John Paul 'offering his Church not merely as a silent sanctuary but as an alternative pole of moral and social authority.'[28]

So to an end-game between the Communist party and Solidarity. In 1980 major protest in the Gdansk shipyards, Lech Walesa, a devout Catholic, its inspirational leader, led to Solidarity being recognised as an independent trade union. A link had been made with the Catholic Church. Here was a rupture in the party's monopoly of power: 'Solidarity was doomed to arouse the ghosts of Budapest and Prague.'[29] But on 13 December 1981 General Jaruzelski imposed martial law and the battle had to be fought all over again. There was the murder of the radical priest, Father Jerzy Popieluszko in 1984. Another counter-society had to emerge. In 18 December 1988 a Solidarity Citizens Committee was formed. On 6 February 1989 the government entered into talks and, as Judt puts it, it led to 'a negotiated termination of Communism in Poland.'[30] On 27 January 1990 the Communist party was dissolved. What had been the response of the composers to this political change?

Characterising the Polish Renaissance

Here I am in part relying on the rich material provided by a conference on post-war Polish music at Canterbury Christ Church University 28 April-2 May 2009, attended by all its expert interpreters.[31] In the early days of the regime Polish composers were threatened by the same decrees of Zhdanov as in the Soviet Union. At the Wagow conference of 1949 the Composers Union came into line. Composers were invited to enter a prize competition in celebration of the merger of the Socialist party and the Socialist Workers party and Panufnik, for one, submitted three songs. Stalin's 70th birthday was likewise to be celebrated. In 1951 there was a Festival of New Music and some 300 new works were submitted, once again with Panufnik to the fore with his Peace Symphony, later recycled as Symphony Elegiaca. Just as in the Soviet Union the Party saw every advantage in patronising music, and this put composers in an impossible bind, rewarded by accommodation and educational and health privileges if they cooperated, by their loss if they resisted. But the Polish composers were unusually resilient and fought back over the content of their music. By 1955 the Government were ready to compromise. And so we enter the period of Khrushchev's thaw and the breakthrough of the Warsaw Autumn festivals.

Can one generalise about the composers of the Polish Renaissance? How much, for example, do they owe to Karol Szymanowski (1882-1937)? He is not always recognised as an influence. Interestingly, he was more a mystical than a religious composer, not a Catholic, though attracted to other faiths, especially Islam. A work, for example, that looks forward to the mysticism of Górecki is his *Stabat Mater* (1925-6), and indeed is seen by one commentator as 'a more varied and more satisfying work' than Gorecki's Symphony No.3, and seen as 'infused with an ecstatic spiritual intensity, drawing on Eastern church music and on inflections of folk song in the vocal lines.'[32] At the Conference Charles Bodman Rae tried out a number of generalisations about the composers. Theirs was an individualism, a dislike of system, their whimsy, sardonic humour, their spiritualism, a deep seriousness, expressiveness, extreme emotional turbulence. Another generalisation was the role of memorialisation in their music, their sense of history. More tricky is any definition of the nature of their modernism. Was theirs a deliberate attempt to cock a snoop at the Soviet ideology of socialist realism by aping the modernism of the Darmstadt school? The point is made, however, that the true ideological opponent at the time was East Germany, still seen as ruled by an unreconstructed Stalinist, Walter Ulbricht, rather than the Soviet Union. Yet in some ways their modernism was subtler than this and sought something distinctively Polish. Possibly the authorities turned a blind eye just because it did not follow the Darmstadt line, the West's Cold War answer to Soviet ideology. My own sense in listening to the modernist pieces played in the Sounds New festival that ran alongside the Conference was of a music which reflected an imprisoned culture, a music that had the feel of a caged animal, restless and angry. Only later did the music open to the spiritual. Pope John Paul argued that Poland had never ceased to be part of a wider Europe and that under totalitarian rule it experienced a spiritual maturation, one that will determine the face of the new Europe. But maybe all this can only be grasped by looking at the composers in their particularity.

Andrzej Panufnik and Witold Lutoslawski

Both these composers from an older generation are seen as metaphysical, but Panufnik more evidently concerned with the spiritual and poetic, Lutoslawski more secular. Jacobson differentiates: 'where Panufnik is metaphysical, Lutoslawski is empirical: looking outwards rather than inwards, he is the sophisticated, cosmopolitan man of reason.'[33] Both survived the war as café pianists. Both went underground to raise money for Resistance Jewish artists. Panufnik's cousin, Anton died at Auschwitz, his brother, Mirek in the Warsaw uprising of Autumn 1944. If Panufnik became Poland's leading composer by 1950 his music was branded as alien to Socialism, and to escape the torment of being a creative artist under Communism he escaped in 14 July 1954. Some saw this as an act of betrayal. In 1954 he was appointed Director of the City of Birmingham Symphony Orchestra. In music oscillating between the visionary and the angry he is seen as having a kinship with Górecki and Pärt. Most germane to this project was his *Sinfonia Sacra* (Symphony No.3 1963), celebrating the millennium of the Polish state and its Christianity. It was commissioned by the Kosciuszko Foundation and awarded 1st prize in a competition sponsored by Prince Rainier of Monaco. Jacobson sees in it 'a spiritual grandeur rare in our times.'[34] There followed his *Sinfonia Mystica* (Symphony No.6 1977) and *Sinfonia Votica* (Symphony No.8 1988), dedicated to Pope John Paul's special icon, the Black Madonna. His *Bassoon Concerto* commemorated the murdered priest, Father Jerzy Popieluszko. Panuknik stated: 'for me personally music is an expression of deep human feeling. I never regard the technical side of a musical work as an end in itself.' Although he eventually returned to Poland his exile inevitably counted against Panufnik.

Witold Lutoslawski's family likewise fell victim to politics. His father had fled to Moscow to escape the German advance in World War 1, only to be trapped by the terms of the Brest-Litovsk treaty and to be shot as a counter-revolutionary. If he himself was captured but escaped, in 1939 his brother

Henryk was captured by the Red Army and later died in the gulag. He had already made a name for himself as a composer pre-war, in neo-classical music influenced by Stravinsky and Bartok, but this inevitably put him at risk from post-war Soviet ideology and his First Symphony was banned as formalist after its first performance in 1948. He ate humble pie and acknowledged it 'was not leading him anywhere' and that he had 'to begin again – to work from scratch on my sound language.' The answer, after a prolonged period of composing, was his Concerto for Orchestra (1950-4), premiered 26 November 1954. Interestingly, he had completed it but 18 days after Panufnik's defection. But he had played safe and made a tactical retreat into children's folk music, all perfectly acceptable to the authorities, and with its success he assumed Panuknik's mantle as Poland's leading composer. In the permissive climate after 1956 he was more boldly modernist, influenced by John Cage. He said of his Concerto that his folk music 'was merely a raw material used to build a large musical form of several movements which does not in the least originate either from folk songs or from folk dances.'[35] In his notebook for 1973 he wrote: 'I regard creative activity as a kind of soul-fishing, and the "catch" is the best medicine for loneliness, that most human form of suffering.'[36]

Krzystof Penderecki and Henryk Górecki

In their mid 20's, Penderecki, born 23 November 1933, and Górecki, 6 December 1933, with the nightmare of Nazism and Stalinism behind them, in Jacobsons's account, they faced a new situation. He summarises: they lived 'in a country where despite periods of national misery on the socio-political front, the arts in general were allowed to flourish with more freedom that at any time since 1939.'[37] They were to benefit from Polish exceptionalism. Their embrace of modernism during the early years of the Warsaw Autumn festivals – and an identikit mitteleuropa modernism shapes these East European composers at this stage – quickly gave way to an underlying, more conservative religio-spiritual music, and here again the regime was permissive. 'Despite the continuing pressures of Communist (and materialist) ideology in Polish life,' says Jacobson, 'the authorities began to realize that a ban on religious subjects could no longer be effectively imposed on artists of their status.'[38] But theirs was to be a different experience of Jaruzelski's dictatorship, Penderecki coming through it a good deal more lightly than Górecki.

Yet, despite Jacobson's caveat, both were haunted by memories of Nazi and Stalinist crimes. During his childhood in Debica, east of Krakow, Penderecki witnessed the round-up of Jews and wrote movingly of the liquidation of the Lodz ghetto in his *Kadisz*. Górecki visited Auschwitz as a school-boy aged 12 and there is no more harrowing response in music to Auschwitz than Górecki's *Symphony of Sorrowful Songs*.

In interpreting their music we come up yet again against that borderline between the religious and the spiritual. Only a fifth of Penderecki's music can be classified as explicitly religious, and even less so in the case of Górecki. But both were devout Catholics.

Penderecki decided in 1958 he would have to start from scratch. He had been educated at the Jagellonian University in Krakow and at the Krakow Academy of Music, 1954-8. He had been isolated from the west by Stalinism and was now suddenly exposed to the likes of Stravinsky, Messiaen, Luigi Nono. At this point, though, he was unable to get a passport to visit Darmstadt. He was to win immediate recognition for his *Psalms of David*, his prize submission in 1958, a work much influenced by Stravinsky's *Symphony of Psalms*. It was also influenced by electronic music. Other early works included the harrowing *Threnody for the Victims of Hiroshima* and *Anaklasis*. Performers, however, took against the way his compositions to their ears abused the instruments. Originality was seemingly all and he turned away from the Polish school that derived from Szyman-owski. And then in 1963 he did visit Darmstadt, only to leave bored after three days. He was in contrast attracted to Bach and sacred music, though of course Bach wrote the Passion story in a Lutheran and Protestant tradition, Penderecki to do so in a Catholic.

So to the work that really established his reputation, his *Passion and Death of Our Lord Jesus Christ according to Luke*, to give it its full title. Why St Luke? More than the other gospels it is seen as dwelling on the experience of the Cross, on the conversation at Golgotha with the criminals, as a gospel of despair, if ultimately one of salvation for the faithful. It was premiered in Munster Cathedral in 1966. I was privileged to hear it performed in Canterbury Cathedral, conducted by the composer, as part of the Sounds New Festival, 2 May 2009. In some ways I was more held than moved yet cannot imagine the nave of the cathedral being filled again by a sound of such magnitude. The Guardian critic observed: 'its moments of extreme violence remain profoundly unnerving.' Here is an 'angry avant-gardiste work,' 'its aim was to redefine the Bach-based tradition of passion music in the aftermath of mid-20th century genocide.'[39] And it was a modernist piece. To quote Paul Griffiths: 'Penderecki speaks a trenchantly modern musical language, exploring all the cloudbursts of woodwind figuration, the brassy eruptions, the searing string clusters and the irrepressible percussion outbursts that had entered the orchestral repertory in the works of Schoenberg, Berg and Webern fifty years before and then been further developed by such composers as Stockhausen, Xenakis and Penderecki himself in the 1950's and early 1960's.'[40] But it is also seen as heralding the new Penderecki: 'its meditative sections, however, are strikingly prophetic of the conservatism of Penderecki's more recent music.' Another commentator sees within the work 'the opposition of two contrasting, semantically differentiated sound worlds,' one, 'the prayerful quasi-ritual nature of this world links it with the mysterious sphere of the sacred,' the other, 'contemporary techniques dominate. This works symbolizes the sphere of darkness, hatred and evil.'[41] Was this, in fact, a portrayal of the conflict between the Catholic Church and Communism? Was this as much a commentary on the cruelty of the 20th century as on the Passion of Christ?[42] Materially, Penderecki did well from the work and by 1967 owned a Mercedes.

Penderecki saw *St Luke's Passion* not in terms of his Catholicism but of his response to Auschwitz and Hiroshima. In a conversation in 1967 with Jacobson he stated: 'I am concerned with these things in an essentially moral and social way, not in either a political or sectarian religious way.'[43] It signalled his parting of the ways with the avant-garde – the avant-garde music in *St Luke's Passion* represented evil – and modernists began to treat him with contempt. He was drawn to Bruckner and loved romantic and tonal music. His music certainly takes on a more ritualistic character. The second half of *St Luke's Passion* is itself seen as a liturgical account rather than a narrative one of the gospel story. In 1979 his *Paradise Lost*, a huge unwieldy opera, was performed before Pope John Paul in the Vatican. Jacobson intriguingly summarises his later music: 'in his most cataclysmic vein, Penderecki can conjure up through his music all the elemental power of a battle between the gods and giants, but it is a battle frozen somewhere in time – we can never know the result.'[44] He was not, however, to be discomfited by martial law – the regime overlooked his religious music. Even *Lacrimosa*, a piece composed to memorialise the Gdansk dockyard workers who had died in the uprising of 1970, and subsequently part of his *Polish Requiem* (1984), escaped the censor.

Górecki's was an altogether more troubled life than Penderecki's.[45] He was born into a peasant background of some poverty in Czernica, near Rybnik, in a coal-mining area near Katowice. His father worked on the railways. His piano-playing mother died when he was two. All his life he endured poor health. In childhood a neglected fall, a hip injury, led to tuberculosis, a tumour on the brain and a permanent limp:

no doubt it would have been worse but for treatment by nuns in a German hospital in Bytom. He had to struggle to obtain a musical education, his father and step-mother forbidding his playing his mother's piano, though in 1943 he was allowed violin lessons with a local teacher. Eventually he made his way in 1955, via a two year period in a teacher training col-lege in the Intermediate School of Music in Rybik, to the State Academy of Music in Katowice. All his life, when he did not escape to Chocholow, near Zakopane and his beloved Tatra mountains, was spent in this bleak industrial city, its steel mill Stalin's gift to the Poles.

Górecki more than any other Polish composer of the Renaissance reflected the history of his times: 'the war, the rotten times under Communism, our life today, the starving, Bosnia – what madness. And why? Why? The sorrow, it burns inside me. I cannot shake it off.'[46]

Even so, Górecki, as Penderecki, was recognised young. On 27 February 1958 the Silesian State Orchestra in Katowice performed an entire concert of the music of this 24 year old composer. Then his *Epitafium* was performed at the Warsaw Autumn Festival in the same year. This was a setting of a poem scribbled on a serviette hours before his death by a young poet, Julian Tuwim.

> *For the sake of economy, put out the light eternal if it were to shine on me.*

In 1961 he attended a summer course at Darmstadt. Of greater significance was the time he spent in Paris where he regularly heard Messiaen perform at La Trinité, though was far too shy to introduce himself. They were only really to speak together in 1980. 'After Messiaen,' he stated in a TV interview in 1993, 'it's all finished for me':[47] Was it Messiaen, together with Charles Ives, with their shared 'mystical extremism,' who inspired the new Górecki?[48]

Then came his Second Symphony, premiered in Warsaw in June 1973. This was a commission from the Kosciuszko Foundation to mark the 500th anniversary of the birth of Copernicus. Here was a two movement work, setting to music a 15th century hymn and texts of Copernicus. Jacobson sees the message of the work as 'quintessentially Góreckian in its untroubled juxtaposition of scientific with traditionally religious concepts.'[49] Adrian Thomas, his biographer, sees Górecki discovering 'a theme in which he could fulfil one of his abiding passions: the contemplation of the cosmos.' He writes of a sustained crescendo in the second movement 'as if to embrace the universe and bathe it in light.' But ultimately Thomas sees it as a tragic symphony, for had not Copernicus destroyed an earlier way of thinking: 'we were no longer the centre of the universe, we became nothing.'[50] Here is a spirituality that leads well into the Symphony no.3.

The *Symphony of Sorrowful Songs*, quite unlike anything he had so far written, was premiered in April 1977 at the Festival International d'Art Contemporain in Royan, France. It made no immediate impact. It was only with the release of a CD recording of a performance by the London Sinfonietta, under David Zinman, with Dawn Upshaw the soprano, that it became the best selling classical disk of all time. His obituarist writes of its spirituality filling 'a God-shaped space in an era bereft of previous certainties.'[51] This success was compounded by Tony Palmer's film (1993) of a performance, set against simply appalling images of Auschwitz, the Ethiopian famine and violence in Bosnia. Possibly no more charged film has ever been made of a piece of music. The fine and uplifting face of Dawn Upshaw just about makes it possible to watch. It was at a showing of his documentary to an audience of the Sounds New Festival that Tony Palmer insisted that all great art is political. I heard the Symphony live for the first time in April 2010, played by the London Philharmonic under Marin Alsop. In fact, it replaced the premiere of his 4th, he was too ill to complete it, and that sady remained the case at his death. The performance was dedicated to the 96 dead of the Polish aircrash en route to

Smolensk to commemorate the atrocity at Katyn. Tim Ashley observed: 'this was a reminder of just how gut-wrenching it can be.'[52] It was superbly sung by a Polish soprano flown in at short notice. I felt that, delinked from those horrific images of the Palmer documentary, the music stood out all the more and was even more moving.

There are three songs. The first, *Where has he gone, my dear young son?* is taken from a collection that celebrated the Silesian uprisings against the Germans, 1912-21. The second was taken from a graffito, scrawled on a prison wall, *mam, do not weep*, written, we now know, by the 18 year old Helena Blazusiakowna, a prisoner, though to be a survivor,[53] in the Gestapo Zakopane HQ. Górecki had come across a photo of the graffito in a collection of photographs on Zakopane under Nazi rule during one of his holidays in the Tatra mountains. The third is a folksong from the Opole region on Poland's South West border. Górecki's childhood visit to Auschwitz had left an indelible impression: 'I had the feeling that the huts were still warm ... the paths themselves – and this image has never left me – the paths were made from human bones, thrown onto the paths like shingle. We boys – how to walk on this? This is not sand, not earth. We were walking on human beings.'[54] Górecki revisited the camp for the documentary and there is a poignant shot of him, with his marked limp, walking into the distance alongside the railway of death. The second song becomes increasingly Marian: 'Support me always Mama, support me always, Hail Mary, full of Grace.' Górecki believed that he had to act as a witness, that music had the power to convey the suffering, and, indeed, in this work one feels that music can achieve what Adorno felt poetry could not do, adequately address the Holocaust.

Yet Górecki did not want too narrow a political reading of the Symphony: it was 'not about war, it's not a Dies Irae.'[55] Jacobson, rising to that expectation, interprets it as 'philosophically, the theme of suffering in its most unchanging aspect.' The music proceeds slowly, somehow relentlessly, and with the utmost gravity. He was much in debt to Schubert. 'It is ironic that, in a work like the Third Symphony,' concludes Jacobson, 'Polish music found a universal language by rejecting the facile orthodoxies of modish modernism on the one hand and dogmatically programmed "social realism" on the other.'[56]

Górecki was always much more caught up in politics than Penderecki. As he himself observed, Silesia, as an industrialised area, was far more oppressed than Krakow and Warsaw. 'Górecki's battles against the party were,' Thomas argues, 'symptomatic of a prolonged malaise in Polish society and culture.'[57] In his job as Principal of Katowice Academy of Music – he was appointed in 1975 – he was always at risk. In resolving to write a piece for Cardinal Wotyla on the 900th anniversary of the death of St Stanislas – recalling a highly symbolic quarrel between Church and State in which the Saint was executed for his rebellion against King Boleslaw – he incurred the ostracism of his colleagues and he chose to resign. It's a story that anticipates the murder of Father Jerzy Popieluszco. In the end the piece, *Beatus Vir*, was performed in the Cathedral of Krakow, with Górecki conducting, to mark the occasion of the first pilgrimage to Poland of the recently elected Cardinal as Pope in 1979. Pope John Paul spoke of 'a profound experience.'[58] The Pope's third visit in 1987 was the occasion for *Totus Tuus,* music devoted to the Virgin Mary.

Under martial rule, Górecki became a recluse. Early on there was an overtly political piece, *Miserere* for unaccompanied chorus, to commemorate those who were injured in a clash between the police and Rural Solidarity, sister organisation to Solidarity, at Bydgoszez, 19 March 1981. Górecki, however, would not let it be performed, for fear this might be taken as a compromise with the new regime. It was only performed in 1987 in the town of Wloclawek where Father Popieluszco's body had been found.

Between 1985 and 1988 Górecki is seen as moving 'ever closer to the musical and spiritual world of the Church.' He drew heavily on the 1878 *Church Songbook* but he always insisted, to quote Thomas, 'neither in these songs nor in any of his compositions does Górecki consider that he is writing religious music.'[59] Nevertheless, when he was awarded 28 February 1995 an Honorary degree by the Catholic University of America in Washington, he quoted Pope John Paul's belief that an authentic work of art 'tries to bring closer the mystery of reality' but 'no matter how strong the charm of their music and words, they know that their words are only a distant echo of God's Word.'[60]

So how to interpret Górecki's spirituality? Both Jacobson and Thomas resist seeing any correspondence with New Age minimalism, the music of Arvo Pärt and John Tavener. Jacobson asserts: 'his powerful sense of concentration has nothing to do with the mental languor, the relentless relaxation of "New Age" music.'[61] Górecki looked to Messiaen and Ives and further back to Bach, Haydn and Mozart, but, above all, to Schubert. But parallels are also seen with the music of Szymanowski, especially in his *Stabat Mater*. Both composers are seen as demonstrating that sacred and folk music are one and the same. One commentator refers to 'a certain maximalism in his work,'[62] which would, of course, make for interesting links with that tradition of the spiritual in music advanced by Richard Taruskin. Jacobson sees him as a greater composer than Penderecki: 'whereas Penderecki's ceaseless search for new creative stimuli seems to have diminished his own artistic size, Górecki, by burrowing ever more deeply within himself, has grown to world stature.'[63] And in his inwardness Górecki is seen as exploring Jungian archetypes.

Neither composer radically changed direction after the fall of communism, Penderecki still exploring his neo-romanticism, Górecki concentrating on small scale works. One supposes that in the manner of an Anthony Page or the Matthews brothers there will be a construction of his 4th Symphony.

Let Górecki's biographer have the last word. 'He is a truly striking, thoughtful and passionate individual who throughout his eventful life has single-mindedly pursued his own musical goals, remaining true to himself and his musical ethos, constantly searching for that state of body and soul so eloquently penned by Tuwim in "Song of Joy and Rhythm"':

> *Slowly –inside – I am restored to myself*
> *To intense joy and profound rhythm ...*
> *Enough. No need for words.*[64]

Notes

[1] Tony Judt, *Postwar: A History of Europe since 1945*, London: Pimlico, 2007, p.117.
[2] Judt, *Postwar* p.145.
[3] Judt, *Postwar*, p.191.
[4] Judt, *Postwar*, p.195.
[5] Judt, *Postwar*, p.188.
[6] Dominic Sandbrook, 'The Year that changed the World,' *The Observer*, 23 October 2006.
[7] Judt, *Postwar* , p.318.
[8] Judt, *Postwar*, p.322.
[9] Judt, *Postwar*, p.425.
[10] Alexander Ivashkin, *Alfred Schnittke*, London: Phaidon, 1996, p.119.
[11] Quoted Judt, *Postwar*, p.443.
[12] Judt, *Postwar*, p.447.
[13] Neal Ascherson, 'When hope faded in the streets of the East,' *The Observer*, 20 January 2008.
[14] Judt, *Postwar*, p.620.
[15] Quoted Judt, *Postwar*, p.604.
[16] Neal Ascherson, 'A time when hope replaced repression,' *The Observer*, 2 October 2009.
[17] Judt, *Postwar*, p.633.

[18] Judt, *Postwar*, p.628.

[19] Neal Ascherson, *The Observer*, 2 October 2009.

[20] T Garton Ash, '1989!,' *The New York Review of Books*, 24 October 2009.

[21] T Garton Ash, 'It was Europe's finest hour. It changed the world. So where now?,' *The Guardian*, 5 November 2009.

[22] Seamus Milne, 'The real lesson of Berlin is that nothing is ever settled,' *The Guardian*, 12 November 2009.

[23] Bernard Jacobson, *A Polish Renaissance*, London: Phaidon, 1996, p.86.

[24] Timothy Snyder, 'Holocaust: The Ignored Reality' *New York Review of Books*, 18 July 2009, subsequently a monograph, *Bloodlands: Europe between Hitler and Stalin*, London: Bodley Head, 2010.

[25] See Neal Ascherson, 'An Accident of History,' *The Guardian*, 17 April 2010.

[26] Judt, *Postwar*, p.102.

[27] Judt, *Postwar*, p.172.

[28] Judt, *Postwar*, pp.586-7.

[29] Judt, *Postwar*, p.589.

[30] Judt, *Postwar*, p.607.

[31] 'Polish Music since 1945,' 30 April-2 May 2009, Department of Music, Canterbury Christ Church University.

[32] Mark Morris (ed.), *The Pimlico Dictionary of Twentieth Century Composers*, London: Pimlico, 1996, p.303.

[33] Jacobson, *Polish Renaissance*, p.107.

[34] Jacobson, *Polish Renaissance*, p.120.

[35] Quoted in notes by Calum Macdonald, 'Proms Programme,' 8 August 2009.

[36] Jacobson, *Polish Renaissance*, p.100.

[37] Jacobson, *Polish Renaissance*, p.123.

[38] Jacobson, *Polish Renaissance*, p.127.

[39] Tim Ashley, *The Guardian*, 7 May 2009.

[40] Paul Griffith's Programme Notes, Sounds New Contemporary Music Festival 2009, for the performance of 'St. Luke Passion' in Canterbury Cathedral, 2 May 2009.

[41] Regina Chlopicka, *Conference programme, Polish Music since 1945*, p.19.

[42] It is instructive to compare it to Roman Maciejewski's (1910-98) monumental Requiem, dedicated to 'those who died in wars of all times.' It is a colossal piece, 110 minutes long. It was recently performed in Westminster Cathedral and one critic found it seriously wanting: 'it's patchwork, fatally lacking the sense of necessity that impelled Maciejewski to write it.' Andrew Clements, *The Guardian*, 8 February 2010. For all its grandiosity and that hugely inflated last movement I have to agree. Maybe Penderecki's modernism acted as a check against similar tendencies in his own work.

[43] Jacobson, *Polish Renaissance*, p.153.

[44] Jacobson, *Polish Renaissance*, p.205.

[45] A major source for his life is Adrian Thomas, *Górecki*, Oxford: Clarendon Press, 1997. See also his obituary by Keith Potter in *The Guardian*, 13 November 2010.

[46] Quoted Jacobson, *Polish Renaissance*, p.174.

[47] Quoted Jacobson, *Polish Renaissance*, p.178.

[48] As Jacobson suggests, *Polish Renaissance*, p.178.

[49] Jacobson, *Polish Renaissance*, p.182.

[50] Thomas, *Górecki*, pp.74-8.

[51] Keith Potter, *The Guardian*, 13 November 2010.

[52] Tim Ashley, *The Guardian*, 21 April 2010.

[53] See a follow up to Górecki's obituary by Bob Bibby, *The Guardian*, 26 November 2010.

[54] Quoted Jacobson, *Polish Renaissance*, pp.171-2.

[55] Quoted Jacobson, *Polish Renaissance*, p.191.

[56] Jacobson, *Polish Renaissance*, p.194.

[57] Thomas, *Górecki*, p.100.

[58] Quoted Thomas, *Górecki*, p.100.

[59] Thomas, *Górecki*, p.106.

[60] Quoted Thomas, *Górecki*, p.107.

[61] Jacobson, *Polish Renaissance*, p.302.

[62] Andrzej Chlopecki, quoted Jacobson, *A Polish Renaissance*, p.203.

[63] Jacobson, *Polish Renaissance*, p.206.

[64] Thomas, *Górecki*, p.149.

8. *Arvo Pärt, Alfred Schnittke, Sofia Gubaidulina*

All three composers had gone into exile before the collapse of the Soviet Union. That was a time when Gorbachev, who had so remarkably rejected the Brezhnev doctrine and left the satellite states to sort out their own future, felt unable to do the same as the Soviet Union itself unravelled. He was ready to resort to violent repression to deal with rebellion in the Baltic States. At home he was squeezed between Russian protest led by Boris Yeltsin and an attempted counter-revolutionary coup, but, as Judt emphasises, the old guard 'were losing their crucial asset, fear.'[1] Though restored to power, Gorbachev resigned 24 August 1991. The Soviet Union was dissolved 31 December 1991. But it is less these events than the earlier, the thaw under Khrushchev and then the long dreary Brezhnev years, that impacted on the three composers under review.

Arvo Pärt

Often compared to Górecki, despite disclaimers by interpreters of Górecki, Pärt is another example of a Soviet composer who flirted with modernism, only to change direction entirely and seek an engagement with the spiritual. If Lutheran by upbringing, in 1972 he converted to Russian Orthodoxy and it was its liturgy, together with Gregorian chant, that was his inspiration. Born 11 September 1935 he lived through the appalling experience of the war in the Baltic States, though Pärt clams his memories only extend back to the long night of post-war Soviet occupation. But once again, to read his music we have to set his composition in its political context.

Estonia was part of those killing fields that Timothy Snyder has portrayed from the Baltic States to the Ukraine. During the war it had to endure both Soviet and Nazi occupation and, in aiding the Germans against a second Soviet occupation after 1941, some Estonians fatally colluded with the holocaust. Just because it had already experienced freedom from Russian (Tsarist) occupation between the wars, Soviet occupation was all the more bitterly resented, and with Russian occupation lasting so much the longer after the war, Communism came to be seen as a greater evil than Nazism. And, of course, any visitor to Tallinn will be aware of how deep a German acculturation Estonia underwent through membership of the Hanseatic League. Even so, Estonian participation in the Einsatzgruppen atrocities is a stain on its honour, however much SS veterans try to pass it off as patriotism.

Life under Soviet occupation was grim. To quote Judt: 'by 1953 rural conditions in hitherto prosperous Estonia had deteriorated to the point where cows blown over in the wind were too weak to get back on their feet unaided.'[2] The Baltic States were worse off than the satellite. Such had been the scale of Estonian deportations and Russian immigration that by the 1980's only 64% of the population was ethnically Estonian. Pärt, who had reluctantly gone into exile in 1980, was not to witness the rebellion against Soviet rule. It began with demonstrations in Tallinn, Riga and Vilnius, 23 August 1987 on the anniversary of the Molotov-Ribbentrop pact. Then 23 August 1989 there was that extraordinary human chain, spread across 400 miles, with some ten million people, a quarter of the entire population, demanding a restoration of pre-war independence. Estonia was to be spared the violence that preceded independence in Latvia and Lithuania: Gorbachev, far too late, realised he'd set in motion the break-up of the Soviet Empire. Estonia's was seen as the Singing revolution. From the late 19th century, from 1869, every five years there had been a Singing Festival, and Estonian patriotic songs once again inspired this, its third national awakening. However, one wonders what Pärt, who has since returned to Estonia, would make of Sofi Oksanen's novel *Purge*, with it bleak account of Estonia's conflicted past and messy present, its revelations of earlier betrayals to the secret police and current settlements of old scores.[3]

It took time for Pärt to discover himself as a composer. His leading interpreter, Paul Hillier, begins with the striking observation that his music was not Estonian, 'yet it is unlikely that the composer's unique musical and spiritual identity could have been created anywhere else.'[4] He entered the Tallinn Conservatory in 1957. He soon displayed exceptional powers of assimilation of a modernist style. There was *Nekrolog* (Obituary), honouring those murdered by fascism: 'the music's character is bleakly depressive, offering no hint of relief or escape, still less of resurrection.'[5] Its serialism led to condemnation by that arch-enforcer, Tikhon Khrennikov, head of the Soviet Composers Union A series of modernist works followed but Pärt was struggling to find his true self: 'by 1966 his was a music that chronicled despair yet no longer feels that this is sufficient purpose.'[6] But Pärt, even less committed to experimentation than the Polish composers of the Warsaw Autumn Festival, looked back to the tonality of Bach and the baroque. So he moved towards *Credo* (1968): 'it is a hymn not only to the splendour of Bach's music but also to the splendour of tonality and finally to the splendour of religion itself.'[7] The last was, of course, sufficient to condemn it in the eyes of the Soviet authorities and it was banned for ten years. Hillier hears it as a study of good and evil, 'not as separate blocks of energy but as linked – with a continuum of gradual disintegration.'[8] In fact Pärt had written himself into a cul-de-sac, had reached a point of complete despair, and fell silent.

Tintannabulism

Hillier sees this silence more in terms of a pressure cooker: 'hardly the meditational calm we might suppose – rather the frustrated immobility of an engine fully revved up, but unable to set off.'[9] One release was conversion to Orthodoxy in 1972. Nor was he exactly silent, for there was the Third Symphony of 1971, seen as 'a transitional work,' 'an underlying searching out and stripping away of all that was alien.'[10] The years 1968-76 are seen as 'purification of musical roots.' More than just a personal quest it sought the reorientation of western culture; 'a culture that attempts to live without the sustaining power of myth is a culture that is not whole, that has no connection with the past.'[11]

Pärt, aided by Andres Mustonnen and the Hortus Musicus, a society founded in 1972, turned to Gregorian chant and early music. In 1978 Mustonnen initiated a Festival of Old and New Music. Pärt now turned to religious texts. A distinctive feature of the new style was a response to the sound of bells, to the small tinkling bells of the tintinnabulum. Given the banning of the ringing of bells of orthodox churches, the *zvov*, by the Soviet regime, this was an act of political protest. Yet the ringing is no sense a summons to the church, 'it remains open to those who seek it, nothing more. The same may of course be said of Pärt's music.'[12] Pärt himself put it this way: 'tintinnabulism is like this. Here I am alone in silence. I have discovered that it is enough when a single note is beautifully played. This one note, or a silent beat, or a moment of silence, comforts me. The three notes of the triad are like bells.'[13]

One of the first works in an astonishing new phase of creativity was his 1977 *Cantus in Memoriam Benjamin Britten.* David Fanning wrote: 'rarely has the distance between the simplicity of technique and the expressive potency of its effect been as great as in this haunting piece.'[14] There is reference here to Britten's own use of bells in *Peter Grimes.* Pärt and Britten are alike in their both being so responsive to the written word. Britten had died in 1976 and this tribute was written in part out Pärt's sense of guilt that they had never met. I have to admit to a worrying sense that this might prove to be music of but a passing phase.

Pärt's break with the regime came in 1979. Sporting a long-haired wig he slated the Estonian Composers Union for the constraints on the playing of his music. Might he have emigrated to Israel? His second wife was Jewish. In fact, he left for Vienna, where Alfred Schnittke, on a short visit, was able to help him, before settling in Berlin.

Passio

Then in 1982 came *Passio, Passio Domini Nostri Jesu Christi Secundum Joannem*, to give it its full title, variously rated as 'the *ne plus ultra* of the tintinnabuli style,' 'the acme of the style, its most perfect realisation.'[15] Hillier sees it as 'a large prose text of very special significance.'[16] Musically it looks back to Bach and Schütz. My own response to the music, hearing it a late night prom – and the Guardian correspondent rightly saw it 'as the perfect piece for the subdued atmosphere of that late night slot'[17] – was as follows. It sounded like an intoned ritual. There was a feeling of abstract timelessness. Here is a parallel in music to Matisse's extreme reductionism in the Chapel of the Rosary in Vence. There was no inflexion in the chanting. This was a music for believers. Might we see this as Minimalism's answer to Maximalism? Within the text I picked up on a certain determinism, to quote, 'that the sayings of Jesus might be fulfilled, which he spake, signifying what death he should die.' And there is no reference in the text to Christ's agony of doubt: why has thou forsaken me? All Christ says is, 'it is finished.'

Ivan Moody has a very interesting if worrying comment on its character as ritual. The text is 'treated according to a hierarchy of values that negates any possibility of unwanted rhetoric, by underscoring it syntactically.' Why it should be so moving 'is apparent to anyone with an inkling of the power of ritual. Pärt would have been more than aware of not only of the powerful beauty of apparently "abstract" early polyphony, but also the reasoning behind intoning Gospel and other readings in both Western and Eastern liturgy, that is, to avoid any possibility of the reader interpreting the text in a way foreign to the mind of the Church.'[18] This feels menacingly dirigiste and is a pointer to the way religion can act as a barrier to the spiritual and the mystical. It is some consolation though that Pärt always denies that he is writing liturgical music. As Hillier explains, 'His music is sacred in subject matter and tone, but remains concert music.'[19]

His was always an intense engagement with texts. His *Litany* was a response to the writings of St John Chrysostom (c.347-417) *Prayers for Each Hour of Day and Night.* He became immersed in Archimandrite Sophrony's account of the life and teaching of the staretz, Silouan (1866-1938), a monk of the monastery of St Panteleimon on Mt Athos, the source of his *Silouan Songs.* Hillier denies that this is somehow Edenic music, a retreat into paradise: 'it carries an oppressive weight on its shoulders, and is written if anything from a post-Edenic position. It is not ignorant of evil. Obliquely perhaps, but nonetheless profoundly, it recognizes the bitter waste of human failure, the anxiety and loneliness of our condition.'[20]

4th Symphony

His 4th Symphony received its world premiere at Los Angeles 10 January 2009 and its British premiere at the Proms, 20 August 2010. It was a return after 37 years to the symphonic form. Peter Quinn writes: 'but the impression of hearing the symphony as a single expressive arc – one continuous breath that starts from and returns to a point of celestial timelessness – is quite overpowering.'[21] Pärt has the endearing idea that we are all constantly in the presence of angels, but fail to see them. In part the symphony is political, a protest at Putin's imprisonment of his opponent, the oil tycoon Mikhail Khodorkovsky. Andrew Clements was not impressed. If he heard echoes of Shostakovich's late quartets and the bleakness of Sibelius, he continues, 'but none of it at all substantial or comes close to justifying the scale on which Pärt presents it.'[22] It is scored for a large orchestra. I found it relentlessly unaccommodating. It reminded me of those demanding, almost action-less films of Straub. You were forced to listen.

Hillier is anxious that we do not confuse Pärt the person with the grimness of his music. We should not overlook 'his delightful sense of humour.' There is 'a balance between light and dark, so that what might otherwise be sheer heaviness of soul is transformed from an earthbound into a spiritual lightness of being.'[23] But is there sufficient stringency? Is he not a little too close to the whimsicality of minimalism and the softness of New Age style music?

Alfred Schnittke

In many respects Schnittke is exactly the composer one might expect to encounter during the Brezhnev years, a time when the sclerotic Soviet system was breaking up from within and Schnittke's conflicted and fragmented music was its odd simulacrum. In terms of this project, Schnittke is a transitional figure, both following on from Shostakovich's humanist spirituality, a continuing protest at the dead hand of Soviet ideology, as well as a breakthrough into a revived expression of the religious and the spiritual in music. So transmuted though be the religious, it is more pertinent to think of it as the spiritual. Just how great a composer he was remains in doubt. Isolated from the mainstream of modernism, Schnittke's initial experimentation can seem ill-digested and the eclecticism of the style he called his own, polystylism – in fact also derivative – can uncomfortably suggest a lack of originality. Was he in fact a provincial composer? But he was extraordinarily popular in the Soviet Union, his music one powerful expression of dissidence, and the exceptional range of his music, turning from the conflicted into something more simple and direct following his strokes, makes him one of the most intriguing composers of the spiritual in the 20th century. His friend and biographer, Alexander Ivashkin sums him up: his music 'reflects the very complex, peculiar and fragmentary mentality of the late 20th century.'[24]

Schnittke was not Russian at all. On his father's side he was
Jewish, Baltic Jews from Kurland in Latvia, who had fled
in 1910 to Germany. They had exchanged their family name
of Katz for that of a German priest, Schnittke. His father
Harry (1914-75) had been born in Frankfurt am Main. Alfred
was to be exposed to anti-Semitism by crass fellow students
at the Moscow Conservatory in the 1950's. Technically
he was not Jewish at all, for his mother, Maria Iosifovna
Vogel (1910-72), came from the Volga German community,
German colonists invited to settle in Russia by Catherine
the Great. They had been recognised 19 December 1924 as
the Autonomous Soviet Republic of Volga Germans, its capital, Engels, only, with the outbreak of war, to be dissolved 28
July 1941 and its population exiled to Kazakhstan and Siberia. Here the Jewish part of his identity came to Schnittke's
rescue for Jews were exempted from this deportation. Alfred's paternal grandparents had returned to Russia, to Moscow, in 1927. Harry had then run away to Engels, too poor to
enter a Russian University but with hopes of doing so in
German Engels, hopes to be belied. But here he met and
married Maria Vogel, and Alfred, one of three children, was
born 24 November 1934.

All this leads Schnittke scholars to see him as 'between two
worlds.' German was his first language. His father, Harry, a
fluent German speaker, made his career as journalist and
interpreter. His mother spoke a Volga German dialect, indeed one that went back to the 16th century as Alfred was to
discover when he came across it in the letters of Mozart. This
German ambience does much to explain why he was increasingly drawn to the music of the Austro-German tradition.
During the war his father joined the army and in 1946 was
posted to Vienna to be an interpreter. Ever after Alfred spoke
German with a Viennese accent. Vienna became his 'cultural
motherland.' He heard many concerts, especially memorable
Otto Klemperer conducting Bruckner's 7th. The family returned to Russia in 1948 but to Moscow not Engels, living
in a wooden house in the village of Valeninovka, formerly

occupied by German POWs. Maybe he was assimilated as a Russian but his German cultural loyalties were the stronger.

Dissidence

Dissidence was rooted in political and social changes apparent by the 1950's. The breakthrough came with Khrushchev's secret speech 25 February to the 20th party Congress – and not secret for long, published in the New York Times 4 June. This dates 'the slow demise of the Terror system that has ruled the Soviet people since 1917.' In Figes's interpretation, 'young people now turned away from politics and took up the pursuit of personal happiness, stimulated by the economic boom of the Khrushchev years. There was a new emphasis on individual and private life.'[25] It signified the emergence of a Russian middle class, only to be belatedly recognised by Gorbachev. But Russian intellectuals soon discovered that the freedom of the private sphere had to be won by a continuing struggle with the Stalinist state. The thaw was but partial and short and with Khrushchev's dismissal in 1964 by the hardliners there followed the long nightmare of the Brezhnev years. As Judt puts it: 'the Soviet Union was settling in for an indefinite twilight of economic stagnation and moral decay.'[26] There was a profound degradation of the public sphere.

Was Schnittke politically minded? He came of age during Khrushchev's thaw. Yet his family inheritance was one of loyalty to Communism and the regime. Both his paternal grand-parents had been revolutionary communists and in Germany had joined the radical Spartacist faction of the Social Democrat Party. Both his parents were party supporters, his mother working for the Young Pioneers, the children's division of the Komsomol. His mother lived with him till her death and we must assume acted as a constraint on any active resistance.

During the thaw, resistance, utterly stifled by Stalinism, surfaced, led by the towering figure of Alexander Solzhenitsyn. A key figure, Alexander Tvardovsky, editor of the dissident journal, *Novy Mir*, in 1961 called on writers to tell the truth about the era of the personality cult of Stalin. Somehow Solzhenitsyn's *A Day in the Life of Ivan Denisovitch* slipped through the censor and appeared in the journal, November 1961. Anna Akhmatova saw him as 'the bearer of light.' This was the time of exposure of the gulag system and few regimes would have survived such moral onslaught. But the Brezhnev regime put paid to any further publication in the Soviet Union. Solzhenitsyn fought back with an open letter to the Writer's Union against censorship in March 1967, only to be expelled in 1969 in the aftermath of the Prague Spring. Publication of *The Gulag Archipelago* abroad in January 1973 was the signal for his deportation in 1974. But I'm not sure he was an appropriate role model as dissident for Schnittke. Already in his Political Manifesto of 1973 he betrayed his markedly conservative and Slavophile outlook. Solzhenitsyn's deep Orthodox Christianity was of an anti-modernising and authoritarian nature.[27]

Others in a more minor key contributed to the dissident movement. There was the arrest and imprisonment of Andrei Sinyavsky and Yuri Daniel, seven years for the former, five the latter, for no more serious a crime than publishing abroad a critical essay on Socialist Realism. Here were the beginnings of the dissident movement, with its underground samizdat (self-publication) literature. Maybe this was not the Terror of the 30's. After all, whereas Osip Mandelstam perished en route to the gulag, Solzhenitsyn survived, if as an exile. Judt observes, however: 'By any standard save those of its own history, the regime was immoveable, repressive and inflexible.'[28]

Other than through his music Schnittke was only marginally involved in the dissident movement. By chance in his Moscow flat he lived opposite the later dissident physicist, Andrei Sakharov, though they never met. His biographer,

Alexander Ivashkin, reflects: 'there is something highly symbolic in the fact that perhaps the two most significant men in Russian culture in the late twentieth history lived in the same house and were separated by just one wall.'[29] But he did know the dissident poet, Joseph Brodsky, notoriously imprisoned in psychiatric hospitals, and in Schnittke's *Five Aphorisms* his poetry was read between the preludes. Schnittke's relationship with the musical establishment was strained and Khrennikov, jealous of the attention the west paid to Schnittke, was always ready to blackball his music. It was very difficult to get a visa to attend any foreign performance of his music. In 1980 he had the courage to abstain from voting Khrennikov back into office as Secretary: 'an unprecedented breach of protocol; according to totalitarian morality his behaviour was completely unacceptable.'[30] All the perks of being a composer, of course, depended on the patronage of the Union. Khrennikov's deputy, Vladimir Panchenko, tried to liberalise the system after Gorbachev came to power. Under *perestroika* Schnittke was indeed far freer to travel, even if the Composers Union remained hostile to his music.

Tragically, though, just at the moment when he could enjoy greater international recognition he was struck down by the first of his strokes and travel was seriously impeded. Schnittke, along with everyone else, did not anticipate the unravelling of the system and he left in 1989 for Germany, after being offered a year long scholarship to study in Berlin. With the reunification of Germany many Volga Germans followed suit. By October 1990 he had moved to Hamburg. He did not, however, break off relations with the Soviet Union. Indeed, he was offered the Lenin prize in 1990. Also, he had to return to Moscow for medical treatment for the strokes. He died in Hamburg 3 August 1998.

Yet just listening to his music was a form of dissidence. Ivashkin makes the crucial point that only through art and music could Russians find 'a substitute for reality.' 'No other life was possible.'[31]

Religion

In what ways was he religious? Both his parents were atheist. It was to be through his pious maternal grandmother, Eliseveta, that he acquired some understanding of Catholicism, though Catholic Volga Germans were scandalised by her reading a Lutheran bible, be it the only one she could obtain. Had that listening to Bruckner in Vienna in 1946 been a turning point? But we know little of how Schnittke came to be baptised a Catholic in the Hofburg chapel in 1982. Even so, he normally made his confession to an orthodox priest, Father Nikolay Vedernikov.

His music goes some way to close the gap in our understanding. A liturgical music was banned under Soviet ideology so Schnittke had to smuggle it in by some other route. The *Requiem* he wrote on his mother's death in 1972 was inserted as music for a production of Schiller's *Don Carlos*. My response to listening to Valeri Polyansky's CD performance was of a music deeply recessed, coming out of infinity, almost the voice of alien beings. At one time I heard the sound-world of Tibetan Buddhism, another of the Carmina Burana. It is highly charged and the Deus Irae is almost accusatory. But it ends on a contemplative and highly melancholic note.

Other works, noticeably his 2nd St Florian's Symphony have a more overtly religious character. On his return to Vienna in 1977, he visited St Florian's, the great baroque monastery where Bruckner had worked and is buried, and this is how he described the visit: 'The cold gloomy baroque church had a mystical air about it. Somewhere behind the wall a small choir was singing the evening mass – Missa Invisibila.' On entering the church he writes of feeling 'the cold and powerful void surrounding our privacy.'[32] Here was his inspiration for the Symphony. It follows the outline of the Latin Mass. Once again I listened to a recording by Polyansky. In the Kyrie there is the strange splintering noise of clashing cymbals. In the Gloria I wondered if Schnittke was recreating the sound that he heard on his visit. But in the Credo there is a panic-stricken feel to the voice, echoing that God-forsaken look on Christ's face in some paintings of the Crucifixion. But once again in the Sanctus and Agnus Dei, despite some jarring sound, it ends on a clear note, tranquil and resolved.

Yet it all felt multi-layered and somehow camouflaged. I-vashkin suggests 'the hidden meaning in the depths of the music is partly determined by the tradition of Christianity to which Schnittke belongs.'[33] 'It is in early Christian culture in which myths and history are perfectly combined, that one finds irrational movements, sometimes impossible to explain.'[34] If this symphony has a Catholic feel his *Choir Symphony*, premiered 9 June 1986, inspired by the Book of Lamentations of the Armenian St Gregory of Narek (951-1003), has a strongly Russian Orthodox feel to it. But Schnittke's music always has an oecumenical feel. His 4th Symphony drew on melodies from Catholic, Protestant and Orthodox music.

But Taruskin will have none of this. He certainly questions whether the religious impulse is primary 'because more than anything else it nudges him over the edge into banality and bluster.' He writes off the 2nd Symphony as 'an unbearably maudlin six-movement meditation on the Latin Mass.' He is far more enthusiastic about the 4th, whose 'oecumenical reach and its harsh spirituality seems a post-modern manifesto and a master-piece.'[35]

The Faust Motif

Another way of exploring Schnittke's religious beliefs is through the Faust motif, so prevalent in his music. It began with his reading in the late 40's Thomas Mann's *Doctor Faustus*. In 1959 he planned an opera on the Apocalypse akin to Adrian Leverkuhn's, the anti-hero of Mann's novel, Lamentations of Jeremiah, but nothing was to come of his engagement with the Faust legend till the 1983 *Faust*

Cantata. This was to be incorporated into the eventual opera, *The History of D. Johann Faustus,* premiered at the Hamburg State Opera 22 June 1995. In the end the story of Faust owes little to Mann's novel and is based on Johannes Spies's 1587 text, *Das Volksbuch vom Doctor Faust.* The first performance of the Cantata went ahead despite every attempt of the establishment to stall it: the programmes, for example, were holed up in the warehouse of the Ministry of Culture awaiting shredding. It was seen as a religious work. Would evil be overcome? It can be a truly frightening experience. One is warned against listening to the cantata in the dark. In Mann's novel Adrian Leverkuhn signs his pact with Mephistopheles in exchange for creativity, metaphor for the selling out of German culture to Nazism. In the 16th century text, Faust's reward for the bargain is expertise in magic and sorcery. Faust himself becomes a devil, but the pact soon palls and Faust is forced to sign two pledges in blood to stand by the deal. The story is far more of an old-fashioned morality tale, for if Faust's body is doomed, there remains a chance that his soul can be saved. There is, indeed, to be a truly gruesome physical death, but the opera ends on an optimistic note, with all the four main characters, centre-stage, rather as at the end of a Mozart opera, averring that if you do not give into the devil, all will be well.

The character of Mephistopheles is divided into two, a seductive figure, sung by a counter-tenor, and a chastiser, who seeks his death, sung by a contralto. In Ivashkin's interpretation, Schnittke's version of the Faust story reflects 'the balance between the rational and irrational, between the human and the devilish, which is found in every man's soul.' 'A struggle between polarities, or irregular pulse, a Faustian multiplicity of meaning that is the quintessence of his music in this period.'[36] You had to grapple with evil. It was a very personal battle. Schnittke identified with Faust and felt that his strokes were 'retaliation because he had dealt with evil forces.'[37]

It led Schnittke into reading alternative spiritualities, Rudolf Steiner, I Ching, but answers were not found. In the *Peer Gynt* ballet music (1986), and his story has affinities with Faust's, for Gynt also travelled and met evil spirits, Schnittke is seen as trying to find a fourth dimension 'which "shimmers" in our real life but which is not yet given to us in full.'[38] 'Frightened by the occultism of all these systems,' Ivashkin argues, 'he felt the need for a proper Christian faith.'[39] If mortally wounded by his encounter with evil, he remained optimistic: to quote his own words, 'that in a human being there is always manifest an essence that is good and that never changes.'[40]

Schnittke and Shostakovich

One way into understanding Schnittke's music lies in his relationship to Shostakovich. At the personal level, this was a failure. Shostakovich had been his examiner for his graduation piece and if it seems a minor matter, Schnittke had been late for a meeting: he had been delayed through having to act as a witness to a charge of homosexuality against his piano teacher; on both sides of the Cold War homosexuals were being persecuted. Shostakovich, always a stickler for punctuality, never forgave him. The piece in question was *Nagasaki* and Shostakovich was going to sign a form recommending its performance. Intriguingly, the piece may well have influenced Shostakovich's *Babi Yar* Symphony, both profound humanist statements. Schnittke always felt Shostakovich had been corrupted by the Soviet system and both spoke and wrote in party officialese.

If at this stage his music owed little to Shostakovich, Ivashkin argues that from Shostakovich Schnittke seems to have assimilated 'a kind of inner energy which he was to reveal fully only in the 1970's and 1980's when critics started to regard him as Shostakovich's heir.'[41] Certainly Schnittke made a point of attending all the performances of Shostakovich's late works. Both composers were embattled with the

Soviet system, Shostakovich more and more overtly in these late works, Schnittke through his experimentalism. David Fanning writes of his 'unflinching confrontationalism,' of works 'that capture something of the glaring contradiction between appearance and reality in the last phases of the Soviet Union.'[42] Much is made of the way Schnittke in his Concertos sees a losing conflict between the soloist as the individual and the orchestra as the mass, evident in his *Concerto for Viola* (1985). Indisputably Schnittke inherited Shostakovich's mantle as the leading Soviet composer. Both are seen as sharing a certain pessimism: 'many of their works have the effect of "dying", dissolving out of the world, fading into the distance of time.'[43] There is a strong resemblance in their lush music for strings.

Taruskin reflects on the Tolstoyan conscience at work in both composers, though here is a higher ethical purpose that risks bathos: 'the wonder of it all,' he reflects, 'is how often Schnittke, like Shostakovich before him, manages to skirt the pitfall and bring off the catharsis – a catharsis a mere hairs-breadth from blatancy and all the more powerful for having braved the risk.'[44]

Nagasaki

Nagasaki is a fascinating pointer to Schnittke's eclecticism. It is based on Japanese poetry together with what one critic sees as Soviet doggerel. One could be unkind and indeed see it as agit-prop art, a Soviet version of CND. Initially Schnittke had wanted to write a piece on Russian POWs in Germany. But the authorities were happier with a piece memorialising war victims and endorsing the Peace movement. And they also insisted on a happy ending and here Andrew Clements's claim that the music might just as well have been written 'to celebrate a bumper year for tractor production' has some justification.[45] And if this is public art, Schnittke had yet to learn from Shostakovich how to communicate with a private voice. In the first section, evoking Nagasaki as 'the city of grief, the city of anger,' you can hear the influence of Orff's *Carmina Burana*. In the third section, where Schnittke incorporates the sound of the atomic explosion, there is a powerful echo of the cracking of the ice under the weight of the Teutonic knights from Prokofiev's cantata, *Alexander Nevsky*. Here is huge agonised protest, utter rejection of any military justification for dropping the bomb. In the fourth section there is a quite different mood, the music fading into an eerie silence, as the Japanese mother laments the loss of her baby's childhood, sung by the mezzo soprano, accompanied on the celeste. The fifth section, an evocation of peace, brings Richard Strauss's vision of the dawn in *Zas Sprach Zaruthustra* to mind. Here is a piece in that tradition of humanitarian spirituality of both Prokofiev and Shostakovich. Clements's account of it as a 'totally anodyne piece of Soviet tub-thumping' is way off the mark.

Eclecticism

Following *Nagasaki,* influenced by the Romanian, Philip Hershkowitz, a former pupil of Webern, Schnittke composed serialist music in the manner of the second Viennese School. At some point this changed in the direction of quotation and pastiche, a style he named polystylism, Schnittke an early post-modernist. Of the music he wrote in the late 70's and 80's Schnittke claimed: 'I am just fixing what I hear. It's not me who writes my music. I am just a tool, a transmitter.'[46] Ivashkin paraphrases this: 'a composer in Schnittke's opinion should be a medium or a sensor, whose business is to remember what he hears – and whose mind acts a translator only. Music comes from some sort of "divine" rather than human area.'[47] I am not sure that I heard this in his *Concerto Grosso No 1* (1977), a polystylist piece that made his name. Certainly I do not hear it in his hugely controversial Symphony No.1 that had to be performed in Gorky, significantly the city of Sakhorov's exile, if it were to be played at all. It was only played in Moscow in 1986. Ivashkin sees it 'as not just music, but also meditation on music, presenting a montage of various types of music.'[48] But I did hear it in the religious music already described.

Much is made of the impact of Schnittke's three strokes on his music, the first, January 1985, the second 19 July 1991, the third 2 July 1994. Various accounts are given of his late music, laconic, quite enigmatic, very ascetic. For the last four years of his life he could not speak and 'was searching for a new musical language.'[49] Certainly the music is simpler and more austere. Here the idea of composer as somehow a transmitter is more easily grasped. The third movement of his 2nd Cello Concerto, for example, has been described as written in 'a special unreal mystical mood, full of ephemeral illusion and ghostly timbres.' There is that same conflict between soloist and orchestra. At the very end the soloist, despite playing fortissimo in a very high register, 'is completely inaudible and practically "killed" by the massive brutal orchestra.'[50]

Assessment

Maybe it is too early to take to the music of Schnittke. Andrew Clements, reflecting on the South Bank Schnittke Festival as a whole, writes of 'the unnerving impression that he lacks a recognisable voice. Like any iconoclast he suffers when wrenched from a context that gives us the focus of his rebellion. And some of his music isn't actually very good.'[51] Taruskin sees him, like Shostakovich, as mainly a 'public orator.' Beneath the avant-gardism, he 'at bottom always conformed, for better or worse, to the customary outlook of the Soviet composer.' You have to be ready 'to regard music as a sweaty, warty human document.'[52] But ultimately his assessment is highly positive: 'with a bluntness and immodesty practically unseen since the days of Mahler, Schnittke tackles life-against death, love-against-hate, freedom-against tyranny, and (especially in the concertos) I-against-the world.'[53]

Can we come to any conclusion about the spiritual in his music? At the outset, Taruskin sees in 'the world of early Schnittke, Dostoyevsky's world without God, where everything is possible and nothing matters.'[54] Claims are made, however, that through his varied origins, influenced by Jewish, German, Russian culture, he 'grew up something of a mystic.'[55] Interestingly, that conflict in the concertos between soloist and orchestra has been interpreted in a Jungian sense as a conflict between the individual and his shadow. To a surprising degree in the late 20th century, so smashed in its feeling for religion and the spiritual, despite all his self-mockery, Schnittke does hover on the expression of both the religious and the spiritual, and is probably the most surprising of all the composers under review.

Sofia Gubaidulina

My first encounter with Gubaidulina was at a Proms performance, 25 August 2002, of her *St John Passion* and *St John Easter*. I was overwhelmed and that experience did much to inspire this project. I recorded in my diary at the time: 'if ever music conveyed the divine, this was it. One really felt the drama of the opening of the seven seals. Here was God face to face.' Then I heard her *The Light of the End* at a prom August 2005: 'it was wholly mesmerising and completely accessible.' But my most prolonged encounter was during a Total Immersion weekend devoted to her music, 12-14 January 2007, at the Barbican. It might be sensible to begin with the critical response to *A Journey of the Soul,* as this event was entitled. Michael Kurtz ends his rather dry biography by quoting her claim: 'art originates in man's spiritual essence, and it can return mankind to that origin.' Does her music live up that ambition?[56]

Gubaidulina divides her critics. Adverse response to the Barbican event was pretty damning. Anthony Holden, whilst recognising 'that her deeply religious soul finds a wide variety of robust, often violent outlets for its suffering,' and sees her as 'a technically clever composer,' is pretty repelled by her 'hectoring religiosity': 'she seems scarcely to have modulated her authorial voice since the downfall of the Soviet Union.' He found the music 'highly derivative and reeking of incense,' the weekend, 'a peak into the recondite mind of a gifted woman dancing almost wilfully to her own line, contentedly out of step with the modern world.'[57] Tim Ashley was equally alienated: 'the more one listens to Sofia Gubaidulina's music, the less one likes it.' Whilst recognising in her extremes of despair and elation comparison with Dostoyevsky, he concludes; 'the overall effect is wearing: you feel you've been in contact with sermonising rant rather than the visionary spirituality.'[58] Geoff Brown is rather more generous: 'the music, jointly haunted by the ancient east and the modernist west, by folk traditions and Russian orthodox chant, spirals and thuds with an intense mystical impulse. With luck you sit hypnotised and uplifted by the ritual: without, you plummet, chafing at the motivic constipation, the repetitions.' 'But all praise to Radio 3 for its ambition; rather this hairshirt experience than something safe and dull.'[59] Paul Griffiths sees her as part female shaman, part holy simpleton, the paradigm Russian fool, and now 'one of the most deeply appreciated artists of our time.' 'She does not offer easy solutions,' he believes, 'or calm, or the vision of a better past. She is at war with the present, but on behalf of the future. She is at war with herself, casting off artistic decorum, throwing doubt into the wild mix that almost any work of hers will contain.'[60]

I admit personally that at first I had mixed feelings. After we'd applauded her to the rafters, though in a half-empty Albert Hall, that August day I encountered her in a nearby café. I recorded: 'she seemed minx-like and cunning.' I am sure this was unfair but this controversial response to the Barbican weekend of her music points to a huge challenge in the communication of the spiritual.

Biography

She was born 24 October 1931, in Chistopol, an industrial town on a reservoir of the Volga, in the heart of the Republic of Tatarstan. The Tatars are, after the Russians, the second largest ethnic community in Russia; interestingly, Gubaidulina shares Schnittke's background from a non-Russian minority. Much is made of her Tatar father, to become a skilled surveyor in the People's Commissariat for Agriculture in Kazan. He was the son of an Imam, one who had trained in Bukhara, a moderniser who had set up a Society for Progressive Muslims. This religious ancestry and their kulak status, however, proved fatal for her father's family, many of whom died in the gulag. Her father kept a low profile and survived. In 1927 he met Fedosia Elkhova, trained as a teacher and member of Komsomol, already married and divorced, and they were not to marry till 12 February 1932. Technically, all three daughters were born out of wedlock. Sofia was the youngest. Kurtz observes: 'it was an act of courage for a Tatar to take a Russian for a wife.'[61] She was close to her father, if in silence she accompanied him on his long walks as a surveyor. Clearly Gubaidulina was to draw on her Tatar background though her use of folk music was always universal rather than local. German culture, however, was always a greater influence. Her childhood was spent in Kazan, in a quiet back street and in 'a world of grim poverty.'[62] And here she stayed till her musical career took her in 1954 to Moscow.

Three marriages lay ahead. The first was to Mark Liando 22 January 1956, by whom she had a daughter, her only child, though the marriage broke down and they divorced in 1964. The second in 1965 was to the dissident, Nikolai Bokov, but whilst remaining on friendly terms, they were to part in 1972 and he emigrated in 1975. Her third was to fellow pianist and music theoretician, Pyotr Meshchaninov. They met in 1972 and lived together from 1979 but did not register their marriage until emigration to Germany in the 1990's.

Religion

In what ways is she religious? In the Kazan of her childhood,
by 1932 all but two of its 60 orthodox churches had been
closed. Neither of her parents were religious. Was there a
Eureka moment when on a holiday in the village of Nizhny
Usslon she saw in a farmhouse one of those icons that the
peasantry kept in their icon corner and this connected with
prayers she was already making? Her parents were horrified
and tried to hush it all up. However, when Gubaidulina fell
seriously ill from malaria in 1945, and her behaviour was so
erratic that the doctors thought of sending her to the Kazan
Psychiatric Hospital, her mother made a promise that, should
she recover, she would have her baptised, and, indeed, in the
hospital she did receive a consecrated wafer. In the event, all
attempts to find her a priest for baptism fell through. Another
Eureka moment was attending a concert in Kazan 12 Novem-
ber1951 by the deeply religious pianist, Mariya Yudina –
Shostakovich had found her piety bothersome – and Gubaidulina had seen her bow her head and make a sign of the
cross. This strengthened her private religious beliefs. Much
later she visited the pianist in hospital in Moscow in early
1964, a friendship began, and they met intermittently till
Yudina's death 19 November 1970. It was Yudina's example
that led to Gubaidulina's baptism in the Church of the
Prophet Elijah 25 May 1970. But had there been another
Eureka moment when she attended a mosque in Leningrad in
1967, the mullah reading from the Koran, and as she recalled, 'the silences between the passages created an almost
ecstatic mood'?[63] Maybe, appropriately, her flat in Moscow
was in Transfiguration Square.

All this was to influence her music. Gubaidulina saw art as
re-ligio, the means of connection with God. In 1978 Meshchaninov brought back from a foreign tour the Proper of
the Catholic Mass, with its Introit, Offertory, Gradual and
Communion, and this underlay a cycle of her works, *De
Profundis, In Croce, Offertorium, Descensio, Seven Words of
Jesus Christ on the Cross*. But there was always a tension in

Gubaidulina's orchestrating choral music, for the Russian Orthodox Church laid down that the liturgy should be choral only and to set it to music was heretical. When she visited in late 2002 Father Vassily, a monk in a *sket*, a hermitage attached to the Monastery of the Transfiguration of the Saviour on the island of Valaam, Lake Ladoga, -she had been visiting the island since the 1970s – she raised these doubts but he gave his consent only to her composing music that was not for specific church use.[64] Clearly here was a barrier that she had to overcome and she was always more than a mere practitioner of Orthodoxy. The true dynamic of her music is to be found in the spiritual.

Spirituality

So how to define that spirituality? Finnish composer, Kalevi Aho, in a conversation he recorded in April 1984, raises doubts as to its discreteness from religion: 'she talked about her mystical – "liminal" – experiences which appear to be religious in nature.'[65] Maybe these were there from the beginning, in that grim back street of Kazan: 'how I used to sit there in that bare courtyard staring at the sky – and I began to live there. The earth disappeared some place else and I seemed able to walk across the sky.'[66] As a student in the Moscow Conservatory she was reading Herman Hesse and Rilke. Later she read Meister Eckhart. She was predisposed to the mystical. In the sacred hours, as she saw them, between seven and ten in the morning, practising the piano, the rooms empty, put her in 'a state of pure meditation.'[67] Crucial was her reading of Berdyaev and from him she learnt the ambiguous idea that God was evolving, that through our creativity we assist in that evolution, though the divine inspiration always fails in the compromises of actual creation.

Gubaidulina believes that every seven years she endures some personal crisis from which she emerges enriched. In 1972 at the age of 42 her intellectual and rational side diminished and her spiritual-intuitive expanded: 'I opened a door

to God.'[68] In July 1990 she attended the Scandinavian An-
throposophist Congress at Tampere in Finland. Was there
here another influence? Somewhere in all this she formed a
dominant idea that there is a tension between the horizontal,
in which we are tied to clock-time and the worldly, and the
vertical, our experience of sacred time, time outside time.
We can also experience this in sleep and in the Eucharist.

We need to link this to her interest in folk music. She asserts:
'I have strived to absorb into myself as many varied national
cultures as possible in order to fertilize the soil in which I
myself, my unique individuality, could thrive ... And to reveal in music, in sound, the truth that I discovered deep down
in myself.'[69]

And, of course, the true test of the spiritual lies in the music.
In a conversation she had with Christopher Cooke at the
Barbican event she claimed to hear music all around her.
Everyone gives off music – you just had to listen. Here she
was suggesting an affinity with St Francis but also playing
the Russian Holy Fool. But she added a far greater complexity in her pre-prom talk at the August 2004 proms when she
referred to Jung and to the way she was tapping into the dark
side, the way the light came out of that dark side. In many
ways, in the easy manner she spoke of her spirituality, she
reminded me of the rather garrulous Michael Tippett.

Dissidence

Inevitably, through her religious belief and all the more so
her spirituality, she was in conflict with the Soviet regime.
During her childhood there was a constant fear that her father
would be arrested: 'today it seems to me that our fear was
even worse than imprisonment – because it paralyzed and
eventually killed the spirit and any kind of creativity.'[70]
Through the Zhdanov decree she had to distrust her liking for
the music of Shostakovich. But it was to be his advice, acting
as her examiner in the Symphony she submitted at the

Conservatory, which proved crucial: 'Be yourself. Don't be afraid to be yourself. My wish for you is that you should continue on your own, incorrect way.'[71] Even so, she saw fit to become enrolled as a member of the Composers Union: failure to do so would have left here branded as a parasite, the fate that befell Brodsky through not joining the Writers Union. Did she become an active dissident?

Through her relationship with Nikolai Bokov, or Kolya as he was known, she was an active participant in the samizdat movement. In their flat such banned literature as Akhmatova's *Requiem* and Solzhenitsyn's writing was printed. After she had separated from Kolya the KGB in June 1974 turned her flat upside down but they did not find the incriminating writings of Avtorkhanov, an early critic of Stalinism. She listened to Evgeniya Ginzburg, in the author's Moscow flat, reading her memoir of the purges *Into the Whirlwind*. Inspired by listening to Schnittke's 1st Symphony she set to music poems by Marina Tsvetaeva, seen as a companion spirit. The poet had briefly visited Chistopol. After a truly tragic life, yet another exile who had fatally returned, she had committed suicide in 1941: 'that life story and the extremity of her poetic voice, seem to be invoked by Gubaidulina's music.'[72]

She was to be more harassed by the system than Schnittke. A cultural ice-age gripped Russia after the invasion of Prague in August 1968. Tikhon Khrennikov took a particular aversion to her music and at the Sixth All Union Congress of the Composers Union November 1979 she was branded one of seven Russian composers whose non-conformist music played up to the west. It was all but impossible to get a visa to hear her music abroad and it was all but ignored at home. Her biographer sees her as especially victimised through 'her hard-headed unwillingness to compromise: from the very start, she never made the slightest concession in return for favours.'[73] In the ideologically dogmatic Brezhnev years the highly charged spiritual music she was writing for the violinist, Gidon Kremer, was 'a potential powder-keg.'[74] Still,

her music was being performed by Gennedy Rozhdetven-
sky's Orchestra for the Ministry of Culture, set up April
1982, seen as a watershed for contemporary music in the
Soviet Union. And she did finally get out to attend the
Helsinki Festival in 1984, only to upstage both Khrennikov
and Schnittke. Through the Gorbachev reforms travel restrictions were considerably eased and she embarked on extensive journeys, not just within Europe but to America, Japan
and Australia. Oddly, it was out of fear at the breakdown of
law and order as the system unravelled that in 1992 she
decided to emigrate and now lives in the village of Appen
outside Hamburg.

Music (Playful)

It is a paradox of the Soviet system that so dirigiste a regime
nurtured so independent-minded a composer. Through time
at the Children's Music School in Kazan, on to the Tatarstan Graduate School of Music and so to the Moscow
Conservatory, Gubaidulina herself uncertain whether to be a
concert pianist or composer, only resolved by 1957 in favour
of composition, this very idiosyncratic voice took shape. In
much the same way as the Polish composers and Schnittke,
initially she responded to western modernism, Stockhausen,
Nono, Berio in her sights. She experimented in the Scriabin
Museum's Experimental Studies of Electronic Music. Yet
something of her true nature comes through in her strange
observation: 'twelve -tone music is like a heavy chain that
composers lay upon themselves in the manner of Russian
Orthodox ascetics to surmount pain and suffering.'[75] Was it
being involved in Kolya's *samizdat* activities andits journal *The Chronicle of Current Events* that led to a more
inward music: 'I need to write miniatures, miniatures in a
whisper.'?[76]

One cannot here discuss all of her extraordinarily large body
of music. I want to see it under two headings, the essentially

playful, Gubaidulina acting the Holy Fool, and the more highly rhetorical, the religious and spiritual.

Much of the former was on display in the Barbican weekend. Of her *Five Etudes* (1965), along with *Chaconne* (1962), music that made her name, we are told she was 'keen to find the magic, the humour and the emotional powers of new sounds,' with 'an awareness of what Berio, Lutoslawaki and Xenakis were up to.'[77] Her String Quartets are often just bizarre. Of the 1st (1971) she wrote: 'the idea of disintegration, dissociation, lies at the heart of the First String Quartet.'[78] I heard it as a dialectic of hope and despair. At the end the players all pull away from each other, seemingly signalling the failure at transcendence. In the 3rd she entertained the lugubrious idea of what Martians might make of our musical instruments. Initially they'd just pluck or strike but then they'd pick up the bows and ravishing music would ensue. In the 4th, even more outrageously, rubber balls are bounced off the strings, creating a mandolin-like sound, and the quartet's own playing weaved in and out of the recording by two other quartets. In time, again, the music turned lyrical. Then the music of the quartet on stage connects with their recorded counterparts: 'visible, they attained the delicacy of the invisible, and with it the light blue of the open sky.'[79]

Another playful side of Gubaidulina is her writing music for a range of highly unusual instruments eg the tar, an Azerbaijani drum. This was her way of connecting with folk music, world-wide. And there was something very distinctive in her relationship with her soloists. Whereas as Schnittke suggested some kind of battle to the death between soloist and the orchestra, she favoured a dialogue of equals and she sought to incorporate the personal resonance of her soloists in her concertos. It was the brilliant success of her Violin Concerto (1980), as played by Gidon Kremer, the *Offertorium*, that put her on the international map. Since her special joy in childhood at hearing a neighbour play the *bayam*, the Russian accordion, and rather in the way Vaughan Williams composed for the tuba, another ungainly instrument, she wrote for the *bayam,* an instrument peculiarly suitable for the way her music swoops. In the Barbican weekend there was a brilliant performance by Friedrich Lips of her *Under the Sign of the Scorpio* (2003). In 1982 she had composed *The Seven Last Words for Bayam, Cello and Strings.* 'Do you know why I love this monster so much,' she asked, 'it breathes.'[80]

Music (Rhetorical)

Gubaidulina's claim to the spiritual in music lie in her large-scale, rather top-heavy works. She was much moved by Shostakovich's late symphonies and quartets, already discussed. But their approach to death could not have been more different, Shostakovich, resigned, stoical, Gubaidulina, a passionate exponent of resurrection. She was a close friend of Arvo Pärt – they first met on her visit to Tallinn in December 1975 – but again his quietism is off-set by her explosiveness. Here a narrative approach will be adopted to her compositions.

Early indication of future large-scale works were her *Night Memphis* (1968) and *Rubaiyat* (1969), both reflections on the inevitability of death and suffering. Then came *Steps* (1974), a seven step descent into death, inspired by Rilke's *Das Marienleben,* and her first large-scale work for orchestra. In 1975 came an Oratorio inspired by Czech humanist, Amon Comenius. There followed a series of religious works, already mentioned. Then her Symphony *Stimmen ... verstummen,* (Voices ... Silenced), premiered in Berlin 4 September 1986, with its echoes of Stockhausen and Nono. 'Sofia's music clearly comes from another world, from entirely different circumstances of life,' observes Dutch conductor, Robert de Leeuw. He continues: 'People like to refer to the Russian soul. Perhaps that means each note is filled with meaning and significance like Shostakovich's last quartets. Perhaps ritual is a part of it, the ritual quality of Gubaidulina's music.'[81] Then came *Pro et Contra* (1989), composed

around a Russian alleleuia chant: 'it as if we were being
shown a holy place – a ruined chapel, perhaps, or a shrine
with an oil lamp burning in front of it – in the middle of a
storm.'[82]

Simon Rattle conducted the premiere of her *Alleluia* in
Berlin, 11 November 1990. This in seven parts is her tribute
to the Orthodox liturgy: in Paul Griffiths's words, 'together
they make not so much a journey from darkness to light as a
journey through different kinds of light, darkness being
one.'[83] And here Gubaidulina shows herself Scriabin's successor, for she uses colour, from blue to yellow, orange and
green. It was performed at the Barbican weekend. 'In four of
the first five movements the choir sings out the title, over
and over, as if from different regions of some vast space.'[84] It
is a work filled with Gubaidulina's characteristic crescendos.
And here is a forerunner of *St John Passion*.

But the question is raised, was her music in response to her
conflict with the system? Would her creativity rise to the
same level in exile? Hamburg was chosen in part because
Rilke's *The Book of Monkish Life,* inspiration for the Cello
Concerto that she was working on at the time, had been
written there.

Her next major choral work was *Canticle of the Sun*, a cello
concerto, written for Rostropovitch and premiered in Frankfurt 9 February 1998. It is based on the deeply moving prayer
of St Francis. This was also performed at the Barbican weekend. I recorded: 'this is ritual. And here there is no doubt we
are listening to the music of the divine – we have eaves-
dropped on paradise. The role of the cellist becomes increasingly extravagant – is he performing a priestly function? At
one point he puts down his cello, walks across stage to strum
the drum – great rolling waves of sound. And then he uses
his bow to make benediction over the choir. Something very
strange happens in this piece and it is wholly transcendental.'
It is interesting that Gubaidulina had also responded very

184

powerfully to a reading of T S Eliot's *Four Quartets*. So we move to her greatest work.

The International Bach Academy of Frankfurt commissioned Gubaidulina in February 1996 to compose an oratorio, one of several, on Christ's Passion to mark the 250th anniversary of Bach's death, to be performed at the Stuttgart 2000 Passion Festival. It was premiered 1 September 2000, conducted by Valery Gergiev. Gubaidulina chose St John's Gospel, its idea of Christ as the embodiment of Logos the closest to Russian Orthodox faith. If *St John Passion* appeared some years before *St John Easter*, premiered in St Michael's Cathedral, Hamburg, 16 March 2002, they were ineluctably linked: in Orthodoxy death and resurrection are inextricable. Jonathan Stedall, to quote, illustrates this in his account of the Easter festival.

The tremendous climax of the festival comes in the first few minutes after midnight when the sorrow of Good Friday and the silence of Saturday give way to Easter Sunday – from death to resurrection. The Church has been in total darkness. Then a frail light is carried from the altar through the centre door of the screen and out to the people. And so the light starts to spread as each person's candle receives light from the next. It is a powerful reminder of our interconnectedness.[85]

In her own interpretation of this music Gubaidulina refers to a conceptual framework of the horizontal and the vertical, the marriage of the horizontal events of the Passion, its temporality, and the vertical of the Resurrections or Apocalypse, its spiritual eternity. She saw *St John Easter* 'as the opening up of our soul, its transition to another dimension.[86] One commentator on the performance in St Michael's Cathedral reflected: 'looking back I am still struck by the spiritual power of the work. In its deeply sincere and highly charged spirituality as well as its frank piety it projects a voice that is unique in contemporary music.'[87] In my own response to the proms performance 25 August 2002 I recorded: 'the wonderful counterpoint of the bass narrating the Passion and then the Resurrection, almost flat, vacant, offset by the sheer drama of evoking Revelation.' No music was quite so overwhelming in all that I've heard for this project. But its force can only be appreciated if we recognise, as in much of the music of Scriabin, here is music suffused with millenarianism.

Then came her *The Light of the End*, premiered by the Boston Symphony Orchestra 17 April 2003. In her pre-prom talk of the performance of this work Gubaidulina spoke of the tragedy of music itself, music unable to sound its natural self, constrained by the dictate of the octave. This echoes Barenboim's idea of music's tragedy, the ephemerality of its sound. In this work the tuba all but disappeared in the playing of its lower notes, but then fought back. For the conductor Kurt Masur, 'the work is a mirror image of her beliefs and what she presents in it is, so to speak, the ebb and flow of life with its obligations and passions. But at the end there is the prospect of hope and light – just as the title of the piece suggests, the light that will shine for each of us at the end.'[88]

One other piece might be mentioned, her *Nadeyka Triptych*, memorial to her daughter, receiving its world premiere at the Barbican weekend. Here was music as quest, Orpheus searching for Eurydice, but never to find her, and Gubaidulina sees her mysticism as quest. The piece is in three panels. In the first Gidon Kremer on the violin holds Orpheus's lyre. In the second, The Beautiful Face of Hope and Despair, words taken from T S Eliot's *Ash Wednesday*, the quest is taken up by the flautist, on this occasion, Sharon Bezely. I heard her contest with three other flautists in terms of St Sebastian, the arrows of the final chords thudding into her. It was a piece of unbearable tension, possibly ending on an upbeat note. The third took its title from Pushkin's *A Feast during the Plague* and is seen by Paul Griffiths as 'addressed to an age beset by plagues, not only of the body but of the mind and the soul.'[89] If I could detect little connection with Pushkin's story, the theme of death and resurrection was

always present. I recorded: 'here was an attempt to storm
heaven and at one point it looked as if the gates would open
– but then it all collapsed, signified by the flat notes of the
double basses. Then came a strange intrusion of some jazzy
music, rather as if some pirate radio station has taken over
a car radio playing classical music – a kind of inter-galactic
struggle. It was all a bit chaotic but the trumpets kept up a
dominant assertiveness and the piece just fell short of teeter-
ing into chaos – and then it all faded at the end.'

Some of Simon Rattle's humorous observations convey Gubaidulina the best: 'she is a really crazy woman, of course
in a completely positive way ... I would call her a "flying
hermit" because she is constantly in orbit, only occasionally
touching terra firma.' This well conveys the Holy Fool side
to her music. But he adds: 'she seems like someone who fil-
ters an unendurable spiritual ecstasy into her music.'[90] Hers
is a key place in any claims for the spiritual in 20th century
music.

It reflects both the triumph of the human spirit but also the
limits of Soviet totalitarianism that three such different dissident composers emerged in the twilight of the Soviet
system. But it had been at a human cost. Paul Griffiths brilliantly suggests a sadness in all three. In Pärt's music, looking at Mediaeval and Renaissance music, there is 'a strong
sense of the distant past – as well as separation from that
past, of loss and absence,' though he recognises that music 'so ageless is thoroughly modern in conception.' 'Pärt's
sacred settings,' he perceives, 'exist beyond belief. Their
church is the church of the abandoned.' [91] In Schnittke's
case, he senses 'a wild hilarity in much of the 1970's seems
to hold despondency in check,'[92] and later, his fate, 'perhaps
wished for fate, to be on the brink.' There is a desperation in
his music, reflecting his own ill-health and the collapse of the
Soviet system, panic at 'a culture passing from tight control
into unchecked freedom.'[93] If 'contortion, parody and extremity' may reflect protest at the persecution of religion,
'equally the music laments the loss of divine community,

of the social order, that sustained the individuality that all Schnittke's music pursues through labyrinths of intensity, disaffection and black comedy.'[94] Gubaidulina's music looks back to Scriabin, to symbolism, but lacks symmetry: 'its characteristics instead are abrupt, ripped change, a finish that is often rough, raw and ragged, and a variety equalling Schnittke's.'[95] Hers is music that comes out of Russian suffering. In *St John Passion*, 'big and overwhelmingly dark,' she is drawing on traditions of sacred oratorio that are broken: 'the work seems to be hammering at the door of plausibility, questioning itself in all its magnificence and drama.' It's as if in reaching out to a religious experience, 'she takes holds of a ghost.'[96] But is there not a breakthrough, her Violin concerto, for example, in her more recent music?

Notes

[1] Judt, *Postwar*, p.655.
[2] Judt, *Postwar*, p.170.
[3] 'History repeating,' Review by Maya Jaggi, *The Guardian*, 21 August 2010.
[4] Paul Hillier, *Arvo Pärt*, Oxford: Oxford University Press, 1997, p.23.
[5] Hillier, *Arvo Pärt*, p.36.
[6] Hillier, *Arvo Pärt*, p.52.
[7] Hillier, *Arvo Pärt*, p.63.
[8] Hillier, *Arvo Pärt*, p.59.
[9] Hillier, *Arvo Pärt*, p.66.
[10] Hillier, *Arvo Pärt*, p.74.
[11] Hillier, *Arvo Pärt*, p.74.
[12] Hillier, *Arvo Pärt*, p.22.
[13] Quoted Hillier, *Arvo Pärt*, p.87.
[14] David Fanning, Programme notes, Proms, 17 August 2010.
[15] Noted by Ivan Moody and Peter Quinn in the Proms programme, 17 August 2010.

[16] Hillier, *Arvo Pärt*, p.122.

[17] Andrew Clements, *The Guardian*, 19 August 2010.

[18] Proms programme, 17 August 2010, p.5.

[19] Hillier, *Arvo Pärt*, p.80.

[20] Hillier, *Arvo Pärt*, pp.178-9.

[21] Peter Quinn, Proms programme, 17 August 2010.

[22] Andrew Clements, *The Guardian*, 23 August 2010.

[23] Hillier, *Arvo Pärt*, p.207.

[24] Alexander Ivashkin, *Between Two Worlds*, p.6. This was the programme accompanying a season of Schnittke's music at the Southbank Centre, 15 November -1 December 2009. It was played by the London Philharmonic under Vladimir Jurowski.

[25] Orlando Figes, *The Whisperers*, pp.594, 561.

[26] Judt, *Postwar*, p.425.

[27] See Michael Scammell's Obituary, *The Guardian*, 8 August 2008. I reread Solzhenitsyn's, *First Circle*, (London: Collins and Harvill, 1st English translation 1968). Here he portrays how those outside the gulag were more oppressed by the police state than those inside. Prisoners believed themselves to enjoy the freedom, despite the risk of betrayal by stool-pigeons, to criticise the system. Still, this was the story of a highly privileged prison, designing high-tech electronic bugging equipment, and hardly typical of the usual labour camp. But it does suggest the rather idiosyncratic moral attitude of the author.

[28] Judt, *Postwar*, p.425.

[29] Ivashkin, *Alfred Schnittke*, p.77.

[30] Ivashkin, *Alfred Schnittke*, p.162.

[31] Ivashkin, *Alfred Schnittke*, p.83.

[32] Quoted in notes for the Chandos recording of St Florian's Symphony, performed by the Russian State Cappella, conducted by Valery Polyansky.

[33] Ivashkin, *Alfred Schnittke*, p.135.

[34] Ivashkin, *Alfred Schnittke*, p.138.

[35] Richard Taruskin, *Defining Russia,* p.103.

[36] Ivashkin, *Alfred Schnittke*, p.154.

[37] Rick Jones, 'Settling Old Scores,' *New Statesman*, 9 November 2009.

[38] Ivashkin, *Between Two Worlds*, p.20.

[39] Ivashkin, *Alfred Schnittke*, p.158.

[40] Quoted Ivashkin, *Alfred Schnittke*, p.151.

[41] Ivashkin, *Alfred Schnittke*, p.60.

[42] David Fanning, Notes in Proms programme, 24 August 2009.

[43] Ivashkin, *Between Two Worlds*, p.23.

[44] Taruskin, *Defining Russia*, p.102.

[45] Andrew Clements, *The Guardian*, 26 August 2009.

[46] Quoted, *Between Two Worlds*, p.6.

[47] Ivashkin, *Alfred Schnittke*, p.92.

[48] Ivashkin, *Alfred Schnittke*, p.123.

[49] Ivashkin, *Between Two Worlds*, p.8.

[50] Ivashkin, *Between Two Worlds*, pp.26-7.

[51] Andrew Clements, *The Guardian*, 28 November 2009.

[52] Taruskin, *Defining Russia*, p.102.

[53] Taruskin, Defining Russia, p.101.

[54] Taruskin, *Defining Russia*, p.100.

[55] Malcolm Macdonald, Notes on Choir Concerto in Ivashkin (ed.), *Between Two Worlds*, p.15.

[56] Michael Kurtz, *Sofia Gubaidulina: A Biography*, Bloomington: Indiana University Press, 2001, p.266.

[57] Anthony Holden, *The Observer*, 21 January 2007.

[58] Tim Ashley, *The Guardian*, 16 January 2007.

[59] Geoff Brown, *The Times*, 17 January 2007.

[60] Paul Griffiths Programme for *A Journey of the Soul: The Music of Sofia Gubaidulina*, p.4.

[61] Kurtz, *Gubaidulina*, p.5.

[62] Kurtz, *Gubaidulina*, p.11.

[63] Quoted Kurtz, *Gubaidulina*, p.60.

[64] All this was in a film, *A Life's Passion*.

[65] Quoted Kurtz, *Gubaidulina*, p.180.

[66] Quoted Kurtz, *Gubaidulina*, p.11.

[67] Quoted Kurtz, *Gubaidulina*, p.42.

[68] Quoted Kurtz, *Gubaidulina*, p.107.

[69] Quoted Kurtz, *Gubaidulina*, p.131.

[70] Quoted Kurtz, *Gubaidulina*, p.14.

[71] Quoted Kurtz, *Gubaidulina*, p.45.

[72] Paul Griffiths Programme for *A Journey of the Soul: The Music of Sofia Gubaidulina*, p.34.

[73] Kurtz, *Gubaidulina*, p.177.

[74] Kurtz, *Gubaidulina*, p.155.

[75] Quoted Kurtz, *Gubaidulina*, pp.65-6.

[76] Quoted Kurtz, *Gubaidulina*, p.69.

[77] Paul Griffiths Programme for *A Journey of the Soul: The Music of Sofia Gubaidulina*, p.44.

[78] Quoted Kurtz, *Gubaidulina*, p.97.

[79] Griffiths, *A Journey of the Soul*, p.32.

[80] Quoted Griffiths, *A Journey of the Soul*, p.39.

[81] Quoted Kurtz, *Gubaidulina*, p.190.

[82] Griffiths, *A Journey of the Soul*, p.29.

[83] Griffiths, *A Journey of the Soul*, p.39.

[84] Griffiths, *A Journey of the Soul*, p.40.

[85] Stedall, *Where on Earth is Heaven*, p.295. He was attending a service in one of the painted monasteries in Bukovina, Romania.

[86] Quoted Kurtz, *Gubaidulina*, p. 256.

[87] Richard Armbruster, Quoted Kurtz, *Gubaidulina*, p.258.

[88] Kurt Masur, Quoted Kurtz, *Gubaidulina*, p.264.

[89] Griffiths, *A Journey of the Soul*, p.13.

[90] Simon Rattle, Quoted Kurtz, *Gubaidulina*, pp.228-9.

[91] Paul Griffiths, *Modern Music and After* (3rd Edition), Oxford: Oxford University Press, 2010, pp.258-60.

[92] Griffiths, *Modern Music*, p.184.

[93] Griffiths, *Modern Music*, p.270.

[94] Griffiths, *Modern Music*, p.272.

[95] Griffiths, *Modern Music*, p.273.

[96] Griffiths, *Modern Music*, p.397.

III.

France and Germany

Olivier Messiaen

Hans Werner Henze

Francis Poulenc

9. *Olivier Messiaen*

Olivier Messiaen is the pivotal figure in any exploration of the spiritual in 20th century music. For Richard Taruskin he is the successor to Scriabin's Maximalism. Yet, more acutely than for other composers under review, Messiaen raises the issue of a tension between religion and the spiritual. Was he too much the theologian?[1] We should resist an earlier temptation to see him as an apolitical and other-worldly composer and, instead, accept a revisionist view of him as man of his times. This opens up the leading question as to where on a spectrum of a this-worldly and the transcendental his spirituality lies. The strongest dynamic in fact came from the personal and in his relationship with three women, his mother, Cecile Sauvage, his first wife, Claire Delbos and his muse and second wife, Yvonne Loriod. Here was an anguished ex-pression of a merely all too human rather than divine love. He escaped from this torment into a spirituality derived from Nature, landscape and birdsong. But the real weight of his music lay with the religious and a contrast can be drawn between an earlier and more conflicted with a later, more dogmatic and bombastic. This will be to look at the music out of a narrative context.

Messiaen and the Political

One of the premises of this project is the impossibility of escaping politics in the intensely political 20th century. Of course the predicament of the creative artist in France and other western democracies was inherently different from those under totalitarian regimes but a greater freedom threw them back on an even greater moral responsibility. But in France, as elsewhere in Nazi occupied Europe, Messiaen was threatened by conditions akin to those experienced by artists under Soviet rule and here was to be a bruising test of his values. One of the paradoxes of this seemingly apolitical composer was his writing in the very depths of the greatest political crisis of the century that supremely iconic composition of 20th century music, the *Quartet for the End of Time*. Just how this-worldly was his music?

Messiaen came of age in the dying fall of the Third Republic. Various combinations of the centre ground had permitted its long-term survival but an increasingly rancorous divide between republican and nationalist put it at risk. It was caught between a threat from a Communist party that only allied with other leftist parties at the dictate of the Comintern and the Soviet Union and a frightening array of fascist organisations that threatened a putsch from the right. No civil order can long survive the spread of para-military organisations. Historians always raise the question, did the Third Republic collapse from within or only as a consequence of military defeat? The seemingly other-worldly Messiaen was revealingly tough-minded during the 1930's.

For a start, after graduating from the Paris Conservatoire in 1929 with his Diplome d'études musicale supérieur, he quickly made his mark as a composer with a performance 22 July 1930 of his *Le Banquet Céleste* and later with his first major orchestral work, *Les Offrandes oubliées*, premiered 19 February 1931. He played his cards very carefully in securing the post of titular organist at La Trinité in 1931, at 22 the youngest organist ever to hold such a post. By 1933 he was teaching at the École Normale de Musique, a post he held till 1939. Messiaen was always canny in promoting his own career. Then in 1933 came military service, Messiaen teaching lessons in harmony to officers and men. In setting up in 1936 the musical group *La Jeune France* – André Jolivet was one of its founder members – Messiaen contributed to the intense pluralism of the Third Republic. In the more interestingly interpretative of Messiaen's biographies, Christopher Dingle comments: 'the fault line that he identified running through the nation's musical life merely reflected the fragmentation in French life as a whole during the 1930's.'[2] Messiaen set himself against Satie and Cocteau and 'this feverish century, this crazy century ... nothing but a century of laziness.'[3] The group was on the side of 'emotional sincerity, put at the service of the dogma of the Catholic faith, expressed through a new musical language.' 'We await the great anticipated liberator of the music of the future.'[4] But at a time when so much of the rhetoric of the Maurassian right was on the decadence of the Third Republic and the need to sweep away the present so as bring about national renewal, this was a regrettable rhetoric. Still, Dingle stresses the eclecticism of *La Jeune France*. And was it so compromising to seek out a peculiarly French spirituality in the music of Berlioz?

But there is an alternative way into his music of the 1930's, its content of violence. Messiaen wrote of a concert given at Boston, Koussevitsky conducting *Les Offrandes oubliées*, 16 October 1936: 'as the conditions of life become more and more hard, mechanical and impersonal, music must always bring to those who love it, its spiritual violence and courageous reactions.'[5] More will have to be said of the violence present in the early religious music. Here is a this-worldly Messiaen. As one critic of *Le Jeune France* put it: 'They are human and want to be musicians above everything else but the musician in them are inspired by their pursuit of the human.': Messiaen was 'not at all other-worldly.'[6] Does his music reflect the conflicts of the dying Third Republic?

Messiaen was already a nationally recognised composer. He was invited to contribute to the 1937 Paris exhibition, the Exposition Internationale des Arts et des Techniques appliqués, and did so in his *Fêtes de belles eaux*, no doubt paying lip-service to the exhibition's technical theme through the role of the electronic ondes Martenot. Likewise, he was acquiring an international reputation, and besides America, in 1938 he visited London, though there the traditionalists were uncomprehending. Messiaen was always robust with critics: 'I say to them simply I am not dissonant: they should wash their ears out.'[7] At this point I want to bypass his period as a POW and look at his experience of Occupation.

How can a creative artist work under a regime such as Vichy? Alone of the occupied states France was granted an Armistice (if not a peace treaty) and legally it remained a sovereign state, even after the Nazi takeover of the Unoccupied Zone. Till the end Vichy claimed to be defending France's interests, however skewed its version of patriotism. Yet this was a brutal police state, one masterminded rather by the Vichy police than by the German Gestapo and one that willingly and quite independently carried out an appalling persecution of the Jews.

The Catholic Church was the strongest institution left in France after defeat. As a profound and seemingly unquestioning Catholic, we have to ask, just how far did Messiaen go along with the official policy of the Church? Admittedly any disquiet the French hierarchy might chose to express could always be stifled by a Vatican obsessed by the threat of communism. Already in 1939 Pope Pius XII had revoked the interdict on Action Française, whose ideology, fashioned by Charles Maurras, was so unduly to influence Pétain's regime. The Papal Nuncio saw Vichy as the Pétain miracle. Its ideology of Travail, Famille, Patrie received the Church's unqualified endorsement. Here was atonement for France's republican anti-clerical past. Communism not Fascism was seen as the real threat and Cardinal Baudrillart happily blessed the Legion of French Volunteers, 31 July 1941, as it set off to join the German army on the Eastern front. There was no question of supporting De Gaulle as here would be the entrée of communism into France. Did the church in any way question Vichy's anti-Semitism?

Obviously the long tradition of Christian anti-Semitism, from St Paul through to Thomas Aquinas, shaped the Church's response to the Holocaust. Vichy moved quickly with its October 1940 Statut des Juifs, which applied to all Jews, though Vichy was never to abandon the lie that it sought to protect French Jews at the expense of foreign. It is disturbing the extent to which Catholic belief infiltrated Vichy anti-Semitism. The first Commissioner of Jewish Affairs, Xavier

Vallat, was a militant Catholic driven by the rabid Catholic anti-Semitism of the journal *Le Pèlerin*; Joseph Darnand, head of the Milice, France's Gestapo, was, to quote Carmen Cahill, 'a staunch, even a fanatical Catholic';[8] Philippe Henriot, a Vichy Minister of Information and Propaganda, shared this outlook. Cahill sees Vallat's anti-Semitic regime as 'the most elaborate and the most severe in Europe.'[9] Already under the Third Republic, but to target the left, some 52 internment camps had been set up and these became the infrastructure for the Holocaust, though the key camp, Drancy, was only set up July 1941. The Catholic hierarchy kept quiet: Cardinal Gerlier of Lyons did express concern 'but his humanity was always drowned by obedience to the Vatican.'[10] The first train departed for Auschwitz in March 1942. On 16 July 1942 came the notorious rounding up in Paris of 12, 884 Jews, more women and children than men, in the Vel' d'Hiv, the winter cycling stadium, and so blatant an event that any Parisian had to know what was going on. If Archbishop Suhard deplored the round-up he only did so in private to Pétain. But the Archbishop of Toulouse, Jules Salège, did eventually speak out, 23 August 1942: Jews 'are part of the human race; they are our brothers, like so many others. A Christian cannot forget this.'[11] And ordinary Catholic clergy did protest. Even so, Cahill summarises: 'in general, however, fewer than half the prelates in the Vichy zone publicly objected to the deportation of the Jews and none in the Occupied Zone.'[12] Unsurprisingly, Cardinal Suhard was not invited to attend the service of Liberation in Notre Dame Cathedral. We have at least to raise the question, how did Messiaen respond to the role of the Catholic Church and to anti-Semitism under the Occupation?

There had to be two kinds of input into cultural policy under the Occupation, but whereas a presumption might be one of a struggle between a resistant French and an oppressive German, the outcome was different, a lenient German and a collaborative French. Frederic Spotts has persuasively explored the way in which Germany calculated that the most effective way of keeping French hostility at bay would be to make considerable gestures towards cultural freedom.[13] France was to be 'anaesthetised' by means of a rich cultural life: 'French artists were to enjoy a preferred status, be cultivated, even feted, but largely left to themselves.'[14] 'Never before in history,' assesses Spotts, 'had a victor framed a cultural policy for a people it has just vanquished, much less one that aimed to make them happy.'[15] Nevertheless it was barbed: the French were to be persuaded of the superiority of German culture. They had to be disillusioned of their own *mission civilatrice*. This was to be a one way cultural exchange with German artists a constant presence in France. The hub of the cultural programme was Ambassador Otto Abetz's German Embassy in Paris and the German Institute. As Spotts interprets, 'in the cultural as in the political field collaboration was a swindle.' French artists became 'in their own way prisoners.'[16]

Music was seen as peculiarly suited to this policy. More than the other arts it brought occupiers and occupied together. The Germans were perfectly happy for the French to administer musical life and ardent Germanophile, the brilliant pianist, Alfred Cortot through the Cortot Committee (modelled on the Reich Music chamber briefly headed by Richard Strauss) became all but musical dictator. He even fantasised at becoming in the manner of Paderewski head of state. Anyone who wanted to perform had to be licensed by the Committee and it rigorously excluded Jews. Amongst composers banned was Messiaen's teacher, Paul Dukas. Both the Opera and Opera Comique became 'the great show-cases of collaboration,'[17] though the Occupiers tended to get more seats. 'And so' to quote Spotts, 'musical life went along essentially as it had before 1940.'[18] Might a French musical tradition yet withstand exposure to Wagner and German romanticism? There was a revival of Debussy's *Pelléas et Mélisande* at the Opera Comique 12 September 1940 and several performances thereafter: there was a memorable performance of Berlioz's *Requiem* at the Opera in 1943. Messiaen, a great advocate of both composers, would have approved. But then he also admired Wagner and the Berlin State Opera was to perform *Tristan und Isolde* in May 1941. How did he accommodate to this scene?

Did he gain from the privileged status of artists under Vichy? Certainly he was fortunate to be released from prison shortly after the performance of the Quartet in January 1941 on the spurious grounds that as a musician he had not been carrying a gun. Captain Karl-Albrecht Brull, Commandant of the camp, as ever his guardian angel, had released him. Fellow POW and cellist Étienne Pasquier forged the papers. But clarinettist, Henri Akoka, a Jew, was not released. By 10 May Messiaen was reunited with his family in his wife's family home at Neussargues, Cantal, in the Unoccupied Zone. On his return he accepted a Vichy commission to compose two *a capella* choruses for *Portique pour une fille de France*, a musical show on Joan of Arc, performed in Lyons 11 May 1941. Was this just out of political naivety? Ever the careerist, Messiaen reclaimed his post at La Trinité and finally secured a post at the Conservatoire as Professor of Harmony, at 32 its youngest professor. Somehow or another, by December 1941 travel restrictions between the two zones were overcome and his wife and son joined him in Paris. He had an established reputation and his music was performed. The Quartet received its French premiere 24 June 1941. In December 1941 he gave organ recitals in the Palais de Chaillot. His work was also performed in the Concerts de la Pléiade at the Galerie Charpentier, organised by Denise Tual, and by invitation only, seemingly to escape German control over French music. In fact the Gallery was in the forefront of a revisionist policy on French art, emphasising its link with Romanticism at the expense of Modernism, a policy that earned the praise of leading collaborationist art critic, Lucien Rebatet, so it was not much of a resistance gesture.[19] Spotts argues that Vichy, rather surprisingly, showed little preference for the religious or traditionalist in music, but Messiaen's style of modernism was also unacceptable to the authorities. He received no further commissions from the state: 'so while never banned, he was marginalized.'[20]

But this is to overlook the way he continued to compose. Inspired by the brilliant pianist Yvonne Loriod who joined his class at the Conservatoire he composed for two pianos *Visions de l'Amen*, premiered 19 May 1943, and commissioned once again by Denise Tual, who organized the Concerts de la Pléiade, the *Trois petites Liturgies de la Présence Divine*, completed 15 March 1944, though its performance was delayed till April 1945. During the time of the Liberation Messiaen was preoccupied with composing the monumental *Vingt Regards sur l'Enfant Jesus*, completed 8 September 1944 but not performed till March 1945. The *Turangalila* symphony was already in his mind's eye. So under Vichy Messiaen was highly creative. By late 1944 he had also become a highly controversial composer, in the main part through those long theological commentaries he attached to his music. But these need to be looked at in considering his sacred music.

Can we see inside Messiaen's mind during the Occupation? Some composers, such as Darius Milhaud, who was Jewish, had wisely left. Another, Arthur Honegger, thrived under Vichy. What was the creative artist supposed to do? Henri Matisse chose to stay: 'if everyone who has any value leaves France, what remains of France?' he wrote to his son, 1 September 1940.[21] 'How else was France to regain its self-respect?' In Michèle Cone's words: 'to rediscover a common identity and a shared culture was the sine qua non of moral rebirth.'[22] Were creative artists somehow different? André Breton put it this way: 'what appears to me as the task of intellectuals is not to let this purely military defeat, for which the intellectuals are not responsible, attempt to carry with it the debacle of the spirit.'[23] This is a very unconvincing piece of special pleading. And clearly not all artists trod their paintings underfoot in disgust as did Robert Delaunay. Did artists indeed just persuade themselves that 'their work was more important than the circumambient ideological environment of Occupation'?[24]

So should we see guilt by association? Messiaen was in Paris by the time of the first systematic round up of foreign and stateless Jews, 14 and 26 March 1941, the first trainloads of Jews from Drancy 27 March 1942, and the Val' d'Hiv event. Is there anyway of knowing how he responded to anti-Semitism? His one aim had been to return to France – he never considered exile. Did he see his composition as restoring national self-respect? All such questions profoundly relate to any account we might make of a this-worldly spirituality. Was he somehow special and apart?

One answer as to where Messiaen stood in regarding Occupation lies in his Gaullism. If detached from Resistance, he consistently supported De Gaulle, seeing him as someone 'who truly loved France, who personified France, who symbolized France and who was a part of French mythology,' – though this was his looking back in 1973 – an opinion which allows his leading biographers Hill and Simeone to see him as 'politically engaged and fiercely patriotic.'[25] In fact his *Chant des déportés,* performed but once, 2 November 1946, was possibly unique as a politically engaged work. He welcomed De Gaulle's return to power in 1958 and thereafter became part of the cultural establishment. In 1958 he was nominated an Officer of the Légion d'honneur and thereafter regularly promoted. André Malraux, De Gaulle's Minister of Culture, 15 November 1963, commissioned a work to memorialise the war dead, and his *Ex Expecto resurrectionem mortuorum* 'set the seal on Messiaen's rise to becoming a figure of national importance.'[26] Its first performance was in the Sainte Chapelle, its second, 20 June 1965, in Chartres Cathedral, De Gaulle in attendance. In the autumn of 1965 he signed an appeal in support of De Gaulle's re-election: 'it was perhaps the only instance of Messiaen voicing a political opinion in public.'[27] Seemingly his only preoccupation during 1968 was over the delay in preparations for the performance of his *La Transfiguration de Notre – Seigneur Jésus-Christ.* Any doubts on whether or not to take up Liebermann's request – he was Director of Opera de Paris – for the massive project on Saint Francis was resolved by attendance at an Élysée dinner party, 28 September 1971: 'I couldn't refuse in front of the President of the republic.'[28] In another account Pompidou pontificates: 'Messiaen, you will write an opera for the Opera de Paris.'[29] By 1987 he reached the Grand Croix of the Légion d'honneur. It is hard not to see in this Gaullism and public endorsement one source for the giganticism and bombastic character of his late music.

Was he drawn into the Cold War? In post-war France French intellectuals were drawn into a politics of commitment, supported the French Communist party, were sympathetic to the Soviet Union, and anti-American. It is impossible, though, to see Messiaen as part of this intelligentsia. Into this mix came the CIA, set up 26 July 1947, successor to the OSS (Office of Strategic Service), which through its various front organisations, above all the Congress for Cultural Freedom took on the Comintern's championing of Socialist Realism. It assumed the role of patron of Modernism and defended Formalism. In terms of music, this meant Schoenberg and the Darmstadt School (in Art, the New York School of Abstract Expressionism). The leading figure in this musical propaganda was the Russian émigré Nicholas Nabokov. It was he who humiliated Shostakovich at a meeting of the Cultural Scientific Conference for World Peace in New York in 1949. If Messiaen was godfather to that radical generation of post-war composers, Boulez, Xenakis and Stockhausen, all his students, he never closely identified with Darmstadt. Indeed, at one stage Boulez saw him as betraying the cause and branded a performance, 14/15 February 1948, of the three central movements from the future Turangalila Symphony, *Trois Tala,* 'bordello music.' (Later he relented of this judgement.) Did Messiean make amends with *Chronochromie*, premiered 13 September 1961, certainly a highly modernist work, yet 'a sun-drenched protest against twelve-tone music'?[30] Admittedly Messiaen was always a friend of America. In 1949 he made his first visit and to Tanglewood. Even so, and maybe significantly, he was not one of the composers featured in Nabokov's Festival of Masterpieces of the Twentieth

Century in Paris, April 1952. It is hard to see Messiaen as a Cold War warrior.[31]

Quartet for the End of Time

Was this a political piece?

The circumstances of its composition are well known and the story does not need to be retold in detail. Maybe not enough attention has been paid to the sheer physical toll on Messiaen. Conscripted at the outbreak of war in September 1939, he was assigned, highly unsuitably, to the Engineers – 'my grazed and blackened hands, using a pickaxe, the flies, carrying unbelievably heavy weights,'[32] 'these labours are beyond my strength.'[33] Later, on appeal, he became a medical orderly. Following capture near Verdun, he was frogmarched some forty miles to a field outside Nancy, kept there for ten days, dispatched in a sealed cattle truck to Gorlitz in Silesia, some fifty-five miles east of Dresden, with nothing to eat or drink. He was a prisoner in Stalag VIII, a prison camp with some 30 barracks, 40,000 French prisoners, 80,000 Belgian, Polish POWs, from July 1940 till his early release January 1941, enduring a bitterly cold winter. Messiaen went down with dysentery – he spent a month in hospital cared for by Polish nuns – and it is hardly surprising he had hallucinations and mistook the Aurora Borealis for the Apocalypse. In some ways the Quartet was a result of a psychosis.

It was in these dire circumstances that Messiaen, on the piano, together with Étienne Pasquier, his Commanding officer at Verdun, the cellist, Henri Akoka, an Algerian-born Jew, whom he met on that field at Toul, the clarinettist, and Jean Boulaire, whom he met in Stalag VIII A, the violinist, on the night of 15 January 1941, performed the Quartet, in prison hut 27 to some 400 fellow prisoners. For Alex Ross this is 'the most ethereally beautiful music of the twentieth century.'[34] 'Never have I been listened to with such attention and understanding' recalled Messiaen, but, in fact, a subsequent review in *Lumignon*, the camp's French language newspaper, wrote of 'both fervent enthusiasm' and 'the irritation of others.'[35] As ever, Messiaen divided his audience. By all accounts Messiaen in the camp was in a very strange state of mind, acting as if he was some Hindu anchorite: 'despite his hunger, despite his thirst, he seemed far away, he seemed to be thinking of something else, of something very pure and brilliant, something which moved very slowly in the distance, something which unceasingly absorbed his gaze, full of life and love.'[36] Fellow prisoners would queue for therapeutic consolation from Messiaen. Out of their recognition that he was an extraordinary human being they gave him extra rations and arranged for lighter duties. One is left with a sense that this whole experience was a lasting trauma and maybe it is not so odd that he misrepresented the event, claiming defective musical instruments, that the cello had but three strings, that his audience was 5000 strong and sat outside in the freezing cold. It may explain his refusal to meet the quasi-angelic Karl-Albert Brull, who had done so much to facilitate the composition, on his attempt to meet up again later in Paris. When Messiaen repented, it was too late, he had been killed in a road accident. Intriguingly in 1981, on moving to his new retreat near Bourges, he discovered that a neighbouring priest, Père Rene Bobineau, had been a fellow inmate in Stalag VIII.

So how to read the spirituality of the Quartet?

One critic has written of its 'heart-on-sleeve' spirituality.[37] For Messiaen himself it was inspired by the 10th chapter of Revelations, by the mighty Seventh Angel, 'clothed with a cloud, a rainbow upon his head,' (there are artistic images of the Angel in a tapestry in Angers and in Durer's lithographs), who announced the end of Time, that God's mystery should be finished. Messiaen was always preoccupied by the Apocalypse. In Jouvenel's account the Christian mysticism is mixed 'with an utterly pagan violence, an abandonment to sensuality such as we no longer find except among "primitive" peoples still living at one with nature.' It is in seven parts. In the second, when the Angel announces the end of Time, Ross writes 'of the gentlest apocalypse imaginable.' As I've listened to it[38] I've wondered if this is playing on a theme of war and peace and to what degree its tranquillity had been fought for or had it just been given; in the third section, an utterly haunting solo for the clarinet, we hear birdsong: for Messiaen, birds 'are our desire for light, for stars, for rainbows and for jubilant songs.' But what birds other than crows would he have seen in the camp? But here was music from the Abyss. In the fifth, Praise to the Eternity of Christ, it seemed impossible that this serenity could have come out of the camp: the praise felt expository, a self-expression of Christ, rather than deferential and adulatory. In the sixth section, Dance of Fury of the Seven Trumpets, I wondered what these mad creatures, these hobgoblins, could be. Was this, at last, a human and infuriated protest, a sense of outrage at the desecration of it all? In the Seventh, Clusters of Rainbows for the Angel who announces the End of Time, I sensed a world falling apart, no real pathway here. In 'the swords of fire, these outpourings of blue-orange lava, these turbulent stars,' was there weirdly some anticipation of the gas chambers? It conjured up images from Pasolini's terrifying film *Salo*. In the final section, Praise to the Immortality of Christ, through the haunting lyricism of the violin, we do reach tranquillity, if hard fought for, a Buddhist detachment. The clarinettist, Robert Plane, told me it was a piece utterly draining to play, though he was recalling a performance in Trinity church, New York, a stone's throw from Ground Zero.[39]

The question remains, is this a response to the terrible times in which he lived, or an escape into the transcendental? In Alex Ross's rich interpretation, it has to be seen as much a product of the prison community as of individual genius. Messiaen addresses matters of fear and faith. His response to hate is love. Through the music he suggests an escape from Time: 'Messiaen no longer wanted to hear time being beaten out by a drum-one, two, three, four: he had had enough of that in the war. Instead, he devised rhythms that expanded,

contracted, stopped in their tracks, and rolled back in sym-
metrical patterns.' For Messiaen, 'the end of time also meant
an escape from history, a leap into an invisible paradise.' But
Messiaen's was a sensuous, almost sexual love of God and
there is a continuum between human and divine love, the
this-worldly and the other-worldly. 'In the end,' interprets
Ross, 'Messiaen's apocalypse has little to do with history
and catastrophe, it records the rebirth of an ordinary soul in
the grip of extraordinary emotions.' Curiously, this is just
how one might interpret the music of Shostakovich.

But all great music reflects both the times in which the composer lives and the eternal. Dingle sees the Quartet 'as a beacon of hope in the face of the most desolate circumstances'[40]
though he also reminds us of Messiaen's Catholic theology:
'death was a beginning not an end.'[41] In part this has to be
seen as political, Messiaen's response to a blighted Europe.

The Tristan Music

Messiaen rarely discussed his domestic life yet the private
sphere was far more the source of his music than the public,
and three women, his mother, Cécile Sauvage, his first wife,
Claire Delbos, and his muse and second wife, Yvonne Loriod, inspired what can be seen as a kind of secular and humanist spirituality, music inspired by carnal rather than divine
love. But Messiaen was far too good a Thomist not to see the
first as subsumed within the second, though possibly not so
good a Freudian as to realise that the frustration of Eros led
him into Thanatos. The music of a love that spills over into
death in Wagner's *Tristan und Isolde* lies behind Messiaen's
Tristan music.

His mother was a distinguished poet – Léon Daudet after her
death saw her as far and away France's best woman poet –
and dedication to her craft set a life-time example of hard
work for her son. But the extent of her influence is a matter
of guess-work and it has the feel of a burden. She was a

distant mother. And he was never close to his father. Pierre Messiaen, Shakespeare scholar and translator, never really understood his son. His parents married 9 September 1907, he was born 10 December 1908. Famously, she wrote whilst pregnant a collection of twenty poems, *L'Âme en bourgeon* (*The Soul in Bud*), forecasting his interest in birdsong and Japan, as well as his role as teacher. Messiaen believed the poems 'influenced my entire destiny.'[42] But his mother was subject to depression and Messiaen's was a lonely childhood. Shortly before her death 26 August 1927 from tuberculosis at the age of 44, she wrote: 'I've got to find again this poetry bordering on the supernatural which is a reason for being, something bright blue and bright red like the stained glass at Chartres.'[43] It was a way of thinking wholly akin to her son's. Messiaen told his student, George Benjamin, that, ever after, his mother watched over him like an angel.[44] But with her depression and keeping her distance it has the feel of a negative inheritance.

The prolonged illness of his first wife and his adulterous love for his second to be is the anguished context of the Tristan music. He married 22 June 1932 violinist and composer, Claire Delbos. They were to give frequent concerts together. She was the daughter of Victor Delbos, a Professor of Philosophy at the Sorbonne. One of the perks of the marriage was access to the family home, the Château St Benoît at Neussargues, in the Cantal region of Auvergne. We can get some idea of their love from the song cycles she inspired, above all the 1936 *Poémes pour Mi*. Originally scored for voice and piano, he made an orchestral version. Intriguingly, at the same time there was a performance of his wife's setting of his mother's poems, *The Soul in Bud*. Messiaen's own poetry for the song cycle suggests a pretty strange marriage. The wife's role was wholly subordinate, 'the wife is the extension of the husband,' she has given herself 'in obedience and in the blood of your cross'; marriage is analogous to that between the Church as bridegroom and Christ. It seems odd that a woman should be singing a song cycle that resonates with the authorial voice of the husband. There is an idyllic account of their newly acquired retreat at Petichet in the mountains of the Dauphiné. But then comes a truly weird anticipation that this marriage will fall apart, 'we shall leave our bodies too,' together with a terrifying image of his wife's death, 'bleeding tatters will follow you into the darkness like spasmodic vomiting.' When I heard this sung as part of the Messiaen Festival, *From the Canyons to the Stars,* 3 October 2008, here was music that evoked Schoenberg and Bartok – shades of *Erwartung* and *Bluebeard's Castle* – a truly terrifying glimpse into the abyss. There follows another moment of horror: 'your eye and my eye among marching statues, among the black howls, it rains sulphurous solids.' It helps to know that Messiaen was much influenced by the surrealists. But there is also a passage of sexual lyricism: 'ah my necklace, little living cushion for my weary eyes': in the programme notes, this is seen as 'the arms of a lover wrapped around her beloved neck.'[45] And the work ends on an upbeat note: 'Behold your day of glory and resurrection! Joy has returned.' Yet, as I heard it, the music belies the words, this felt like a desperate appeal, a terrible unspoken doubt, and the orchestra plunges almost into gloom at the end. It is an extraordinarily dramatic piece with its chiaroscuro of mood, but it is surely a telling insight into the strangeness of their marriage.

On his return from prison in 1941, still traumatised, reunited with Claire but then separated by the line of demarcation, newly appointed to the Conservatoire, there he meets in his Harmony class, Yvonne Loriod, young (born 20 January 1924), beautiful. A childhood prodigy, she was a brilliant pianist. Thanks to the Occupation her first two teachers, Lazare Lévy for piano, André Bloch for harmony, had been deported. At that stage she had yet to choose between being a composer or a concert pianist. Immediately they were drawn together. Her exceptional pianism was to inspire *Visions de l'Amen* (1943) and *Vingt Regards sur l'Enfant-Jésus* (1945). At least nine future orchestral scores were to contain major roles for the piano.[46] In 1943 Claire began to show the first signs of dementia. Had she apprehended something had happened?

In some ways parallels can be drawn with the personal life of a comparable composer, Vaughan Williams. For years he had endured an unfulfilled marriage with his seriously sick wife Adeline, then he met his Yvonne Loriod in Ursula Wood, 3 March 1938 and they soon became lovers. It now seems probable that the violence expressed in works such as his 4th Symphony reflected less outrage at the rise of Nazism than anger at the frustrations in his marriage. But the option of an affair was not open to Messiaen with his deep catholic commitment to the sacrament of marriage. While Vaughan Williams, Adeline and Ursula lay three to a bed during the war out of fear of night-time bombing, Messiaen embarked on a long emotional nightmare that would only end with Claire's death 22 April 1959. Out of guilt at this emotional entanglement he was to give up all religious music till the 1960's.

Her illness was not well handled. In 1946 Messiaen arranged a visit to Lourdes. Her increasingly erratic behaviour render-ed his personal life and his composing more and more difficult. In January 1949, she underwent a hysterectomy but the operation was mistakenly carried out with an epidural rather than an anaesthetic, and her health collapsed, she lost her memory and, in time, her sanity. Initially his father Pierre looked after her. Belatedly, in 1953, she was institutional-ised. Messiaen thus became a single parent and a measure of the poor relationship with his son was failure to attend Pas-cal's wedding 2 August 1957. Father and son were to patch up their differences.

Messiaen's domestic life would have been impossible with-out the presence of the practical Yvonne Loriod. It was she, for example, who added more mod cons to the retreat at Petichet. The two women got on well and Claire had been able to attend Yvonne's performance of *Catalogue d'Ois-eaux,* 15 April 1959. Claire was but 52 when she died. At her funeral Messiaen's 'face was extremely pale but also seemed to show a sort of deep peace. He seemed calm, serene, relaxed; he gave the impression of arriving from another world.'[47] At this juncture he had no other choice but to turn to Loriod. He moved into her flat. Out of decorum they delayed the civil marriage till 1 July 1961, the religious, 3 July. Oddly, it was a marriage ceremony without music, though a blackbird sang.

One of the three Tristan compositions, and seen as a farewell to Claire, *Harari (Le)* was to be his last song cycle, for 'never again would he return to a genre so closely associated with his first wife.'[48] Claire was in the audience at its first private performance 26 June 1946. Inspired by Peruvian folk music – Harari is the Quecha word for a song about love that ends in death, another version of Tristan and Isolde, together with a violent decapitation – and is one of Messiaen's darkest compositions. Roland Penrose's painting, *Seeing is Believing,* of a female head upside down, her hair streaming down and neck disappearing into the night sky above, profoundly influenced Messiaen. It is a song of farewell:

> *Farewell to you, my heaven on earth*
> *Farewell to you, desert who cries*
> *Mirror without the breath of life*
> *Of flower, of night, of fruit, of heaven,*
> *of day Forever.*[49]

'Altogether,' interpret Hill and Simeone, 'the music of *Harari* has a ferocity and desperation not found elsewhere in Messiaen.'[50]

The Turangalila Symphony was the major work of the triptych of pieces inspired by Wagner's liebestod from *Tristan und Isolde.* It can only be understood in terms of the maelstrom of Messiaen's personal life. If *Harari* was written for Claire, this was written for Yvonne. It is also seen as a continual rejoicing at his survival of imprisonment. It was commissioned by Serge Koussevitsky for the Boston Symphony Orchestra. The three corps movements *Trois Tala,* were premiered in Paris 14/15 February 1948, the full symphony in Boston 28 November 1948.

The Sanskrit title needs translation. *Lila* means play, 'play in the sense of the divine action upon the cosmos, the play of creation, of reconstruction, the play of life and death. *Lila* is also love.' Often overlooked by interpreters is reference to the Krishna cult, to his *lila*, his sporting with the cow girls, the *gopis*. *Turanga* translates as movement, rhythm, 'time that flows, like sand in an hourglass,' so that the whole work adds up to 'a love song, hymn to joy, time, movement, rhythm, life and death.'[51] It was a work that only evolved gradually, Messiaen writing of himself at the time, 'could a composer be found more isolated, more wretched, more uncertain of himself and of others, and further from the intrigues, selfishness and unreasonableness of the world?' Equally, however, he saw himself as 'the innovator, that liberator who is so impatiently awaited, the composer of love.'[52]

As ever the music had a mixed reception. If Boulez heard *Trois Tala* as bordello music, another heard 'both softness and violence, magic at every level, and an almost irresistible lashing of the senses.'[53] Of the American premiére, Leonard Bernstein its conductor, some wrote 'of the fundamental emptiness of the work,' 'the longest and most futile music within memory,'[54] others were astounded by 'its hectic invention, fearless decibel-level, total lack of inhibition and its joyful excess at every level.'[55] Koussevitsky believed it to be the first new milestone in music since Stravinsky's *Rite of Spring*.

The organisers of the 2008 Messiaen festival ranked it 'as the most astonishing and emotionally charged classics of the 20th century.'[56] A critic of the Promenade performance in the same year by the Berlin Philharmonic under Simon Rattle conjured up parallels with 'the rapture of Chagall's familiar lovers floating in bliss over the rain-bow kissed rooftops of

Paris.' 'When the music required that famed carpet of string sound, as in "Garden of the Sleep of Love", it was there in all its deep-pile luxury.'[57] Another critic, commenting on the relationship between sex and metaphysics in the work, wrote of 'its sense of divinity exuberantly manifested in physical joy,' 'its Debussyan sensuousness.'[58] In this section I heard Krishna playing in the forest. Messiaen is portraying both carnal, indeed orgiastic love, and something more tender and idealised. Dingle sees it as 'a gregarious beacon of joy' but quotes Messiaen as admitting that, if a work about love, it is of 'joy as it may be conceived by someone who has glimpsed it only in the midst of sadness' – (of course exactly his situation) – 'the lovers are outside of time.'[59] If the work of a man in love, it is of someone in the grip of extreme emotion, tortured and confused. Indeed, Messiaen compared the climax to Section 7 to the tortures described in Edgar Allan Poe's *The Pit and the Pendulum*. In the final section, through the swooping glissandos of the ondes Martenot and the music of the piano, there is some resolution; significantly, early performances were by Yvonne Loriod on the piano and her sister, Jeanne, on the ondes Martenot.

The third panel of the Tristan triptych, *Cinq Rechants*, was another song cycle, inspired both by Peruvian folk music and by the mediaeval. It is seen as breaking new ground in choral writing, 'a masterstroke, perhaps never to be repeated.' Hill and Simeone see it as yet another reflection of Messiaen's 'agonizing predicament.' Had Loriod become 'the image of the[60] fateful step, the love potion, the seventh door'?

Can the place of cruelty in Messiaen's composition be attributed to his naivety? Why was he so drawn to so cruel a character as Gilles de Rais, the occult companion of Joan of Arc? Sander van Maas is an apologist: 'the naïve is an implicit recognition of the existence and the power of evil in the world, and of the necessity to constantly counteract its workings.'[61] But it leaves a sour taste.

Landscape and Birdsong

Here were further sources of his more 'secular' spirituality.

Messiaen looked to Nature. He found it all but impossible to compose in Paris and sought the peace of the countryside. Spending his childhood years during World War 1 in Grenoble led to a lasting love of the mountains of Le Dauphiné. On a holiday in Grenoble in 1935 he reported, 'I have seen the most stunning mountain landscape here. The Dauphiné is really one of the great things in France.'[62] In 1936 he found his ideal retreat in Petichet on the shores of Lac Leffroy, off the Route Napoleon, south of Grenoble. In the distance was 'the looming hogsback of the Grand Serre.'[63] It is easy to feel this great slab of a mountain brooding over his music. In the organ work *Livre d'orgue* Messiaen drew on the view of the mountain La Grave and the glaciers of the Meije above.

Another inspirational landscape, and one that lay behind his *Des Canyons aux étoiles*, was the Grand Canyon, in particular the canyons of Cedar Breaks, Zion and Bryce in South Western Utah. He drew inspiration from the red and orange of the sandstone and 'the immense silence.' The piece was by way of dedication to God in all his creation. The locals were to name a mountain after him near Cedar Breaks.[64]

In the 1950's Messiaen retreated from both his appalling personal circumstances and the pressures of modernism into birdsong: 'Nature, birdsong. These are my passions. They are also my refuge.'[65] At the time he confessed to his students: 'We are all in a profound night and I don't know where I am going; I'm as lost as you.'[66] 'In melancholy moments, when my uselessness is brutally revealed to me ... what else is there to do except search for the true face of nature, forgotten somewhere in the forest, in the fields, in the mountains, on the seashore, among the birds.'[67] His mother had forecast his love of birds: his teacher Dukas had told him, 'study the birds. They are great masters.' Messiaen saw them as 'God's songsters.' Had there been a turning point in 1940 at Verdun when he requested the early morning watch to hear the dawn chorus? In the Quartet for the End of Time, in *Abysse des oiseaux*, he looks to the birds: 'birds can escape and fly closer to God.' In1952 he joined Jacques Delemain, producer of brandy but also a noted ornithologist, and in his garden at Branderaie de Gardepée near Cognac, became a systematic recorder of birdsong as the huge number of his *Cahiers* bear witness.

The first outcome was *Le Merle Noir* (*The Blackbird*), in fact composed in 1952 as a test piece for the flute at the Conservatoire: 'it belongs to the most technically progressive period of his career.'[68] In fact, as I heard it played, it struck me as crude and thrusting, with a kind of top-down quality. Here was a received opinion, one we had to bow to. Then came *Réveil des oiseaux*, 1953, tracking the songs of birds from midnight to midday, with two long silences at dawn and noon. Yvonne Loriod only grasped how to play the piece by driving into the forest near Orgeval to hear the dawn chorus for herself. She premiered *Oiseaux exotiques*, Messiaen here turning from the birds of France to those of North and South America, China, Malaya and India: he both listened to recordings and visited the bird markets of Paris. Loriod premiered *Catalogue d'oiseaux* 15 April 1959, all 2½ hours of it, a panoramic sweep of birds in France, one, Le Loriod, the Golden Oriole, included in her honour, ending with the Curlew from the island of Ushant, off Finistère, with the piano 'petering out into the silence of "cold black night" with a dribble of surf.'[69]

Disingenuously Messiaen declared of the birds 'we know each other, but I am not St Francis in talking to them, you understand, I just listen and take down what they have to say.'[70] In fact, Peter Hill suggested in a talk at the Sounds New Festival 2008 that in 80% of cases he took poetic licence, reshaping their sounds. In impossible ways birds from different part of the world sing together. Curiously, there remains that undercurrent of violence: in *Catalogue d'oiseaux* we hear the cries of victims of the tawny owl as if those of a murdered child. Messiaen explained away the mixed response to this music in terms of a conflict between rigour and freedom: '*Freedom!* Doubtless we're afraid of the word. In the end it is freedom that triumphs in my music.'[71] But this obsession with birdsong had been by way of escape. It took a journey to Japan in 1961 and the resolution of his personal tragedy to turn Messiaen back to where the real focus of his music lay, the religious.

Could it be argued that in his absorption in birdsong, orthodox Catholic Messiaen had turned heretical pantheist? But Paul Griffiths will have none of this: 'by endeavouring to reflect back, perfectly, the perfection of creation, Messiaen's birdsong pieces of 1951-60 participate in his spiritual project, even though this period was unique in his output for its lack of explicitly religious music.'[72]

Religion

Given that his religious faith defined the man and his music, it is surprising how uncertain we are about the origin and content of Messiaen's Catholicism. He believed he was born a Catholic. And maybe indeed nature not nurture is the explanation. In his biographies to date neither parents are seen as religious. Despite being educated at the Catholic University of Lille his father was a non-believer and his mother an avowed atheist. In another account, however, in contrast, Pierre is deemed 'a fervently Catholic father.'[73] And they did not discourage his religious beliefs. Messiaen believed that his mother explored through her poetry just those same mysteries of faith that he did through his music and that she always guided his spiritual life. His father's taking him on a tour of the churches of Paris, following his appointment at the Lycée Charlemagne in 1919, also left a lasting impression; his musical response to the colours of the stained glass of Sainte Chapelle was an early sign of his synaesthesia. But probably nothing did so much to make Messiaen a dutiful Catholic than playing every Sunday whilst in Paris at La Trinité. There is a wonderful account by Denise Tual of bearding him in his den: 'I found myself in front of a man of the church, ageless, with a forehead bulging and glasses.' They had to climb five flights of stairs till Messiaen took a key 'to let us into a kind of cubby hole. He genuflected and prayed before a crucifix.' She had come to commission *Visions de l'Amen.*[74]

In the 1930's his music assumed a strongly theological character. He informed his audience for *La Nativité de Seigneur* 27 February 1936 of 'the emotion, the sincerity of the musical work: to be at the service of Catholic theology.' 'Theological subject matter? The best, since it contains all subjects.'[75] At the first concert of *Le Jeune France,* 3 June 1936, he spoke of 'Catholic faith expressed through a new musical language – or at least an attempt to achieve this.'[76] But how well versed was Messiaen as a theologian?

We should see Messiaen as part of a long term Catholic revival, a *renouveau catholique*, both doctrinal and liturgical, that was to come of age in the 20th century through Paul Claudel, Charles Péguy, Georges Bernanos and Francois Mauriac. As a church organist Messiaen was most immediately drawn into that liturgical reform movement in favour of Gregorian chant, initiated by Dom Prospect Guéranger (1805-75), revivor of the Benedictine order in France as Abbot of the monastery of Solesmes, founded in 1832. One of the theologians he quotes in his *Technique de mon langage musicale* (1944) was Dom Columba Marmion, Abbot of the Belgian Benedictine abbey of Maredsous, who summarised Gueranger's 15 volume *The Liturgical Year* in his single *Le Christ dans ses mystères* (1919), a work Messiaen read c.1931. There was always to be a running battle over the liturgical music at La Trinité, Messiaen favouring the Solesmes tradition over attempts to move towards the vernacular over Latin and a polyphonic style over the Gregorian plainchant, reforms favoured by Vatican 11. But there was a deeper theological debate and much of this hinged on the role of Neo-Thomism.

The revival of Thomism owed much to Pope Leo XIII's encyclical *Aeterni Patris* (1879). Here was to be the answer to all the vagaries of philosophy since Descartes, a challenge by the catholic avant-garde to the positivism and historicism of the Sorbonne. The key theologian of Neo-Thomism was Jacques Maritain (1882-1973) and Messiaen certainly read his *Art et Scholastique* (1923, revised 1927). But Maritain took up the music of Eric Satie, also championed by Jean Cocteau, the very style that Messiaen was rejecting in *Le Jeune France*. Interpreters vary on his indebtedness to Aquinas. Certainly he frequently refers to him in his musical texts. One interpreter sees him as striving 'to align his compositional aesthetics with Thomistic doctrine,' aiming, like Aquinas, at a philosophical synthesis of Christian and non-Christian writers, 'attempting to make the invisible real through a superhuman language of praise.'[77] But others see him as moving away from Neo-Thomism, towards a theology of feeling over the intellect. This is evidenced by the alternative theologians he refers to, the 19th century Ernest Hello (1828-85) and his own contemporary, Hans Urs von Balthasar (1905-88). His poet brother, Alain, introduced him c 1933 to Hello's *Paroles de Dieu* (1877). Hello, a major figure in the 19th century catholic revival, indebted to Romanticism, had taken on Voltaire, Rousseau, Hegel and Renan, seeking to convert the *théologique* into the *mystique*. In his *Contes Extraordinaires* (1879) he also took up Poe and the fantastical. Messiaen read von Balthasar's *Welt und Person* (1939). Here was a theologian markedly breaking away from Thomism into a much more shadowy theology of symbolism.

Fascinatingly, links are made between theological symbolism and surrealism, and Messiaen, as we have already seen, was profoundly influenced by surrealism, by the poetry of Pierre Riverdy (1889-1960) and Paul Éluard (1895-1952). Both the theology and the poetry sought invisible symbols, if one in the divine, the other in the unconscious.

There is a strong case for seeing him as moving beyond Thomism. Douglas Shadle concludes that Messiaen side-stepped Maritain's brand of Catholic thinking, and became all the more successful through doing so. Peter Bannister sees Messiaen as taking on secularism by attempting to 'baptize' the language of modernism. Robert Scholl sees Messiaen using shock as a way of bringing 'secular humanity to an encounter with God,' and, if a little portentously, as embracing 'a state of subjective alienation as a springboard to freedom.' He concludes: 'Messiaen's music acts like the lens through which our eyes become accustomed to the radiant and enigmatic beauty of the divine.'[78] Breaking from Neo-Thomism allowed him the better to work out his own personal style, a 'glistening music,' as Shloesser sees it, 'simultaneously both voluptuous and contemplative.'

Messiaen's theological commentaries on his work proved deeply provocative and lead to the so called *Le Cas Messiaen,* the Messiaen Controversy. One critic wrote of his 'abysmal commentaries,' 'elaborate gobbledegook' 'of the musty smell of pious congregations ... the images of slimy bigots.'[79] (I have to say I associate Catholic buildings with the smell of carbolic). In particular this was a response to commentaries on his *Trois petites Liturgies* and here, as Schloesser observes, 'such immanentist effusions' clashed with the mood of a blood-soaked city. Messiaen took note and at the time, from 1945 on, refrained from these theological introductions.

Somewhat perversely Messiaen retreated from the religious at the very time in the late 40's and 50's that France at large was experiencing a Catholic revival. As Judt explains: 'the Catholic Church offered a sense of continuity, of security and reassurance in a world that had altered violently in the past decade and was about to be transformed even more dramatically in the years to come. It was the Catholic church's association with the old order, indeed the firm stand against modernity which gave it special appeal in these transitional years.'[80]

But the theological flooded back into his music in the 1960's. Possibly he felt some disquiet at new trends introduced by Vatican 11, for, in a rare moment of dissent, he continued to set Latin texts to music. But he joined the crowds in Paris to witness the visit of Pope Jean Paul: 'I was on my feet for five hours.'[81] In April 1989 Cardinal Lustiger in Notre Dame conferred on him the Prix Paul VI.

But herein lies the rub. In that tension between the two, did Messiaen's faith stifle the expression of his spirituality? Richard Taruskin implies the problem. He sees him as both 'that unregenerate maximalist' and a 'working church musician.' 'He managed to transform theological dogma into musical dogma and that is why Messiaen always objected to being called a mystic. Rather than a mystic he was a *scholastic*, in the mediaeval sense of the term. Like Saint Thomas Aquinas, he sought to embody the mysteries of faith in a rational transmissible discourse.'[82] Paul Griffiths likewise emphasises the theological at the expense of the mystical. His was not, he claims, a personal vision.[83]

Shenton's recent volume responds to some of these doubts. But in which case, how do we in fact hear the music? Like all maximalist music, it has to be heard live. It needs space. Paul Griffiths makes the interesting observation that Messiaen sought 'not to manifest his faith ... but to make possible a religious experience for his listeners.'[84] Is there a parallel with Mark Rothko who left it to his viewers to discover their own experience of the spiritual in his paintings? His sacred music was in two main phases, the 1930's and early 40's, and from the 1960's onwards. Here I'll focus on music that I myself have heard.

Music

Early Sacred Music

From an early stage Messiaen decided that only his organ music could be liturgical, the rest was for the concert hall. Early on he discovered his style, those 7 modes, 'the modes of limited transposition,' a way of slowing up the music and suggesting timelessness. They are there in *Le Banquet céleste* (1928). His was a conscious rejoinder to the frivolity of the music of Les Six. In *Diptyque* (1930) the useless torment of life is off-set by the peace of Christian paradise.

Dingle sees an early orchestral work *L'Ascension* (1935), subsequently arranged for organ, a meditative work indebted to plainsong, as an example of a musical structure supporting theological symbolism: 'Christ is the Alpha and Omega, the beginning and the end, encompassing everything in the orchestra, from winds to strings.' He comments on the audacity of the way this symbolism is conveyed.[85] In the finale there is indeed an ascent: 'an unadorned silence – punctuated procession, in the way that a colonnade of pillars in a cathedral interior leads the eye gradually onwards and upwards towards the lit spaces of the dome overhead.'[86]

Premiered in La Trinité January 1936, and seen as 'a watershed' piece, *La Nativité de Seigneur* is the point at which Messiaen begins fully to sound like Messiaen. Through Claire's false pregnancies it was a theme of special poignancy for Messiaen. Their only child, Pascal was born July 1937. It is, however, a piece less to do with the family event of the Nativity and more the incarnation of God, of the Word. The third meditation, Eternal purposes, described as 'the abstract yet rapturous masterpiece,' is seen as 'the most timeless of all the meditations,' and 'arguably contains some of Messiaen's finest music.'[87] One of the best known of the meditations is *Dieu parmi nous* (*God amongst us*), often played on its own.

Messiaen, however, believed that the best of his organ works from the 1930's was *Le Corps Glorieux* (1939), inspired by St Paul's essay on life and death, 1 Corinthians 15: 'how the dead are raised up and in what body do they come? Here is the glorious victory of the risen Christ over the powers of darkness.' As I heard it performed by Thomas Trotter in the appropriately cavernous space of St Paul's Cathedral, 27 November 2008, it was tentative, abstracted, distant, until an extraordinary change of mood in section 4, *Combat de la mort et de la vie*. Here was Death stalking the land, shrill and in full cry, here is the suffering of Christ, to quote the programme notes, 'Death snarling on the reeds and thundering out beneath a tumult of discords.' 'After a final cataclysmic thrust of the sword, it seems that Death has won the day.' But then there is a hiatus, the music turns very introspective and 'the Theme of Eternal Death is miraculously transformed into a Theme of Eternal Life.' Here is also an example of Messiaen's obsession with numbers: the work ends with homage to the Trinity, 'every element of this elusive, other-worldly final vision is built around the figure 3.'[88]

Was this a premonition of war? Dingle comments: 'it is hard to regard the unusually stark directness of Messiaen's title for the movement (the fourth) as coincidental, for it could stand as an epithet for the catastrophe that was about to engulf the world: "Combat of Life and Death."'[89]

Yvonne Loriod's pianism inspired his war-time religious works. *Visions de l'Amen* was in part indebted to the theology of Ernest Hello, partly to Revelations. After its first and private performance 9 May 1943 Messiaen took his audience off to attend Vespers at La Trinité. The fervour of the audience at its public performance the next day, one of the Concerts de la Pléiade, it is claimed, 'seemed to challenge the German army.'[90] In fact it was an establishment event, Christian Dior, Colette, Honegger, Poulenc amongst the audience. The second work, its performance delayed till after the Liberation, *Trois petites liturgies de la Présence Divine,* with a leading role for the piano, was deemed a success:

one critic saw it as symbolizing 'the spiritual renewal of France.'[91] But the strongest work, 'the pianistic Everest,'[92] and this to be his last religious work till the 1960's, was *Vingt Regards sur l'Enfant Jésus-Christ.*

'Regards' translates as somewhere between contemplation and adoration. It was written both to illustrate a broadcast of Maurice Toesca's poem on the Nativity as well as a concert piece. Plans for a de luxe illustrated text by Picasso and Rou-ault fell through. In summary, with its leitmotif of God, it is a journey from God the Father and Son to the 'convulsive energy of creation' and to the Spirit, to the events of Nativity, to the glory of the Eternal Church.[93] This two hour marathon for piano was premiered in the Salle Gaveau 26 March 1945. It was to be performed twice in the Messiaen centenary year, by Pierre-Laurent Aimard at the Queen Elizabeth Hall, 13 February 2008 and Stephen Osborne at the Wigmore Hall, December 2008. Did Messiaen succeed, as the notes for the first suggest, in fashioning 'a cathedral of sound out of the piano, a rapt and massive musical contem-plation,' with Turanga-lila like thundering, rises and descents across the piano in the contemplation of the Spirit of Joy?[94] My own notes pick up on 'furioso' passages, colossal chords, violently rhythmical even jazzy music, angels as giants walk-ing, demonic passages. At one point I wondered if Messiaen had any awareness of his audience. Fiona Maddocks had some vivid responses to Osborne's performance. She writes of 'its overt religiosity and heady musical mysticism, thick with smoochy added sixths': 'at the start, the fearful theme of God rumbles low on the piano eventually mingling with the ecstatic Theme of Love via several all embracing Divine ep-isodes.' Osborne played 'with muscularity and sensitivity': 'in his hands, the chameleon piano turns itself into trombone, panpipe, birdsong, cheesy cinema organ.'[95] Dingle writes of 'the violently anarchic passage that immediately precedes the most resplendently ecstatic pages of the work' and speculates if this was a response to Occupation.[96]

Late Sacred Music

By the time he returned to composing sacred works in the 1960 s, Messiaen had become the Grand Old Man of French music. Hill and Simeone see *Et expecto resurrectionem mortuorum* as setting the seal on his rise to becoming a figure of national importance. But the music takes on an evermore monumental form and can prove dogmatic and overbearing. Rather more kindly, Griffiths sees it as 'theatrical,' 'the paradox of a combination of sacredness and showmanship, of grace and grandiloquence.'[97]

The first of these grandiose projects was *La Transfiguration de Notre Seigneur Jésus-Christ*. It was commissioned for a fee of two million old francs by Mme Perdigao of the Gulbenkian Foundation, Lisbon, to commemorate not so much the death of Calouste Gulbenkian as his generosity. It was inspired by a sermon Messiaen had heard in 1961 in the Dauphiné on the feast of the Transfiguration. It was long in the making, gestating from 9 to 14 movements, divided into two Septenaire sections. He experienced the events of May 1968 as disruption to its composition. But it was finished 21 February 1969 and premiered in Lisbon 7 June 1969. Messiaen had written a substantial cello solo role for Rostropovitch, but on the night he had gone down with food poisoning and only the redoubtable Mme Perdigao, dragging him from his hotel room, ailing and feverish, had got him to the concert hall. There was also a substantial piano part for Loriod. We are told 9000 people applauded for half an hour.

The text is in Latin, Messiaen drawing on the Bible, the Office for the Feast of the Transfiguration, the Roman Missal and Thomas Aquinas. The first half dwells on the theme of Light, of Christ transfigured; the second on the filiation of Christ as God's Son and of Christ's adoption of Humanity. Hill and Simeone see it as 'his greatest utterance to date.'[98] Julian Anderson writes of it as 'a massive fresco in sound and word attempting to evoke the dazzling, unimaginable radiance of Christ's transfiguration.' At various points we can hear 'the aural equivalent of a flash of lightning,' 'a smooth carpet of sound from humming choir and strings,' a gesture to Xenakis, together with the sounds of Tibetan ritual and birdsong from the Alps.[99] Dingle writes of it as 'the first of Messiaen's monumental acts of homage,' 'a vast liturgy for the concert hall which determinedly cultivated the mysterious and transcendental at every level.' 'We are beyond the restrictions of reason and are now in eternity.' (And interestingly, Aquinas himself at the end abandoned his proof of faith by reason.[100]) But Dingle also wonders if this was a Gaullist work. In December 1967 he was elected to the music section of the Academie des Beaux-Arts. Had he sold out to the establishment?[101]

The La Trinité organ had been renovated and electrified in the early 60's and this inspired Messiaen to return to the organ after a long break. He did so through a complimentary piece to *La Transfiguration, Mystère de la Sainte Trinité*, composed in August and September 1969, though not performed till 1972. Messiaen had always been fascinated by the decipherment of the Rosetta Stone and in this nine movement set of quotations from Aquinas he devised another secret language, but in musical code. Programme notes on themes for Gillian Weir's performance in Westminster Abbey 15 July 2008[102] indicate its scope: the wheeling of the stars, 'all that we know of God is summarised in these words, so complex yet so simple, HE IS' (Messiaen's own words); 'man overwhelmed by the dazzling light of the sacred; God is eternal – a scintillating radiance explodes into being; God is love, a sublime coda; God is simple; the Wind of the Holy spirit sweeps all before it.' All kinds of familiar and exotic birds feature, the wren, the woodpecker, the so-called Persepolis bird, (heard there but one Messiaen was never able to identify), the Moroccan bulbul, the garden warbler. In the performance I heard, the great chords seemed to drown out the birds. The music encompassed the High Gothic and the Rose Window of the Abbey. At the end it climbed to a new vision, then growlingly subsided in search of calmer waters, though I felt the vision to be more of a searching nature than a confident one. London felt very noisy on leaving the Abbey.

Saint Francis of Assisi

Many of the reservations one might have at the over-rhetorical in Messiaen's late sacred music are wholly suspended for his opera. It was a work written *in extremis*. Messiaen feared it would be his swansong and that he would die before it was completed. Indeed, he endured serious ill-health during its composition and by December 1981 was reduced to weeping in despair at his ever finishing it. His doctor recommended a daily walk and each day he climbed to the Sacré Coeur to attend mass. Superficially, with his love of birdsong, this might seem an obvious choice of subject for Messiaen. But the reasoning was more complicated. He never felt he could do justice square on to Christ's Passion but, through the stigmata of St Francis, he could attempt its nearest equivalent. But what is very revealing, and has seemingly been overlooked by many interpreters, is that the theme of the opera is not so much the connection between the human and the divine as the way music itself accesses the Divine: here is Messiaen's profoundest expression of belief in music as the spiritual.

It was a work long in the making. He first visited Assisi in 1959. His next visit was in April 1970 when he attended a mass in the Basilica of St Francis. In May 1972 he saw Fra Angelico's frescoes in the Convent of San Marco, Florence, the Angel in his *Annunciation* to be the inspiration for the Angel of Music in the Opera. In June 1976 he visited the Hermitage of the Carceri where St Francis preached his sermon to the birds. Meanwhile Messiaen steeped himself in the literature on St Francis, the saint's own writings, the lives of Celano and St Bonaventura, the anonymous *Fioretti* (*Little Flowers of St Francis*): several of these he took on his journey to New Caledonia in September 1975 where he encountered the Gerygone, the theme bird of the Angel. If he completed the libretto by June 1976, it took 5½ years to orchestrate and it was only completed by 22 August 1983. Messiaen is quoted: 'Twilight has arrived. I have finished. I will never write anything else.'[103]

In the thick of all this he retired as Professor of Harmony June 1978: as Dingle bitterly recounts, 'perhaps the greatest musical teacher of the twentieth century stepped put of the Conservatoire for the last time without even a handshake.'[104]

It is an astonishing enterprise. It lasts 4½ hours. It is scored for an orchestra of 119 and choir of 150. A moment of epiphany for the 10 year old Messiaen had been the gift of a score of *Pelléas et Mélisande*, and he had always hoped to write an opera, though recognised that the stage was not his milieu. In fact it can be highly dramatic, as Peter Sellars's 1992 Salzburg production made evident. It was premiered in Paris 28 November 1983 with ten subsequent performances. The Proms performance I heard by the Netherlands Opera 7 September 2008 was highly charged: one critic heard this as 'one of the great operatic achievements of recent years.'[105]

The usual narrative drive of an opera gives way to something more static, Franciscan scenes or eight subjects for meditation, 'physical action is often subordinated to philosophical and theological enquiry.'[106] Two characters dominate, the Angel, sung by a soprano, and St Francis, a baritone, both linked, in the manner of the *daemons* of Philip Pullmans' *Dark Materials,* to birds, the Angel to the Gerygone, St Francis to that warbler Messiaen had heard at Assisi. One theme explored in the opera is that persistent issue within the Franciscan order, the choice between poverty and power, with the ill-tempered Brother Elias, a bearded fellow and a real toughie in the Proms production, much irritated by the questioning of the Angel over predestination, Brother Elias the symbolic representative of the urge to power. But the only way to tease out the message of the opera is to look closely at the libretto itself.

The early scenes address the issue of fear, Brother Leo's of brigandage on the road, St Francis's of leprosy. St Francis deals with fear in terms of 'perfect joy': 'there is the power of overcoming oneself and to bear willingly for the love of Christ, ills, injuries, opprobrium, discomfort.' St Francis then addresses his own demons: 'thou hast allowed ugliness to exist, that the postulating toad, the poisonous mushroom be found alongside the dragonfly and the bluebird.' Can God help him overcome his horror of lepers? The encounter with the leper (one has to suspend disbelief that this was his first such encounter) is extraordinarily dramatic: the leper berating God and the brothers for his infirmity and their 'horrible chit-chat': 'first take way my pustules and then I will do penitence.' In the physical appearance of the leper Messiaen drew on Grunewald's portrait of St Antony in the Issenheim altar piece. St Francis's kissing the leper is both highly operatic and a striking gesture of a humanist spirituality. St Francis strides very deliberately towards the leper: 'Forgive me my son: I have not loved thee enough.' St Francis has at last overcome his fear. The leper does a Turangalila-like dance of joy at his cure. The celebratory music of the xylophone echoes that of the gamelan in Britten's *Dance of the Pagodas*.

Then comes the visionary claims for music. The Angel theme announces his intent to speak to St Francis, the music again charged and electric, the piccolo reminiscent of the tweetering birds in the paintings of Klee. Then comes St Francis's transfiguring vision:

> Ah, God dazzles us by excess of Truth. Music
> carries us to God in default of Truth.
> Thou speakest to God in music. He is going to
> answer thee in music …
> Listen to his music that suspends life from the
> ladders of heaven, listen to the music of the
> unseen.

The Angel plays the viol. And Messiaen here risks a supreme conceit, composing the sound of the music of Paradise. There is the utter serenity of the ondes Martenot, with the orchestra in the background, rather like an Indian drone. Francis is 'overwhelmed, dumbfounded by that music, that heavenly music.'

Somehow the actual sermon to the birds is less charged: 'everything beautiful should lead to freedom, the freedom of glory. Our brothers, the birds, await that day.' 'He allowed you to sing so marvellously that you speak without words, like the speech of the angels.' Through a projection onto the platform in the Albert Hall, the birds form a kind of Cross in the sky, reminding one of those astonishing formations in flight of flocks of starlings or swifts. Here is Messiaen the conveyor of the spiritual in nature.

So to the drama of the stigmata. Was Messiaen here handicapped by an inability to portray pain?: 'I'm not a composer of pain, suffering, but a composer of joy. That is to say the scene was totally contrary to my nature, but nevertheless I composed it with all my heart.'[107] Interestingly, the encounter is with God not Christ: 'it is I, it is I, I am the Alpha and Omega. It is I, it is I who thought time and space ... Who goes from the reverse side of time, who goes from future to the past, and goes forward to judge the world.' This is accompanied by a furious drum role, sharp and violent. But with the appearance of the five blood stains of the stigmata the music turns soft and subdued: 'is there anything painful which we would not bear for Life Eternal?' There follows the prolonged and indeed operatic-style death of St Francis, in the company of the leper and the Angel: 'today, in a few moments, thou will hear the music of the invisible and thou wilt hear it forever.' St Francis cries out: 'Music and poetry have led me to Thee: by image, by symbol, and in default of Truth dazzle me for ever by Thy excess of Truth.' The music ends in a rather jazzy, almost minimalist way. I picked up on other references in the Proms production, to the poetry of T S Eliot,[108] to Japanese Noh plays, to Buddhism.[109]

This is the finest expression of Messiaen's spirituality. Ashley interprets the opera in this-worldly terms: 'the score is sensuous and at times overpoweringly physical, Messiaen's abiding vision of the manifestation of the divine in the material universe reaches its fullest expression in his portrait of Francis.'[110] But, of course, it is equally other-worldly and transcendent. Dingle sees it as 'a testament to the strength of Messiaen's vision of faith, hope, colour and joy. It draws on the entirety of his creativity.' In anticipation of the Prom he predicted, 'in the final pages of the score nothing will prevent all heaven breaking lose in the Albert Hall.'[111]

It was not of course the end of composition. There was another organ cycle, *Livre du Saint Sacrament,* a companion piece to the opera. Very interesting claims are made for this work, as a work of intransigence, as a wilful attempt to break entirely new ground, as a late style, a parallel to the late style in Scriabin.[112] But he was exhausted and it took time to rediscover the self-belief to write *Éclairs sur l'au delà,* 'a sidelong glimpse of eternity.'[113] Here was no barnstorming of heaven in the style of *Visions de l'Amen.* To quote Dingle: 'Rather than overwhelm us with the glory of the Almighty, Messiaen here presents God as the assuager, comforting humanity, in a movement as delicate as the gossamer thread of string trills with which it begins.'[114]

But he was not to hear it performed. He died, following an operation for cancer, 27 April 1992. He was buried in the churchyard of St Théoffroy in Petichet: on his headstone, 'all the birds of the stars.'

Boulez compensated for the rudeness of the Conservatoire at the time of his retirement with this tribute: 'he personally resembles some great baroque building: he fascinates by the diversity of his options and the elaborate simplicity of his choices. Beneath the very complexity of his intellectual world he has remained simple and capable of wonder – and that alone is enough to win our hearts.'[115] Messiaen summarised his own project as: 'true music ... that is to say spiritual music which may be an act of faith, a music which may touch upon all subjects without ceasing to touch upon God; an original music, in short, whose language may open a few doors, take down some as yet distant stars.'[116]

Taruskin brilliantly explores what this might mean in music-ological terms (and this project has not gone along this route). Messiaen sought 'invariance,' one and the same as constancy, immutability, eternity. He did so by off-setting the vertical, those modes of limited transposition, against the horizontal, the non-retrogradable rhythms. (Is there where Gubaidulina got her ideas from?) Here 'is the time-trans-cending truth that religion reveals through music.'[117]

So can we place his music on a spectrum of a this-worldly and other-worldly? Did he rather seek their synthesis? And did his religious faith stand in the way of an expression of the spiritual? In his response to the political, there is ambi-guity, for if the Quartet for the End of Time is one extra-ordinary response to his times, it is hard to see in what ways Messiaen distanced himself from the Occupation and its terrible agenda. Did the conflict in his early religious music though reflect the conflicts of the 30's and 40's? There are moments of a terrifying religiosity in this music. Even so, this has to qualify ascribing a this-worldly spirituality. Yet, if it feels counter-intuitive for so Catholic a composer, it is in his all too human response to his personal life in the Tristan music and to Nature through his delight in birdsong that a humanist or a this-worldly spirituality does shine through. Dingle even suggests, had he died in 1962, apart from his organ music, there would have been little religious music anyway.

It is only thereafter that he wrote music 'that is not just religious, but unashamedly and assuredly theological.'[118] There was indeed to be an ideological aspect to his later religious music, an authoritarian – can we call it Gaullist? – and a dogmatic side, that surely is a barrier to the spiritual. One possible comparison is with another leading contemporary Catholic artist, Graham Sutherland, whose early Pembrokeshire landscapes are steeped in mysticism but whose post-war art, the thorn period, feels somehow hieratic and cold. But in his opera, through responding more to a human being than to Doctrine, and, in the same way as Messiaen saw in medieval stained glass, the religious and the spiritual do come together.

Notes

[1] Fortunately for his project, we now have Andrew Shenton's edited text *Messiaen The Theologian*, Farnham and Burlington: Ashgate, 2010.

[2] Christopher Dingle, *The Life of Messiaen*, Cambridge: Cambridge University Press, 2007, p.33.

[3] *Le Page Musicale*, 17 March 1939, quoted Dingle, *Life of Messiaen*, p.60.

[4] Quoted Peter Hill and Nigel Simeone, *Messiaen*, New Haven and London: Yale University Press, 2005, p.62. Theirs is the bench mark for all Messiaen scholarship.

[5] Quoted Hill and Simeone, *Messiaen*, p.62.

[6] Andre Coeloy, Quoted Hill and Simeone, *Messiaen*, p.64.

[7] *Le Monde Musicale*, 20 April 1939, Quoted Hill and Simeone, *Messiaen*, p.82.

[8] Carmen Cahill, *Bad Faith: A Forgotten History of Family and Fatherland*, London: Jonathan Cape, 2006, p.312. This is a pretty devastating account of the role of the hierarchy of the church under Vichy and of France's contribution to the Holocaust.

[9] Cahill, *Bad Faith*, p.232.

[10] Cahill, *Bad Faith*, p.240.

[11] Quoted Cahill, *Bad Faith*, pp.297-8.

[12] Cahill, *Bad Faith*, p.299.

[13] Frederic Spotts, *The Shameful Peace: How French Artists and Intellectuals Survived the Nazi Occupation*, New Haven and London: Yale University Press, 2008.

[14] Spotts, *Shameful Peace*, p.19.

[15] Spotts, *Shameful Peace*, p.35.

[16] Spotts, *Shameful Peace*, p.47.

[17] Spotts, *Shameful Peace*, p.205.

[18] Spotts, *Shameful Peace*, p.211.

[19] See Michèle C Cone, *Artists under Vichy: A Case of Prejudice and Persecution*, Princeton: Princeton University press, 1992, p.29.

[20] Spotts, *Shameful Peace*, p.219.

[21] Quoted Cone, *Artists under Vichy*, p.51.

[22] Cone, *Artists under Vichy*, p.179.

[23] Quoted Cone, *Artists under Vichy*, p.105.

[24] Spotts, *Shameful Peace*, p.15.

[25] Quoted Hill and Simeone, *Messiaen*, p.140.

[26] Hill and Simeone, *Messiaen*, p.257.

[27] Hill and Simeone, *Messiaen*, p.263.

[28] Quoted Dingle, *Life of Messiaen*, p.196.

[29] Roger Nichols, Programme Notes, Proms, 7 September 2008.

[30] Hill and Simeone, *Messiaen*, p.238.

[31] See Frances Stonor Sanders, *The Cultural Cold War: The CIA and the World of Arts and Letters*, New York: The New Press, 2000.

[32] In a letter to Jean Langlais, 2 November 1939, quoted Dingle, *Life of Messiaen*, p.67.

[33] Quoted Dingle, *Life of Messiaen*, p.68.

[34] Alex Ross, *The New Yorker*, 22 March 2004.

[35] Nigel Simeone, 'Notes From the Canyons to the Stars Messiaen Study day,' Southbank Centre, 3 February 2008.

[36] Recollections of Charles Jouvenet, quoted Hill and Simeone, *Messiaen*, p.95.

[37] George Hill, *The Guardian*, 6 September 2008.

[38] I heard two performances at the time, by the Nash Ensemble and Pierre-Laurent Aimard, Queen Elizabeth Hall, 3 February 2008 and as part of the Sounds New Festival 2008, by the Ensemble Intercontemporain in the crypt of

Canterbury Cathedral 16 April 2008, and hard to imagine a more perfect performance.

[39] Quotations describing each section are from the Wikipedia entry for the Quartet.

[40] Dingle, *Life of Messiaen*, p.74.

[41] Dingle, *Life of Messiaen*, p.102.

[42] Quoted Dingle, *Life of Messiaen*, p.2.

[43] Quoted Dingle, *Life of Messiaen*, p.20.

[44] See Hill and Simeone, *Messiaen*, p.22.

[45] See programme, *From the Canyons to the Stars*, pp.41-4 and Felix Aprahamian's translation.

[46] See the Obituary on Yvonne Loriod, *The Guardian*, 19 May 2010.

[47] Recollections of Antoine Golea, Quoted Hill and Simeone, *Messiaen*, p.229.

[48] Dingle, *Life of Messiaen*, p.109.

[49] Quoted Dingle, *Life of Messiaen*, pp.110-11.

[50] Hill and Simeone, *Messiaen*, p.157.

[51] Malcolm Hayes, Notes Proms programme, 2 September 2008.

[52] Quoted Hill and Simeone, *Messiaen*, pp.153-4.

[53] Fred Goldbeck, Quoted Hill and Simeone, *Messiaen*, p.173.

[54] Cited *From the Canyons to the Stars*, p.15.

[55] Proms programme.

[56] *From the Canyons to the Stars*, p.16.

[57] Stephen Pritchard, *The Observer*, 7 September 2008.

[58] Tim Ashley. *The Guardian*, 4 September 2008.

[59] Dingle, *Life of Messiaen*, pp.106-7.

[60] Hill and Simeone, *Messiaen*, pp.182-3.

[61] Sander van Maas, 'Messiaen's Saintly Naiveté,' Chapter 3 in Shenton (ed.), *Messiaen the Theologian*.

[62] Quoted Hill and Simeone, *Messiaen*, p.56.

[63] Hill and Simeone, *Messiaen*, p.114.

[64] See August Kleinzahler 'Diary,' *London Review of Books*, 2 December 2010.

[65] Quoted Hill and Simeone, *Messiaen*, p.226.

[66] Recollections of Alexander Goehr , Quoted Dingle, *Life of Messiaen*, p.151.

[67] From his introduction to *Catalogue d'oiseaux*, quoted Hill and Simeone, *Messiaen*, p.201.

[68] Programme notes, Sounds New Festival 2008, p.24.

[69] Dingle, *Life of Messiaen*, p.152.

[70] Quoted Hill and Simeone, *Messiaen*, p.187.

[71] Quoted Hill and Simeone, *Messiaen*, p.245.

[72] Griffiths, *Modern Music*, p.134.

[73] Stephen Schloesser in Shenton (ed.), *Messiaen the Theologian*, p.172.

[74] Dingle, *Life of Messiaen*, pp.80-1.

[75] Quoted Hill and Simeone, *Messiaen*, p.59.

[76] Quoted Hill and Simeone, *Messiaen*, p.62.

[77] Vincent P Benitez, 'Messiaen and Aquinas,' Chapter 6 in Shenton, *Messiaen the Theologian*.

[78] See Douglas Shadle, 'Messiaen's Relationship to Jacques Maritain's Musical Circle and Neo-Thomism,' Chapter 5; Peter Bannister, 'Messiaen as Preacher and Evangelist in the Context of European Modernism,' Chapter 2; Robert Sholl, 'Olivier Messiaen and the Avant-Garde Poetics of the *Messe de la Pentecôte*, Chapter 11; Stephen Schloesser, 'The Theme of Impossibilities: Mystic Surrealism as Contemplative Voluptuousness,' Chapter 9 in Shenton (ed.), *Messiaen the Theologian*.

[79] Claude Rostand, though later a convert to his music. Quoted Hill and Simeone, *Messiaen*, p.147.

[80] Judt, *Postwar*, p.229.

[81] Quoted Hill and Simeone, *Messiaen*, p.332.

[82] Taruskin, *History of Western Music*, Vol.4, pp.229-30.

[83] Cited Dingle, *Life of Messiaen*, p.56.

[84] Griffiths, *Modern Music*, p.262.

[85] Dingle, *Life of Messiaen*, p.39.

[86] Malcolm Hayes. Quoted in the programme notes of Sounds New Festival, 2008. And indeed this was reflected in the performance by the Kent County Youth Orchestra in Canterbury Cathedral, 12 April, 2008.

[87] Programme notes, *From the Canyons to the Stars* for Olivier Latry's performance in Westminster Abbey, 22 February 2008.

[88] David Gammie, *Les Corps Glorieux*, Programme Notes, 'Thomas Trotter,' St Paul's Cathedral, 30 October 2008.

[89] Dingle, *Life of Messiaen*, pp.63-4.

[90] Frank Langlois, Notes, *Sounds New Festival 2008*, for a performance by Peter Hill and Benjamin Frith, 14 April 2008.

[91] Serge Nigg, Quoted Dingle, *Life of Messiaen*, pp.89-90.

[92] Dingle, *Life of Messiaen*, p.86.

[93] Summarised by Hill and Simeone, *Messiaen*, p.134.

[94] Nick Breckenfield, Notes, *International Piano Series 2007-8*, Southbank Centre, pp.27-30.

[95] Fiona Maddocks, 'Two Masters, Two Centenaries,' *The Observer*, 21 December 2008.[96] Dingle, *Life of Messiaen*, pp.86-7.

[97] Griffiths, *Modern Music*, p.262.

[98] Hill and Simeone, *Messiaen*, p.263.

[99] Julian Anderson, Notes, Proms performance, conducted by Thierry Fischer, 27 July 2008.

[100] See Armstrong, *The Case for God*, pp.140-2.

[101] Dingle, *Life of Messiaen*, pp.177-8. See also Nigel Simeone, Notes for a performance of, *La Transfiguration*, 16 October 2008. *From the Canyons to the Stars*, pp.24-8.

[102] Notes, 'Summer Organ Festival,' Westminster Abbey, 2008, pp.4-7.

[103] *Libération*, 28 November 1983, Quoted Hill and Simeone, *Messiaen*, p.342.

[104] Dingle, *Life of Messiaen*, p.206.

[105] Tim Ashley, *The Guardian*, 9 September 2008.

[106] Roger Nichols, Notes Proms Programme, 7 September 2008.

[107] Messiaen, *Music and Colour*, Quoted Shenton (ed.), *Messiaen the Theologian*, p.57.

[108] Andrew Shenton explores the Eliot link but with reference to the 'Quartet for the End of Time,' see 'Five Quartets for the Still Point of the Turning World in the War Quartets of T S Eliot and Olivier Messiaen,' Chapter 8 in Shenton (ed.), *Messiaen the Theologian*.

[109] Quotations from the text are from Felix Aprahamian's translation. See Proms programme.

[110] Tim Ashley, *The Guardian*, 9 September 2008.

[111] Dingle, 'Sin isn't interesting. I prefer flowers,' *The Guardian*, 29 August 2008.

[112] Luke Berryman, 'Messiaen as Explorer,' in *Livre du Saint Sacrament*, Chapter 12, in Shenton (ed.), *Messiaen the Theologian*.

[113] Hill and Simeone, *Messiaen*, p.363.

[114] Dingle, *Life of Messiaen*, p.238.

[115] Quoted Hill and Simeone, *Messiaen*, p.322.

[116] *Technique of My Musical Language*, 1944, Quoted Taruskin, *History of Western Music*, Vol.4, p.229.

[117] Taruskin, *History of Western Music*, Vol.4, pp.230-7.

[118] Dingle, *Life of Messiaen*, p.188.

10. *Francis Poulenc*

Poulenc is an interesting foil to Messiaen. He is so immediately personable. Hard to imagine anyone attacking Poulenc in the manner of *Le Cas Messiaen*. Whereas in Messiaen
there was always a tension between the human and the divine, in the early Poulenc there had been a frankly hedonistic
side. But the focus here is on the religious and the sacred
music that followed his reconversion to the faith in 1936.
The hallmark of his subsequent music is an expression of
sexual and spiritual anguish, a sexual anxiety that spills over
into his morbid fear of death and religious doubt. In 1953,
stress in his personal life and the strain of composing his opera *Les dialogues des carmélites*, together with doubts about
his worth as a composer, precipitated a complete breakdown.
And yet the very accessibility of his music leaves a question
mark over its spirituality. Certainly there was to be none of
that grandiosity of Messiaen's music. Poulenc was no more
political than Messiaen though certainly closer to Resistance.
His music can best be divided into song, sacred and choral
music and opera.[1]

Rocamadour

A degree of myth surrounds Poulenc's response to the death
of composer Pierre Octave Ferroud 17 August 1936. He was
not a personal friend, let alone a lover, but a rival composer.
That a contemporary and peer could be struck down in so
grotesque a manner, decapitated, *collation atroce,* in a car
accident in Debrecen, Eastern Hungary, (think of the death of
Jayne Mansfield), proved highly traumatic and was to haunt
his imagination all the way through to the beheading of the
Carmelite nuns in his opera. At the time he was holidaying in
Uzerche with his close friends Yvonne Gouverné and Pierre
Bernac. He asked Bernac to drive him over to the nearby
pilgrimage site of Rocamadour. Here is his own account:

I had just learned a day or two before of the tragic
death of my colleague Pierre-Octave Ferroud.
The atrocious extinction of this musician so full
of vigour had left me stupefied. Pondering on the
fragility of our human frame, the life of the spirit
attracted me anew.

Rocadamour led me back to the faith of my
childhood. This sanctuary, certainly the most
ancient in France, had everything to subjugate
me.[2]

Something happened to Poulenc in the inner chapel with the
image of the Black Madonna. Yvonne Gouverné later recorded: 'outwardly nothing happened, yet from that moment
everything in the spiritual life of Poulenc changed.'[3]

Who was buried here? Was it the publican, Zaccheus, disciple of Jesus and husband of Veronica of the miraculous
cloth, forced to flee from Palestine and preaching the gospel
in Limousin? Or was St Rocamadour some other hermit? In
the 12th and 13th centuries it became one of medieval Europe's most sought out pilgrimage sites. The entire assembly
of buildings is dramatically poised over the Alzon canyon.
Within the Chapelle Miraculeuse, its spiritual heart, is hous-
ed the statue of the Black Madonna.[4] Intriguingly, the figure
itself, sculpted by the Saint, with its thick lips, heavy eye-
brows, beak-like nose and high cheek bones, bears a striking
likeness to Poulenc's great friend, Raymonde Linossier. Her
premature death 30 January 1930 had robbed Poulenc of one
of his closest confidantes. He had seriously hoped for a marriage of convenience. Just as probably, it was her death
rather than that of Ferroud that lay behind his religious
experience.

On the evening of the visit Poulenc began to compose his
Litanies à la Vierge Noire. As he put it: 'in this work I have
tried to express the feelings of "peasant devotion" which had
so strongly impressed me in that lofty place.'[5]

But to explain that spiritual experience one has to explore in a larger context the two leading dynamics in Poulenc's life, his sexuality and his Catholicism.

Sexuality

Poulenc 'had an insatiable appetite for being loved.'[6] To understand his homosexuality is to explain the nature of his religious music. Poulenc was drawn to a down-to-earthness, an ordinariness in his lovers rather than to any flamboyance. He shared Edward Carpenter's ideal of comradeship with the mature working class rather than Oscar Wilde's cult of glamorous youth. In the same misleading way that he acquired a reputation for facility in his composition, so might he be wrongly seen as at ease with his homosexuality. In fact, for all his openness with his friends, he still saw his homosexuality as sinful, though a constant state of anxiety rather than of guilt underlay his sexuality. To make greater sense of his attitude to homosexuality we have to set it in its broader French historical context.[7]

If it was through some rather idiosyncratic reason at the time of the Revolution – Cambacérès, who introduced the legislation, was gay – France enjoyed a legislation that permitted homosexual relations in private. But it was by no means the case that French public attitudes were sympathetic. Julian Jackson, historian of homosexuality in France, puts this strongly: 'the history of same-sex relations in modern France is not so much of social tolerance as a combination of formal legality and deeply embedded cultural hostility.'[8] Even in Paris, seen as so much more permissive than the provinces, in the 1950's, 'cultural norms were extraordinarily hostile to homosexual visibility or homosexual activism.'[9] The law was particularly strict at all displays in public and over relationships with minors. It could be argued that the republican tradition, with its integrationist philosophy, was always hostile to the rights of minorities. In the immediate aftermath of World War 1, at a time when Proust was publishing novels saturated with homosexuality and Gide openly defending pederasty, there had been an aggressive flaunting of a rather exotic homosexuality. By the 1930's, by way of a repressive response, and in ways that demonstrates how the late Third Republic shades into Vichy, 'a conscious or unconscious fascization,' as Michel Duchein[10] put it, took over. Jean Chiappe, Paris Prefect of Police 1927-34, launched a crackdown on all homosexual activity, and there were proposals to make all homosexual relations with minors under 18 illegal. Under the Occupation, the German authorities introduced German anti-homosexual legislation of Article 175 to the annexed region of Alsace and the Moselle, but otherwise left it to Vichy and 'its Christian neo-Puritanism,' to quote Duchein again, to take up where the Third Republic left off. It amended article 334, 6 August 1942, with up to 3 years imprisonment for sex with minors under 21 and between those under 21. The Naval Ministry would have liked to penalize adult homosexuality altogether. Post-Liberation, homosexuals were caught between the hostility of both left and right, for not only did Conservatives perpetuate Vichy attitudes but the Left, led by the Communists, preached its own Marxist neo-Puritan version of a wholesome manliness, and accused Vichy France of succumbing to a hyper-Nazi version of masculinity. And it is true, a number of prominent collaborators were gay, Henry de Montherlant, Robert Brasillach and Marcel Jouhandeau. As Jackson observes, the language of virility was omnipresent in 1945. It was not a time to open up any debate on homosexuality. Catholic sympathisers like Marc Oraison soon took fright, and it was left to a small-scale organisation, L'Arcadie, set up in 1954, to fight a lone battle for a greater understanding. Under the Fifth Republic and de Gaulle, the authorities became even more hostile, with the repressive legislation of the Minguet amendment of July 1960. Homosexuality was seen as a social scourge alongside alcoholism and prostitution. Daniel Guérin, a leading gay activist, wrote of anti-sexual terrorism.

So it was always going to be a strain for Poulenc to come out as a homosexual. Not that he ever seems to have shown any curiosity in its aetiology or take any interest in L'Arcadie. He came of age in the world of the Ballets Russes and the openly gay circles of Diaghilev and Jean Cocteau, though Poulenc, with 'the rough-featured ugliness of a French *pay-san*,'[11] was spared their attentions. Just possibly, though, its ambience explains the choice of his first openly acknow-ledged lover, the artist Richard Chanlaire: 'Poulenc made a thorough job of "coming out", telling his friends about his love for Chanlaire.'[12] Predictably this affair with a middle class intellectual fizzled out, but one of the attractive features of Poulenc's emotional life was that he never rejected his former lovers – compare Benjamin Britten and Lennox Berk-eley – and they remained friends for life.

Poulenc's true preferences were for the working class and the peasantry. It was in all those childhood holidays in his grand-parent's house in Nogent-sur-Marne, to the east of Paris, that he first encountered his preferred sexual milieu: 'a quiet little town by day, it was a popular amusement spot at night ... a cheerful suburban blue-collar atmosphere per-vades the place..'[13] By inclination Poulenc was promiscuous; as Ivry puts it: 'Poulenc's preferred nocturnal prowl was searching among Parisian pissoirs for sexual adventures.'[14] And we also learn from Jackson, for all that repression in post-war Paris, 'for those who were adventurous and con-fident, the possibilities after 1945 were probably as great as they had ever been.' Did he cruise the vespasiennes on Boulevard de Clichy?[15] Poulenc saw 'casual sex as the Holy Grail'[16] for it would lead to his lovers. And, indeed, this was the way that led to the three most important affairs in his life. They were all to exercise a powerful influence on his music.

Following the ending of his affair with Chanlaire and his moving in 1928 to his country home, Le Grand Coteau at Noizay, near Amboise, he met a far more appropriate lover in the bi-sexual chauffeur and ambulance driver, Raymond Destouches. He was the emotional anchor in Poulenc's life, a live-in lover till he moved nearby in 1952 to set up home with his second wife. Variously Poulenc referred to him as 'my dear old wire-haired terrier,' 'my bristly old fox,' 'my loyal dog.' In time, as with all his lovers, he came to look on him as one of his children. He was always very careful to spare Raymond any knowledge of his other affairs. When he met on a train in the spring of 1950 a far more disturbing lover, the 41 year old Lucien Roubert, a travelling salesman, he confided to a close friend, 'I am loved too much in Toulon which frightens me as I am not totally free. Although with Raymond there has been what is referred to nowadays as a transference of feeling on my part to something far more paternal I cannot after 20 years cause any pain and he will always have first place in my life.'[17] Raymond in fact remained his driver, Poulenc often visited the new couple for meals and he was never to know of the affair with Lucien. Raymond was the inspiration, no doubt through his bisexuality, for *Les mamelles de Tirésias*.

Through the affair with Lucien Roubert, Poulenc experienceed entirely new emotional demands: 'I have not had much sweetness in the affairs of the heart, and when for once after gadding around like a dirty old man the right sentiment arrives, the wretched kilometres get in the way.'[18] But it was not just the distance apart, it was the uncertainty of Lucien's affections and Poulenc experienced all the anguish of uncertain sexual fulfilment. How this played into his opera on the Carmelites will be explored below.

There was to be one more great love, Louis Gautier, a 29 year old career sergeant, 'as kind as he is handsome which has brightened up my life considerably after all the disappointments of the last few years.'[19] Admittedly, in his usual anxious way, Poulenc feared he would lose him and this neurosis played into his opera *La voix humaine*, and, indeed, military duties did take him away. But 'my great big peasant' in fact was loyal till the end, if expensive – Poulenc paying for the building of his home. Even here, though, Poulenc reported, 'I now think of him as a child whom I adore.'[20]

Was he bi-sexual? Certainly in 1946 he fathered a daughter, Marie-Ange, by the 39 year old Fréderique, a cousin of Richard Chanlaire's sister-in-law. Posing as her god-father he always took an interest in her career as a ballet dancer. And then there was his friendship with Raymonde Linossier. Their childhoods had overlapped in Paris and Vichy and it was she who introduced Poulenc to Adrienne Ronnier's bookshop La Maison des Livres sometime 1917-18 and to the poetry of the surrealists. She was clearly a very unusual person, a barrister who specialised in briefs for prostitutes, an Orientalist with a keen interest in Japan, and a novelist. So close did they become that Poulenc asked her younger sister, Alice to be a go-between in an offer of marriage: 'the longer I live, the more I feel that she is the only person I would like to share my life with. I've reached the point where the idea of doing without her is intolerable to me and it is out of a dreadful fear of refusal that until now I have kept silent, through cowardice, admittedly.' He continued: 'I am sure she would have an immense and salutary influence on my work. It would mean everything to me – I have just become a machine that produces notes.'[21] She had already inspired his ballet *Les Biches*. Their friendship survived her refusal and he 'never recovered from the loss of Raymonde as a cherished friend and a moral and musical guide.'[22] Death became an obsessive theme in his music.

If we accept Poulenc's homosexuality as his most powerful drive, in what ways and why did it become so powerful an influence on his music and its spirituality? Was it out of guilt? Linossier had turned him down out of contempt for homosexuality, so did he inherit from her a sense of guilt? He certainly shared with Auden a sense of homosexuality as sinful: 'sex and impurity remained synonymous for Poulenc.'[23] Was he oppressed by social prejudice? Given the ages of his lovers he need not have been affected by that hostility against sex with the young. But he was sensitive to social conventions. Unlike Cocteau he did not take his lovers along to society events: 'he had always a strong sense of what was socially acceptable and revelled in gossiping about his private life as if divulging naughty secrets.'[24] On one occasion he did request Marie-Blanche de Polignac to let him bring Raymond to a performance of his cello sonata. But the need to confide his love life with his friends could prove intolerable, and Pierre Bernac, his musical partner, was driven to distraction by the affair with Lucien Roubert. At one stage it all got so desperate that a concert tour in Germany in 1953 had to be broken off. It is clear that Poulenc was far from being at ease with his homosexuality. Ivry might claim that by the age of 50 he accepted 'the intricacies of his own personality,'[25] but, to the contrary, he seems to have become ever more neurotic in the 1950's. Whether this can be attributed to guilt is in question – and his love of gossiping suggests otherwise – but it was certainly the source of a kind of anguish that underpinned so much of his religious music.

Religion

It has been claimed that once religious then there is always a likelihood of a return to the faith in middle age.[26] In his childhood, so important to Poulenc, he had been profoundly affected by the traditional faith of his pious father. He had been a regular visitor to Rocamadour and this will have flooded back in his reconversion experience at the shrine. But Auden, who had a like reconversion in 1940 to his childhood Anglo-Catholicism, raised the question, was there not a subtle change between 'not only to believe *still* but to believe *again*.'?[27] Did Poulenc's Catholicism at this point undergo a change? Equally, Poulenc found consolation in liturgy: 'he loved Church ritual, Romanesque architecture, chalices and other paraphernalia of Catholicism.'[28] Pilgrimage brought spiritual relief: 'I went to Rocadamour last week all alone. It really calmed me down.'[29] During his breakdown he visited Lourdes: 'I had never seen a pilgrimage before. It was at once atrocious and sublime. What moved me most was seeing all those young people, boys and girls, devoting themselves to the sick.'[30] He allowed himself to be seen as a believer. In his radio conversations with Claude Rostand he claimed: 'I am religious by deepest instinct and hardily. As incapable as I feel of ardent political conviction, so does it seem quite natural to me to believe and practice religion. It is my greatest freedom.'[31] In consequence he acquired, as he ruefully recognised, a reputation as 'a courtly abbé, an oozy flattering socialite clergyman, a reputation he spent much of his life trying to live down.'[32] And, indeed, it was grossly inaccurate.

Poulenc's was always a fragile faith. Ivry writes of 'his passionate but unfulfilled desire to believe.'[33] Early in the 1950's he confessed to a friend: 'Unfortunately I am not as religious as I would like to be. Half of me remains quite the opposite. Though I'm not totally pious, I am – alas – as pied as a horse.'[34] In a letter to Bernac during Easter 1958 he confessed: 'my *total* absence of faith this morning at mass is not helping matters much.'[35] In just the same way as he sought a kind of down-to-earthness in his homosexual partners, so he sought in his religious life 'a country pastor' expression of the faith. He backed away from anything too intellectual: 'I beg of you,' he wrote to Bernac, 'pray for me in Assisi that I may meet a simple good priest (like the dean of Rocamadour) who wafer in hand and wine before him will be able to do something for me.' During his breakdown in Avignon he would 'willingly have insulted and clouted' an 'intelligent' priest. But he added: 'my desire for everything to come right shows that deep down I have an atavistic, very real need, a craving for something.'[36] One of his spiritual advisers, Father Carré, saw him as the tumbler Jean in Massenet's opera *Le jongleur de Notre Dame*, who, after entering a monastery, but then accused of blasphemy, dances himself to death in front of a statue of the Virgin. But she blesses him as he dies.[37] Increasing religious doubt was to beset his final years.

Yet it is through that very doubt that Poulenc communicates. All the best sermons, it could be argued, are those that address the frailty of belief. In contrast to Messiaen, there is nothing doctrinaire in Poulenc's religious quest. One might assume he shared Auden's hostility to Manicheanism and a conviction that no religion is valid which does not validate the needs of the flesh. But Poulenc brought to his would-be-faith a morbid obsession with death. Already in his Cantata *Le bal masqué* there is 'an expression of the all pervasive smell of death.'[38] In religion Poulenc sought consolation from deep personal anxieties. The anguish of sexual desire spills over into religious anxiety. It is all deeply personal. But it is in this very fluidity and uncertainty that the religious and the spiritual can much more readily weave in and out of each other.

Politics

Poulenc's apolitical stance can in large part be explained by his social background. He was born 7 January 1899 into the *grande bourgeoisie*. His father Emile, together with his two brothers, had founded the chemical giant, Rhone-Poulenc, and when he died in 1917, he left his son a rich man: 'I am fortunate in not having to do anything other than my music. I have lost both my parents and am quite well off.'[39] Here were the funds to purchase his substantial home at Noizay. (Still, his sister inhabited the even grander Château de Tremblay in Normandy.) But then came the 1929 crash and, through some poor investment in a private bank, Poulenc was forced to earn his living. In 1935 he formed his musical partnership with Pierre Bernac, if 'only to maintain his relatively luxurious life-style rather than merely having to make ends meet.'[40] Wealthy himself, there were social élites all too ready to patronise his music. There were aristocratic families ready to act as patrons, and Poulenc drew close to Vicomtesse Marie-Laure de Noailles and Princess Edmond de Polignac, as well as rather less prestigious Parisian bourgeois families. Was he ever fully aware of his privileged position? It certainly helps to explain his sentimental attachment to *le grand siècle*, the grandiose France of Louis XIV. All this was bound to rub off on his political attitudes.

So did he in any way engage with the political struggles of his times? As with Messiaen this is one way of reading any this-worldliness into his spirituality. Poulenc always privileged the private sphere over the public. Given his background it is not surprising to find a few unpleasant right-wing features. His piano teacher Ricardo Vines was an anti-Dreyfusard. In times of psychological stress Poulenc himself could turn anti-Semitic. One supposes his friendship with Max Jacob was out of a shared homosexuality rather than through his being Jewish. He did not identify with the anti-fascist struggle of the 1930's, was not averse to Franco-German reconciliation, and despised the extreme left and right alike. To Comtesse Jean de Polignac he declared: 'I am not Popular Front. I am an old French Republican who once believed in Liberty. For me you see the Republic was men like Clemenceau, whose maxims I think of so often: on your feet!!!!!' But, he added, 'to believe that I have no leftist leanings is to know little about me.'[41]

But the times did not permit such detachment. He had been called up in World War 1 in June 1918 and was not released till 1921: after a brief spell in prison – overstepping his leave – he had a cushy job in the Air Ministry. Facing conscription again in 1939 he became obsessed about his future reputation. He was called up as a private (second class) in a regiment of farmers in Cahors: 'I am not surprised at what is happening. I have had such a strong sense of foreboding since the beginning of August that I could not help feeling nervous.'[42] But he saw no action and with the surrender returned to Noizay. But Occupation was a different challenge.

Post-war, Poulenc congratulated himself on keeping out of trouble, but clearly he had an uneasy conscience at being so little the hero. In 1940 he tried to console Darius Milhaud who, as a Jew, had gone into exile, by suggesting his own experience was far worse than it actually was: 'Noizay is now free but badly looted,' in fact untrue. He tried to justify his return to Paris and to `the zone of mystery': 'after all I suppose there are spiritual values to be defended.'[43] What did he mean? Poulenc's music was in no way neglected under Vichy. Charles Munch made a point of playing his music. Poulenc later did not blame those who had collaborated. During the purge he defended Jacques Rouché, head of Paris Opera, and Claude Delvincourt, Director of the Conservatory. He did not hold it against Arthur Honegger that he had been so extensively performed under the Occupation. Was his own setting of La Fontaine's fables to music for his 1942 ballet *Les animaux modèles,* with its sentimental regard for rural values and the peasantry, Pétainist? But anger at Occupation showed through in his 1943 song cycle of Éluard's poetry, *Figure humaine,* most famously the poem, *Liberté.* Poulenc gave a private performance on the piano at the home of Marie-Laure de Noailles and another for Picasso and Éluard. But it remained clandestine during the Occupation and only received its first public performance in London in March 1945 and in Paris only in May 1947. His patriotism shone through in his setting of Aragon's poem C, an expression of grief at France's collapse in 1940. A rare response to the Holocaust came with his setting of Robert Desnos' *Dernier poème*, the poet a hero of Resistance, who died in Therezin concentration camp, but this was only composed in December 1956. For the most part Poulenc kept his head down in Noizay during the war.[44]

At one remove, though, he did engage with Resistance. In 1943 he was faced with the nightmare possibility of losing Raymond to forced labour in Germany (compare E M Forster's threatened loss of his lover Bob Buckingham to the RAF). Then there was a moment when Raymond might have been shot. He had joined up with the American troops as they closed in on Amboise, only to face German machine gun fire. To dissuade the Americans from liberating the town by bombardment Raymond had clandestinely entered the town and found that it was defended by only 60 to 80 Germans, hardly worth an American full-scale assault. The citizens of Noizay showed their gratitude by offering to elect Poulenc as their mayor. Poulenc meanwhile had been careful to establish his resistance credentials by displaying his

Cantata *Figure humaine* on his desk, with a French flag at the window of his study. 'I hope,' he wrote to Bernac, 'that *Figure humaine* and *Les mamelles* will prove a sufficient tribute from a Frenchman.'[45]

Whereas in post-war France Messiaen drew ever closer to the political establishment, Poulenc kept his distance. He was indifferent to public honours. On receiving the office of the Légion d'honneur in October 1953 he commented: 'I feel like an old gentleman since they gave me the decoration. I may be exaggerating but it seems to me I have fewer erections since!!!'[46] Nor did he become a cold-war warrior. There is a reference in a letter to meeting Nicholas Nabokov, followed by numerous exclamation marks.[47] What did that signify? And he liked America, 'how much I love America – my best public.'[48] But he was not adopted by those Cold War organisations for cultural freedom.

But political detachment is quite different from a this-worldly engagement. His music was strongly engaged with the sensual, a rich amalgam of both human and sacred. Wilfrid Mellors, by way of qualification, suggests there was always a tension in his music between physical sensuality and metaphysical chastity.

Music

Self-Doubt

As part of that morbid assessment of his worth as a composer at the outbreak of war he looked back on his inter-war music as 'worthless drivel in the main.' In the same vein, reflecting on the success of his war-time ballet *Les animaux modèles*: 'I have suddenly become aware that for all the twenty-five years in which I have been writing music, a whole section of the public has cared very little for what I have been doing.'[49] His serious religious music had been ignored in favour of the frivolous of Les Six. Maybe self-doubt had been there from the start through his lack of formal instruction; he had been turned down for the Conservatoire by Paul Vidal in September 1917. Not that this had stood in the way of recognition. Through Ricardo Vines he had met Eric Satie (1866-1925) and George Auric (1899-1983). Satie he looked on as his spiritual father, though later they fell out. With his ballet *Les Biches* he acquired an international reputation. Belatedly in 1922 he took instruction from the contrapuntalist, Charles Koecklin. He even engaged with the Second Viennese school (indeed he developed a surprising crush on Webern). Admittedly, Les Six was never more than a loose association of composers, but it fatally typecast Poulenc, even if he did not altogether go along with Cocteau's attack on post-Wagnerism and late romanticism: he always admired Debussy, though did criticise his imitators. Charitably, Mellors describes this early music as 'the essence of amorousness.'[50] But he was stuck with a reputation for facility and shallowness. Might he alter this image though his religious and sacred music?

There is a strong case for seeing Poulenc's breakdown in the 1950's as part of a continuing neurosis as to the true worth of his creativity. Was, he worried, as good as his peers, Darius Milhaud (1892-1974) and Arthur Honegger (1892-1955)? Having once been in the forefront of the avant-garde in the 1920's he now found himself looked down on as a conservative by the new generation of serialists, Boulez to the fore. Not even the success of the Carmelites could shake this self-doubt. To Simone Girard he complained: 'Not that I am intoxicated with the idea of being a *grrand* (sic) *musician* but it nevertheless exasperates me to be thought of by so many people as nothing more than a *petit maître érotique.*'[51] He became his own analyst: 'what has often been praised as my charming modesty is fundamentally nothing more than an inferiority complex that has now taken a pathological form.'[52] In the same vein he confessed: 'often, during my fits of self-doubt, alas more and more frequent, I ask myself if it is not sterility that causes me to compose so slowly.'[53] The success of his extraordinary music of the 1950's failed to shake off his morbid self-doubt.

Stravinsky versus Messiaen

One way of characterising Poulenc's spirituality is by connecting his music to the contrasting styles of Stravinsky and Messiaen. In that divide there is a conundrum in assessing his spirituality. In admiring Stravinsky, was he in serious danger of being harnessed to a musical outlook that, it has been argued, led away from the spiritual, or is it just the case that there are variant expressions of the spiritual? Here we will have to reopen the debate on Jacques Maritain and look at Richard Taruskin's punitive critique of Stravinsky.

Stravinsky was his role model. In 1914 he heard Pierre Monteux conduct his *Rite of Spring* and he became a convert. Literally they first met at a music publishers in Paris in 1916: 'when I saw him come through the door, I thought it was God himself arriving.'[54] By September 1919 he was sending him his own compositions and ever afterward it became a mutual admiration society. In response to *Oedipus Rex* Poulenc wrote: 'your art has reached such a height that it would need the language of Sophocles himself to describe it. Heavens how beautiful it is.'[55] In reply to an admiring piece he had written on *Symphony of Psalms* Stravinsky responded: 'I could not have wished for a better Easter present. You are truly good, and that is what I always find again and again in your music.'[56] They lost touch during the war but then came a parcel of Stravinsky's music: 'I was delighted, dazzled – and in particular heartened – by the beautiful present of music. Once again I felt your presence, your genius, your example. You can be sure that I am among those to whom you bring the light.'[57] Stravinsky replied: 'My very dear Poulenc, send me some of your music I beg of you: you know what loyal and tender feelings I have always had for your beautiful music.'[58] Not that Poulenc was always so receptive. He wrote of Stravinsky's *Cantata* (1952), 'what a crushingly boring work it is and how awkward.'[59] By then Poulenc was caught up in a spat between Messiaen and Stravinsky, though one led by Messiaen's disciples. But Poulenc's loyalty was never to be subverted. At the end in 1962 he wrote: 'I consider myself a son of Stravinsky, the kind of son he would no doubt disown, but nevertheless his spiritual son.'[60]

If Poulenc was little interested in polemics he was drawn into the debate over Maritain's ideas. This was in part through association. The Maritains, Jacques and his wife Raissa, had, in 1905, met Poulenc's piano teacher, Ricardo Vines. They also befriended his close friends, George Auric and Jean Cocteau. Just a little oddly, the composer whom Maritain adopted in his exposition of the artist as next to, if subordinate, to God in *Art et Scholastique* (1920) was Eric Satie, Poulenc's spiritual father figure. Cocteau gave a further puff to these ideas in *Le coq et le harlequin*. Arthur Lourié (1892-1966), Maritain's apologist, then embraced Stravinsky into this neo-Thomist canon: 'surmounting the individual element – the animal principle – Stravinsky's music tends more and more towards the spiritual.' But was all this in danger of losing touch with everyday humanity? Maritain himself saw the danger and wrote of 'an angelist suicide' and of the need to recognise physical reality. Lourié followed suit, perceiving a risk of inhumanity in the so-called objective and pure. Lourié remained the leading Thomist apologist of a particular style of sacred music, even if 'he packaged the Gregorian chant in a thoroughly modern harmonic idiom.' It was Lourié who is seen as influencing Poulenc in that all-important breakthrough into sacred music, his *Litanies à la Vierge Noire de Rocamadour*.[61]

But Stravinsky was by far the greater influence. And here we have to engage with Taruskin's critique.[62] If Stravinsky had become an international sensation with the neo-pagan music of *The Firebird* and *The Rite of Spring*, a far greater impact on modern music came from his 1923 *Octet for Winds, for Clarinet and for pairs of Bassoons Trumpets and Trom-*

bones: 'a pronounced general swerve in the arts that reflected a greater one in the wider world of expressive culture.'[63] This was the beginnings of neo-classicism, a phrase coined by Boris de Schloezer, Scriabin's apologist, though before Stravinsky's Octet. Here in Taruskin's analysis was a music in response to the barbarism of World War 1, that rejected pathos in favour of irony, seen as 'the indispensable ingredient in practically all European art ever since': 'it cast a retrospective pall over all serenely spiritual and exalted art the previous century had produced. All rhetoric of hope and glory now seemed a lie.' The preference was for 'the matter-of-fact said over the rhapsodically sung.'[64] One dissenter, Prokofiev, saw Stravinsky's neo-classical music as 'Bach with smallpox.'[65] Taruskin may well confuse the categories of the aesthetic and the political but he is outraged by Stravinsky's admiration for Mussolini: 'I don't believe anyone venerates Mussolini more than I do.'[66] 'Are artists who enjoyed the patronage of this century's blood-soaked dictators,' Taruskin rhetorically asks, 'stained with the blood that soaked them?'[67] He sees little mitigation in Stravinsky's plight as a Russian nobleman driven into exile by the Bolsheviks. Needless to say, Taruskin has little time for Poulenc's music, so evidently under Stravinsky's spell. He writes of his 1944 opera *Les mamelles de Tirésias* as 'sadly lyric music': 'the French music of the post-war period was desacralised art and art brought down to earth.'[68] Poulenc, it would seem, was in danger of being drawn into a music that was highly elitist and authoritarian. Fortunately, the nature of his homosexuality, that search for ordinariness, led him in another direction, both into an all-too-human acceptance of the physical and also into a very particular kind of immediacy and directness in his music.

How sympathetic was Poulenc to Messiaen's radically different expression of a Catholic spirituality? We have to remember that Messiaen was a composer from a younger generation that threatened to eclipse Poulenc's own musical reputation. At the time of his reconversion, his was a positive response to the music of Le Jeune France. 'Messiaen and I do not genuflect in the same way,' he commented, 'but what matters is that we both try to share our faith with the public.'[69] He was 'overwhelmed'[70] by his *La Nativité du Seigneur*. But Messiaen's and Poulenc's paths did not converge. By 1944 he was having to ask Bernac what Messiaen was up to and whether his *Trois petites Liturgies de la présence divine* had yet been performed: 'I have been playing quite a lot of his music again. When he sticks to his own methods and vision, it is truly remarkable: in other more contrived pages the influence of Dukas is irritating. There can be nothing worse – in fact for any of us.'[71] After Bernac had sent him the score, he responded: 'I find it quite simply indescribable, which does not stop me from feeling that he has a lot of talent. Dukas and Dupré are very responsible for its didactic tone, exacerbated by the gentleman's mysticism.'[72] To Milhaud, helping him to catch up on the music he had missed through exile, he reflected: 'either one loves this (Messiaen's) music or one hates it, but it cannot be ignored any more than the paintings of Rouault. It has greatly influenced a whole generation of 25 year-olds, which perhaps is not so fortunate, as they are being systematised.'[73] This was during the bitter attack on Stravinsky by Messiaen's students. He further communicated: 'the rise of Messiaen has been the most important musical event. In fact you will find a fanatical sect surrounding the musician, who for all the impossible musical jargon, is nevertheless remarkable.'[74] To another composer, Henri Sauguet (1901-89), he complained: 'the public always goes for what is easily understood unless, like Messiaen, one lives entirely in the ether – often quite unbreatheable.'[75] He took some satisfaction in reporting from America on the press notices for his concerts, 'I must not complain, compared with Messiaen, who was unmercifully slated by all that lot and who was generally detested by the musical milieu as a whole.'[76] Once more to Milhaud: 'Messiaen is very well placed to do penance in the game of forfeits. He has been deconsecrated.'[77] (No doubt following *le Cas Messiaen.*) Poulenc was evidently ambiguous in his response to Messiaen. There is no evidence of any personal friendship.

Song

Mellors wrote of Poulenc's middle years music as veering 'between animal hedonism and humane sensuality'[78] and that might best describe his music for song. In the same way as Benjamin Britten, Poulenc was at his most natural in setting words to song. Briefly, we have to explore his kinship with the surrealist poets. Pierre Bernac is the best guide. Here was an irrational language drawing on the unconscious and Poulenc had to go beyond that language if he was to discover a spiritual meaning. In Apollinaire, Poulenc encountered a kind of Paris he knew all too well: 'no one understood better than Poulenc the dark poetry of a certain sordid Parisian atmosphere. It is this poetry one must try to recreate.'[79] With Max Jacob there was a double kinship, his homosexuality and his Catholic faith. In 1909 the Jewish Jacob experienced a vision of Christ and, if not baptised till 1915, later chose to live near the Monastery of St Fleury, St Benoit-sur-Loire, where he was arrested in February in 1944 and later murdered. Poulenc had first met him in 1920. Then there was another Resistance poet, Louis Aragon, a Communist, whose poem C, evoking the Exode ...

> *Oh my France O my forsaken France*
> *I have crossed the bridge of Cé*

... Poulenc so memorably set to music. Aragon subsequently came out in a highly dramatic way as gay. But Resistance poet and Communist Paul Éluard, a surrealist poet rare in his love of music, inspired Poulenc's finest composition. Mellors rates *Figure humaine* 'as possibly Poulenc's greatest work.'[80] Then there were those setting of poems by another Resistance hero, Robert Desnos: 'Poulenc succeeds without the least sentimentality in expressing the piercing sorrow, then the mood of rebellion, and finally the despair and resignation suggested by the poem.'[81] There is a homo-erotic subtext to this poem on the parting of friends.

In 1935, in a garden in Salzburg, Poulenc embarked on a musical partnership with Pierre Bernac, all the way through to the latter's retirement at 60. Mellors writes: 'the mutual understanding and the moral and artistic inspiration they afforded one another can hardly be overestimated.'[82] The obvious parallel is with Britten and Pears except that Bernac was exclusively heterosexual. Few grasped better than Bernac the strengths and weaknesses of Poulenc's character: 'he could never restrain himself in any way, he was capriciousness itself.' Above all he feared solitude and boredom. Yet 'his nature was fundamentally gay and happy,' 'he never spoke ill of anyone,' 'there are few composers whose music so faithfully reflects their personality.' 'He followed the impulse of his sensibility and his heart and gave himself up entirely to it.' But, tellingly, he also observes 'at heart he was an anxious man.'[83] Poulenc's constant anxiety state, as we have seen, put enormous strains on their friendship. Some of Poulenc's indebtedness to Bernac comes through in his comments on Bernac's retirement concert 27 May 1959: 'What memories I shall have of 27 May, how I revelled in Pierre's glory. There was not one person who did not salute, hat in hand, that great artist.'[84]

Sacred Choral Music

Poulenc has been described as 'one of the most deeply reverential choral composers of the century.'[85] Ivry, in a more back handed way, suggests, if homosexual Poulenc can celebrate heterosexual love the way he does in setting Éluard's *Tel jour, telle nuit,* it is not surprising 'that his talent was also sufficient to create moving religious music.'[86] Out of his trauma of 1936 came the *Litanies*, the Mass in G, *Quatre Motets pour un temps de Pénitence,* all, in Ivry's estimate, a setting of France's agony to music. On a similar scale was his *Quatres Petites Priéres de Saint François d'Assise* (1948), composed for the voices of the brothers of Champfleury monastery. In 1952 he wrote his *Quatre motets pour le temps de Noel.*

There are four larger works. His secular Cantata, *Sécher-esses,* is seen as one of his failures. Maybe Edward James's poetry failed to inspire in the same way as Apollinaire's and Éluard's, though it is a work of ferocity, if somehow barren and desolate. Not so his *Stabat Mater,* premiered in1951. He wrote to Bernac: 'the *Stabat* is going at such a rate that there can only be a Rocamadour miracle behind it.'[87] Again, a song cycle of Mary grieving at the foot of the Cross might have political overtones of a France and Europe coming out of war. In fact, it was inspired by the premature death of his artist friend, Christiane Bérard, both gay and transvestite. On completion Poulenc reflected: 'the *Stabat* is finished. My nerves were so frayed by the end of it that I wondered if I wasn't deluding myself as to its merits. However a cool assessment of it this morning has convinced me it is good, because it is profoundly authentic.'[88] The work that has proved lastingly popular is his *Gloria,* composed for the Koussevitsky Foundation. During rehearsal he enthused: 'the *Gloria* is without doubt the best thing I have done and it has given me the confidence *that I badly needed.*'[89] To his bio-grapher he confided: 'I know very well that I am not exactly in vogue but I need at least to be recognized. And that has happened.'[90] This was also Poulenc's way of thanking God for coming through the crisis over Lucien Roubert. Here was music that reflected his 'country parson' view of the faith, music that can be both light-hearted and profound, for, as he saw it, 'soccer playing Benedictines could be as devout as a pious churchgoer,' but the 3rd and 5th movements are seen as his most sincere and profound religious music, and in the last 'we are left to ponder no less than life and death.'[91] There was one more choral work *Sept Répons de Ténèbres,* com-missioned by Leonard Bernstein for the opening of the Lincoln Centre in 1962 but, in fact, premiered, posthum-ously, in the Avery Fisher Hall in 1963. He looked on the piece as 'very interior, not at all decorative as the *Gloria.*'[92] Mellors sees it 'as probably Poulenc's greatest religious work,'[93] though it has not enjoyed any popular success. Sid-ney Buckland describes it as his 'darkest large-scale work,' 'most dissonant, audacious, modern.'[94] The first movement looks back to the *Litanies*. There is real anger in the music at Judas's betrayal: maybe as a homosexual Poulenc was particularly angry at such a kiss being a means of betrayal. Did it anticipate his death from a heart attack 30 January 1963? Again, as a homosexual, did he insist on the male voice to sing his elegy? With reference to these last three choral works Poulenc mused: 'I think I have three good religious works. May they spare me a few days of purgatory, if I do narrowly avoid going to hell.'[95] And indicative of his greater self-confidence, and jealousy was alien to his nature, he could write to Benjamin Britten: 'more recently your marvellous *Requiem* has quite shaken that little fortress of religious music in which I am now happily thriving.'[96]

Dialogues des Carmélites

All of the conflicting strands in Poulenc's life come together in his defining work, his opera *Dialogues des Carmélites*. It is the polar opposite of *Les Mamelles de Tirésias*, Poulenc's personal favourite, a work inspired by his long-term lover, Raymond Destouches. Its composition was to drive Poulenc to a nervous breakdown. One factor was the deeply disturbing love affair with a new lover. Lucien Roubert. Another was anxiety as to his true worth as a composer. He also became increasingly neurotic about his health, convinced he was suffering from cancer. Deeper than all these fears was confrontation with death and the truth of his religious faith. The opera was driven by a search for spiritual transcendence. But he was never to lose his crippling sense of inadequacy and, if paradoxically, it is in that all-too-human frailty that lies the secret of its enormous success.

The opera is based tangentially on true events. It is the story of the nuns of the Carmel of Compiègne during the Revolution. In 1789, under the recently elected Prioress, Mother Thérèse of St Augustine, there were twenty one Sisters, three lay Sisters, two external, and sixteen Choir sisters. The Revolution quickly turned against the religious orders. In August

1790 the District Commissioner of Compiègne made an inventory of its possessions. On 12 September 1792 these were confiscated and the nuns forced to leave. On 21 June 1794 they were arrested and imprisoned in the Conciergerie. On 17 July sixteen nuns were guillotined, Sister Constance the first to go, the Prioress the last. On 27 May 1906 they were to be beatified.[97]

But this story was to be radically retold in Gertrud von le Tort's 1931 novel, *The Song at the Scaffold*. She invented the central character, Blanche de la Force, a name echoing her own. Jacques Maritain had it translated into French. Postwar, there were plans to turn it into a film, and George Bernanos wrote the script, completed 8 April 1948, shortly before his death on 5 July. If not a script used for a film, it did become a play, first performed in June 1952 at the Hebertot theatre in Paris. Unfortunately, Gertrud le Tort had granted copyright to an alternative play by the American, Emmet Lavery, *Song of the Scaffold*. Another factor precipitating his breakdown was the horrible uncertainty as to whether his opera would be produced at all, though in time the Arbitration Tribunal gave permission, whilst awarding Lavery substantial damages and insisting that his name appear in all the programme notes. Poulenc met Lavery and they got on well.

His had been 'the frenetic bulimia' of a search for a libretto.[98] Approached by Guido Velcaringhi, Director of La Scala, on behalf of the music publishers, Ricardi, to submit a composition, the eventual choice was Bernanos's script. By weird chance Poulenc had espied a copy in a book-store in Rome. Did he owe it all, he wondered, to Rocamadour? To Bernac he wrote: 'I have prayed so many times for a libretto that the Holy Mother sent me this one to sing her praises with.'[99] Bernanos's confessor, Abbé Daniel Pézeril, believed Poulenc and Bernanos were of one mind; Poulenc had found his way 'into the very heart of the Dialogues – a meeting of souls if ever there was one.'[100] Poulenc himself put it this way: 'his concept of the spiritual is exactly mine and his violent side is in perfect accord with a whole side of my nature, be it in pleasure or in asceticism.'[101]

At the outset Poulenc had been incredibly energised: 'I am completing one scene a week, I hardly recognise myself. I am crazy about my subject, to the point of believing that I actually know these women.'[102] But then his personal life began to engage in a destructive way with its composition. Running parallel with the emotional drama of the opera was Poulenc's deeply troubling affair with the 41 year old travelling salesman, Lucien Roubert. They lived apart, and Poulenc suffered all the anguish of sexual frustration and the morbid fear that Lucien would not be loyal. In despair he turned to Bernac: 'I rely on your tenderness, your strength of mind, your lucidity. I so much want to pull myself together but will I ever manage.'[103] But Bernac was almost ready to throw in the towel, told him to show moral virility and resort anyway to his usual solution for such crises, take another lover. To the Girards, likewise closely involved in the drama, he confessed: 'how ashamed I am to have involved you in this mortifying mental agony.'[104] All of that sexual anguish was poured into the opera.

But then the affair, with Lucien falling ill, originally diagnosed with tuberculosis but then terminal cancer, paralleled the opera ever more closely. Poulenc, exhibiting a distinctly morbid side to his religiosity, began to wonder if Lucien was dying on his behalf. This idea of a sacrificial death was, of course, the moral core of the Bernanos script. As Lucien lay dying at Cannes, Poulenc, lover turned carer, wrote to Bernac: 'I have entrusted him to my sixteen blessed Carmelites: may they protect his final hours since he has been so closely involved with their story. In fact I began the work at his side, in happiness, in Lyons in August 1953. After all the torment, which I need not describe to you, I have just finished the work at his side, during the last days of his earthly life. As I wrote to you once before I am haunted by Bernanos's phrase, "We do not die for ourselves alone, but for, or instead, of each other."'[105] And he did ask the Carmelites at Compiègne to pray for Lucien, for a friend 'who had always been peculiarly interested in my work which alas he will never see staged.' Poulenc reflected, 'this great drama of my life is ending in the most melancholy (dare I say it?) happiness. My morale vis-à-vis Lucien is very high and that is what is needed.'[106] Lucien died 21 October 1955. Did Poulenc seriously believe, convinced of his own imminent death, that Lucien had died in his place?

In 1953, Poulenc – almost certainly as much through the sheer strain of creativity as the emotional demands of the affair – suffered a complete breakdown. 'I have indeed poisoned myself little by little. Too much introspection – emotional as well as intellectual – has been gnawing way at me for months,' he confided to Bernac. 'But can one prevent a lame man from limping?'[107] He entrusted himself to neurologist (I guess psychiatrist) Dr Meillard-Verger and his clinic at Avignon: there he was offered two weeks of sleep to catch up on all his insomnia. He reported to the Girards: 'Stuffed full of sedatives, I am holding out – quite obviously so to the old bag I passed in the corridor who exclaimed "well, well, if it isn't Poulenc!" She should have said the ghost of Poulenc. Alas I am no longer master of my will, of my poor nerves. I am all adrift. It is mortifying.'[108] If he did recover from what he called his menopause, Poulenc was never to be free of neurotic anxiety.

If one must be cautious at over identifying Poulenc with Bernanos's text, clearly, with his sentimental attachment to the Ancien Regime, he was on the side of the Nuns against the Revolution. It is always referred to in the opera as the mob or rabble and, in Mellors's words, it had 'destroyed civilised tradition, human dignity and spiritual grace, without knowing what to put in its place.'[109] Such sentiment explains Poulenc's sympathetic treatment of the Marquis de la Force and Le Chevalier de la Force, Blanche's father and brother.

Two preoccupations of Blanche shape the opera, overcoming fear, not just of the Revolution but of the world more

generally, and her realising a good death.[110] Poulenc identified with Blanche. Reluctantly both father and brother endorse her decision to enter the Carmelite convent at Compiègne. Quite soon Blanche has to witness the death of the
Prioress in great pain and in denial of God. Here was a bad
death. Blanche has assumed the conventual name of the
Prioress, Blanche of the Agony of Christ on the Cross. Poulenc had every confidence in the stark terror of the scene,
'the crux of the whole play': 'You will see,' he told his future biographer, 'the atmosphere is terrifying and I think
when the interval comes, the audience will be in shivers.'[111]
Sister Constance has proposed to Blanche that they die in
place of the Prioress, and this raises the true subject of the
opera: 'it is a play about fear, it is also and above all,' Poulenc explained to Claude Rostand, 'a play about grace and
the transference of grace. That is why the Carmelites go to
the scaffold with an extraordinary calm and faith. For are not
calm and faith at the heart of all mystical experience?'[112]
Now the sub-Prioress, Mère Marie takes on the role of managing Blanche's fear. Initially Blanche resists her brother's
persuasion to return to the family home, choosing subser-
vience to God over escape: 'Poulenc maintains momentum,
perhaps because his heroine's crisis is so deeply involved
with his own.'[113] But the Revolution is closing in and when
the Commissioner breaks into the Convent to announce the
closure of the religious orders Blanche drops a figure of the
infant Jesus: 'God is shattered.'[114] The nuns now have to face
the possibility of martyrdom, and only Blanche desists from
taking a vow, precipitating her flight to the family estate.
Here Mère Marie tracks her down. Blanche admits to being
afraid all her life. Is there in a very personal observation by
Mère Marie, 'the misfortune my girl is not to be despised but
only to despise oneself,' Poulenc's confronting his homosexuality?[115]

Meanwhile the Nuns have been imprisoned in the Conciergerie and there the new Prioress assures them they are ready
for transcendence: 'it would seem the new Prioress is a
redemptive agent, who atones for the dubieties of Blanche

and even of the old Prioress.'[116] So to the Place de la Revolution and the final shattering scene. At the last moment Blanche joins them, just as Constance is mounting the scaffold and smiling radiantly at her. Blanche, finally overcoming fear, follows and so attains a good death. In the thudding sounds of the guillotine did Poulenc finally exorcise the trauma of 1936 of Ferroud's beheading?: 'we may see the final scene of *Les Carmélites* as a desperately private horror publicly attested.'[117] To the Girards, Poulenc wrote: 'I think these terrible nuns, before losing their heads, have wanted me to sacrifice mine. Which is not impossible.'[118]

He had great faith in the opera: 'I do not think I have done anything so good. You will see it is terrifying.' Reflecting on the melodrama with Lucien: 'sometimes these ordeals are necessary. No doubt my Carmelites have required this of me.'[119] It was premiered at La Scala 26 January 1957, in Paris 21 June 1957, Covent Garden 16 January 1958. 'Opera houses worldwide tumbled over one another to perform the work.'[120]

La voix humaine

Then came the 40 minute opera, *La voix humaine,* a coda to the *Carmélites*. Ostensibly it is the drama of a woman at the end of her tether, trying to win back her lover. Here after 40 years of friendship was a belated collaboration with Jean Cocteau. And here is yet another example of Poulenc's appropriation of someone else's text as his own: 'I will send you the music of the atrocious tragedy (my own). It is a musical confession.'[121] For this could equally be read as the desperate attempt by a gay man to hang onto a lover. In his usual neurotic way Poulenc feared he might lose the love of his 'great big peasant,' Louis Gautier: 'just as Blanche was myself so was the woman in the opera, she is again myself in relation to Louis, because life will no doubt deprive me in my one way or another of the angel.'[122] In fact Louis was loyal till the end and Poulenc was really working through the trauma of his love for Lucien. Whereas the sexual anguish had been transmuted in the *Dialogues* here it is painfully explicit. But there is a connection for, as Poulenc explained to Aragon, he 'needed the spiritual and metaphysical anguish of the Carmelites to avoid betraying the terrible anguish of Cocteau's superb text.'[123] The woman on the telephone, having once attempted suicide, now needs to undertake an act of self-sacrifice, equivalent to that of the nuns, 'to face death rather than submit to shame and self-betrayal.'[124] Maybe this was acting out Bernac's advice of displaying a more virile morality, living with dignity rather than attempting suicide yet again. 'This is really music composed,' he wrote to Bernac, 'in a state of trance.'[125] It was premiered in Paris 6 February 1959.

In the performance I heard,[126] possibly through the weaknesses of the soloist as an actress, the woman seemed by the end, rather than resigned, let alone transcendent, desolate and defeated. Given the hysteria required of the role, it was hard not to sympathise with her ex-lover. Bernac's irritability with Poulenc's own neurosis over Lucien comes to mind. But Poulenc's music beautifully matches the fluctuating hope and despair of the abandoned woman.

There was one more richly spiritual piece, his Oboe Sonata (1962): 'the confidences of an oboe are given to us as if at the end of a long day, when someone sits opposite you and speaks frankly of what is in the heart.'[127] His Clarinet Sonata was only to be performed posthumously.

Summary

If his sexuality took precedence over his faith, this interpretation has shown how the conflicts over both come together in his music. A very personal quality of anguish characterises Poulenc's spirituality. A strong strain of humanism pervades his music, obviously so in his early work and in his songs, but in the sacred music as well. That search for an earthy ordinariness in his lovers is carried over into his attitude to religion. Poulenc was largely apolitical in the Third and Fourth Republics and, given the identification of the fearful Blanche of the Carmelites with Poulenc's own cautious temperament, it is hardly surprising that his was but a marginal engagement with Resistance. But this raises, as it does with Messiaen, the uncomfortable question, are you an artist first or a human being, and if the latter, as it is argued here, surely the artist had to respond to Occupation and the Holocaust? In many ways, Poulenc's expression of the spiritual is more emotional and direct than Messiaen's, and this is because it is less cluttered up with theological concerns. Poulenc shares with Shostakovich and Britten their exceptional talent for communicating feeling. But, as a final speculation, given his morbid preoccupation with death, was Poulenc able through his music to overcome his fear of death?

Notes

[1] I have relied on two recent studies, for the biographical, Benjamin Ivry, *Francis Poulenc*, London: Phaidon, 1996, frank and explicit, and, for the interpretation of the music, Wilfrid Mellors, *Francis Poulenc,* Oxford: Oxford University Press, 1993, reprinted 2003, a highly sensitive study. Another invaluable source was, *Francis Poulenc: Echo and Source. Selected Correspondence 1915-1963*, Edited and translated by Sidney Buckland, London: Victor Gollancz, 1991.

[2] From his radio conversations with Claude Rostand. Quoted Pierre Bernac, *Francis Poulenc: The Man and his Songs*, London: Victor Gollancz, 1997, p.28.

[3] Quoted in Sidney Buckland and Myriam Chimènes (eds.), *Francis Poulenc: Music, Art and Literature*, Aldershot: Ashgate, 1999, p.154.

[4] For details on Rocamadour see the Michelin Guide, *Dordogne Périgord Limousin Quercy*, London: The Dickens Press, 1965, pp.149-52.

[5] Quoted Bernac, *Francis Poulenc*, p.29.

[6] Ivry, *Francis Poulenc*, p.70.

[7] I opened up a history of homosexuality in my *Sexual Moralities in France 1780-1980: New Ideas on the Family, Divorce and Homosexuality*, London and New York: Routledge, 1989, but, in the nature of scholarship, there has been much new research. See Julian Jackson's scholarly and remarkably explicit, *Living in Arcadia: Homosexuality, Politics and Morality in France from the Liberation to Aids*, Chicago: University of Chicago Press, 2010.

[8] Jackson, *Living in Arcadia*, p.19.

[9] Jackson, *Living in Arcadia*, p.12.

[10] These were in a series of articles in the journal, *Arcadie, Revue littéraire et scientifique*, first published January 1954, summarised by Jackson.

[11] Ivry, *Francis Poulenc*, p.12.

[12] Ivry, *Francis Poulenc*, p.68.

[13] See Marjorie Wharton's chapter, 'Nogent Music: Poulenc and Dufy,' in Buckland and Chimènes, *Music, Art and Literature*.

[14] Ivry, *Francis Poulenc*, p.153.

[15] Jackson informs us this was a favourite gay haunt, *Living in Arcadia*, p.48.

[16] Ivry, *Francis Poulenc*, p.175.

[17] Letter to Simone Girard, September 1952, Buckland, *Correspondence*, p.396.

[18] Letter to Simone Girard, November/December 1951, Buckland, *Correspondence*, p.194.

[19] Letter to Rose Dercourt-Plaut, 1 May 1957, Buckland, *Correspondence*, p.245.

[20] Letter to Bernac, 26 March 1962, Buckland, *Correspondence*, p.288.

[21] See Sophie Robert, 'Raymonde Linossier: Lovely soul who was my flame,' Chapter Three in Buckland and Chimènes, *Music, Art and Literature*.

[22] Ivry, *Francis Poulenc*, p.74.

[23] Ivry, *Francis Poulenc*, p.71.

[24] Ivry, *Francis Poulenc*, p.151.

[25] Ivry, *Francis Poulenc*, p.103.

[26] So Michael Argyle pronounced in a lecture I attended as a student at Oxford.

[27] See Arthur Kirch, *Auden and Christianity*, New Haven and London: Yale University Press, 2005, p.xi.

[28] Ivry, *Francis Poulenc*, p.147.

[29] Letter to Bernac, 12 July 1945, Buckland, *Correspondence*, p.161.

[30] Letter to Bernac, July 1954, Buckland, *Correspondence*, p.220.

[31] Quoted Buckland and Chimènes, *Music, Art and Literature*, p.159.

[32] The description of him in Emile Vuillermoz's, *Histoire de la Musique*, 1949, Ivry, *Francis Poulenc*, p.153.

[33] Ivry, *Francis Poulenc*, p.91.

[34] Letter to Simone Girard, November-December 1951, Buckland, *Correspondence*, p.194.

[35] Letter to Bernac, Easter 1958, Buckland, *Correspondence*, p.252.

[36] Letter to Bernac, 17 August 1956, Buckland, *Correspondence*, p.242.

[37] See Buckland, *Correspondence*, p.392.

[38] Ivry, *Francis Poulenc*, p.77.

[39] Letter to Paul Collier, 1921, Quoted Buckland and Chimènes, *Music, Art and Literature*, p.210. See Miriam Chimènes, 'Poulenc and his Patrons: Social Convergences,' Chapter 9.

[40] Buckland and Chimènes, *Music, Art and Literature*, p.241.

[41] Letter to Comtesse Jean de Polignac, 15 August 1936, Buckland, *Correspondence*, p.107.

[42] Letter to Comtesse Jean de Polignac, September 1939, Buckland, *Correspondence*, pp.120-1.

[43] Letter to Darius Milhaud, 9 September 1940, Buckland, *Correspondence*, pp.125-6.

[44] I find it odd that Frederic Spotts in his account of music in his *The Shameful Peace*, only uses Poulenc as a witness of events and does not assess his actual response to Occupation.

[45] Letter to Pierre Bernac, 1944, Buckland, *Correspondence*, p.143.

[46] Quoted Ivry, *Francis Poulenc*, p.172.

[47] Letter from Assisi to Pierre Bernac, March 1953, Buckland, *Correspondence*, p.205.

[48] Letter to Doda Conrad, September 1953, Buckland, *Correspondence*, p.211.

[49] Letter to Andre Schaeffner, 1942, Buckland, *Correspondence*, p.129.

[50] Mellors, *Francis Poulenc*, p.22.

[51] Letter to Simone Girard, June 19589, Buckland, *Correspondence*, p.262.

[52] Letter to Pierre Bernac, Easter 1958, Buckland, *Correspondence*, p.251-2.

[53] Letter to Geneviève Sienkiewicz, 21 December 1959, Buckland, *Correspondence*, p.270.

[54] Quoted Buckland ,*Corespondence*, p.324.

[55] Letter to Igor Stravinsky, 30 May 1927, Buckland, *Correspondence*, p.83.

[56] Igor Stravinsky to Poulenc, 6 April 1931, Buckland, *Correspondence*, p.94.

[57] Letter to Igor Stravinsky, 28 December 1945, Buckland, *Correspondence*, pp.165-6.

[58] Letter from Igor Stravinsky to Poulenc, 10 January 1946, Buckland, *Correspondence*, pp.166-7.

[59] Letter to Henri Hell, December 1953, Buckland, *Correspondence*, p.213.

[60] Quoted Buckland, *Correspondence*, p.314.

[61] See Douglas Shadle, 'Messiaen's Relationship to Jacques Maritain's Musical Circle and Neo-Thomism,' Chapter 5, in Shenton (ed.), *Messiaen the Theologian*.

[62] And here it is only fair to point to those who quarrel with Taruskin's judgement. John Tavener, for example, seeks 'to understand Stravinsky's stature by placing his music besides permament and universal truths, essential truths, situated outside time and space.' Even so, Tavener recognises that there was a barrier in Stravinsky's personal definition of the objective in art, 'a non-expressive coldness and a complete lack of sentiment. Stravinsky believed that music could

express nothing at all. Thank God that most of his finest music belies this nonsense.' See 'The Holy Fool of Music,' *The Guardian*, 19 January 2007.

[63] Taruskin, *History of Modern Music*, Vol.4, p.448.

[64] Taruskin, *History of Modern Music*, Vol.4, pp.472-3.

[65] Quoted Taruskin, *History of Modern Music*, Vol.4, p.479.

[66] Quoting Stravinsky in 1930, Taruskin, p.477.

[67] Taruskin, *History of Modern Music*, Vol.4, p.472.

[68] Taruskin, *History of Modern Music*, Vol.4, p.587.

[69] Quoted Hill and Simeone, *Messiaen*, p.65.

[70] Dingle, *Life of Messiaen*, p.57.

[71] Letter to Pierre Bernac, 24 June 1944, Buckland, *Correspondence*, p.136.

[72] Letter to Pierre Bernac, 14 July 1944, Buckland, *Correspondence*, p.137.

[73] Letter to Darius Milhaud, 3 January 1945, Buckland, *Correspondence*, p.147.

[74] Letter to Darius Milhaud , 27 March 1945, Buckland, *Correspondence*, p.153.

[75] Letter to Henri Sauguet, 9 August 1945, Buckland, *Correspondence*, p.163.

[76] Letter to Henri Sauguet, 12 February 1950, Buckland, *Correspondence*, p.180.

[77] Letter to Darius Milhaud, 6 March 1951, Buckland, *Correspondence*, p.188.

[78] Mellors, *Francis Poulenc*, p.34.

[79] Bernac, *Francis Poulenc*, p.58.

[80] Mellors, *Francis Poulenc*, p.66.

[81] Bernac, *Francis Poulenc*, p.191.

[82] Mellors, *Francis Poulenc*, p.61.

[83] Bernac, *Francis Poulenc*, pp.29-36.

[84] Letter to Simone Gerard, June 1959, Buckland, *Correspondence*, p.262.

[85] Keith W Daniel, 'Poulenc's Choral Works with Orchestra,' in Buckland and Chimènes, *Music, Art and Literature*, p.48.

[86] Ivry, *Francis Poulenc*, p.101.

[87] Letter to Pierre Bernac, 19 August 1950, Quoted Buckland, *Correspondence*, p.381.

[88] Letter to Pierre Bernac, October 1950, Buckland, *Correspondence*, pp.186-7.

[89] Letter to Pierre Bernac, January 1961, Buckland, *Correspondence*, p.281 .

[90] Letter to Henri Hell, 2 March 1961, Buckland, *Correspondence*, p.282.

[91] See Daniel in Buckland and Chimènes, *Music, Art and Literature*, pp.65-8.

[92] Quoted Ivry, *Francis Poulenc*, p.210.

[93] Mellors, *Francis Poulenc*, pp.157-8.

[94] Buckland and Chimènes, *Music, Art and Literature*, p.73.

[95] Letter to Pierre Bernac, 26 March 1962, Buckland, *Correspondence*, p.288.

[96] Letter to Benjamin Britten, October 1962, Buckland, *Correspondence*, p.296.

[97] See Claude Gendre, 'Dialogue des Carmélites: the historical background, literary destiny and genesis of the opera,' Chapter 11 in Buckland and Chimènes, *Music, Art and Literature*.

[98] See Denis Waleckx, 'In Search of a Libretto,' Chapter 10 in Buckland and Chimènes, *Music, Art and Literature*, p.267.

[99] Letter to Pierre Bernac, 1 September 1953, Buckland, *Correspondence*, p.208.

[100] Quoted Mellors, *Francis Poulenc*, p.104.

[101] Quoted Buckland and Chimènes, *Music, Art and Literature* .

[102] Letter to Stephanie Audel, 31 August 1953, Buckland, *Correspondence*, p.206.

[103] Letter to Pierre Bernac, September 1954, Buckland, *Correspondence*, p.222.

[104] Letter to Doctor and Madame Girard, October 1954, Buckland, *Correspondence*, p. 224.

[105] Letter to Pierre Bernac, August 1955, Buckland , *Correspondence*, p.234.

[106] Quoted Buckland and Chimènes, *Music, Art and Literature*, pp.306-7.

[107] Letter to Pierre Bernac, July 1954, Buckland, *Correspondence*, p.219.

[108] Letter to Doctor and Madame Girard, October 1954, Buckland, *Correspondence*, p.224.

[109] Mellors, *Francis Poulenc*, p.125.

[110] I have explored the place of a bad and good death in 20th century painting in my essay 'Varieties of Death: A 20th Century Perspective,' in Marcus Reichert (ed.), *Art and Death*, London: Ziggurat, 2008/2009.

[111] Letter to Henri Hell, 14 February 1954, Buckland, *Correspondence*, p.216.

[112] From *Entretiens avec Claude Rostand*, 1954. Quoted Buckland, *Correspondence*, p.390.

[113] Mellors, *Francis Poulenc*, p.117.

[114] Mellors, *Francis Poulenc*, p.120.

[115] Quoted Ivry, *Francis Poulenc*, p.183.

[116] Mellors, *Francis Poulenc*, p.123.

[117] Mellors, *Francis Poulenc*, p.127.

[118] Letter to Doctor and Madame Girard, October 1954, Buckland, *Correspondence*, p.224.

[119] Letter to Rose Dercourt-Plaut, 21 July 1955, Buckland, *Correspondence*, pp.230-1.

[120] Ivry, *Francis Poulenc*, p.189.

[121] Letter to Rose Dercaut-Plaut, 30 January 1959, Buckland, *Correspondence*, p.257.

[122] In a letter to Hervé Dugarde. See Denis Waleckx, 'A Musical Confession: Poulenc, Cocteau and *La voix humaine*,' Chapter 12 in Buckland and Chimènes, *Music, Art and Literature*, p.321.

[123] Quoted Mellors, *Francis Poulenc*, p.128.

[124] Mellors, *Francis Poulenc*, p.137.

[125] Letter to Pierre Bernac, 6 February 1959, Buckland, *Correspondence*, p.254.

[126] Part of a double bill, 'Cocteau Voices,' Linbury Theatre, June 2011, Nuccia Focile the soloist.

[127] Ivry, *Francis Poulenc*, p.216.

11. *Karlheinz Stockhausen*

With Stockhausen and Henze this project comes full circle.
Both emerged from that context of evil addressed at the
outset. Stockhausen confirms Jung's fear of a connection
between the occult and the spiritual. From amongst his
contemporaries, Luciano Berio (1925-2003), Pierre Boulez,
born 1925, Gyorgy Ligeti (1923-2006), Luigi Nono (1924-
90), Iannis Xenakis (1922-2001). Stockhausen selects himself for this study as a self-proclaimed exponent of spirituality. Indeed, he verged on the self-parodic. His biographer
sees him as a 20th century Faust, always in search of the
dynamic in music.[1] Henze broke from Darmstadt and his
fellow modernists and emerged as a Romantic within the
Austro-German tradition. Both composers were drawn to
radical, indeed revolutionary politics, and, in Henze's case,
to the gay movement. Henze was far more a this-worldly
composer and can be placed at this end of a spectrum of
the spiritual. But Myth featured prominently in his music and
if in no way formally religious, Henze seeks the transcendental.

In the Context of Post-War Music

Composers in the aftermath of war saw the need, to quote
Paul Griffiths, our best guide to post-war modern music, for
'not just reconstruction but an alternative paradigm.'[2] Set up
in the summer of 1946, largely to help young German composers catch up with new music they had not heard during
the Nazi regime, the Darmstadt Summer School became the
centre for this quest. Another centre was to be the Donaueschingen Festival. Messiaen was the outstanding teacher
of this post-war generation of composers, largely through his
talent for telling his disciples to follow their own path. Here
was an isolated avant-garde – 'separation from the past became an item of belief – and, by the middle of the 60's, a
fragmented one, 'the pursuit of fashion and the splintering of

factions had together created a turmoil of simultaneous developments.'[3] This was a crisis: for all its variety 'music's existence as expressive thought, as the register of inner experience never registered before, was in peril.'[4] Might engagement with the political save the avant-garde? In the conservative 1970's it disintegrated, one symptom in Griffiths's estimate, the rise of religious music. Post-1989 new music lost its official patronage (for the Soviet system had paradoxically been a patron). If post-modernism was another new expression it 'rapidly forked in its meaning almost to the end of usefulness.'[5] It led to a new Romanticism, to reach its apogee in the 1990's. Yet heterogeneity remained, 'symptomatic of an impending cultural swerve on the scale of the Renaissance.' But it is also a time of stasis: Griffiths concludes, 'the water at the moment looks calm, certainly by comparison with the foam and rush of the decades after 1945.'[6]

If it seems special pleading to claim of a composer who was increasingly marginalised from the 1970's onwards as the central figure in post-war modernism, Griffiths has no hesitation in ascribing this role to Stockhausen. How did his career evolve? One way is to see it in three phases. Firstly the 1950's, with radical innovatory works in terms of the nature of sound such as *Gruppen* and *Gesang der Jünglinge.* Then in the 1960's a second, when, turned in on himself and on a small group of performers, he was ever more willing on aesthetic and mystical grounds 'to open himself to the unexpected' in scores that 'set out only systems of signals, cues and other basic instructions,' best known *Hymnen* and *Stimmung.* These tie into Stockhausen's identification of himself with 1968. And then came a third style with his so-called formula composition or intuitive music, *Mantra* (1970) its first expression, 'sounding like sacred chants from another planet.'[7] He became wholly preoccupied with his opera *Licht.* Should we see him from now on as cut off in his home in Kurten near Cologne with family and acolytes, withdrawing into an increasingly fantastic and megalomaniac world? Alternatively, might we read this third period differently, seeing 'this enormous scenic vista of a universe falling apart, with islands of hope, love and consolation adrift in a merry-go-round of banality,' to quote Griffiths, 'as not so untrue to the world in which we live today.'?[8]

Philip Hensher[9] offers a more useful framework for this project, seeing his career as divided into a Darmstadt Stockhausen and a Sirius Stockhausen, the first running from the 1950's to the mid 1960's, a soberly analytical period, and then a mystical. But Hensher also refers to a middle period, so maybe he and Griffiths are not so different.

But clearly something truly bizarre occurs. Jonathan Harvey conveys this in a matter of fact way:

> I once went to Stockhausen's house in Kurten, Germany. We talked about spiritual matters. He felt he was in contact with the angels, like William Blake, as well as with higher intelligences, beings who had evolved more, maybe on other planets. He talked a lot about Sirius (the planet from which he believed he hailed) I thought of him as a sort of shaman: once or twice I saw strange things in his face – other than his own.[10]

Hensher still admires some pieces from the second phase, *Stimmung, Inori, Trans,* all seen as 'impressively sustained exercises in pure orchestral grandeur.' But his social isolation is seen as fatal: 'it isn't difficult to imagine that this removed any kind of nourishing critique from the processes of composition.' Hensher looks on his opera *Licht* as `a vast folly.' He has a telling comparison with Joseph Beuys. Beuys saw through the absurdity of the idea of guru and genius: Stockhausen failed to do so. Hensher concludes: 'the weakness and the foolishness were the product of someone in love with the idea of his own cryptic authority.'[11]

This project will focus far more on this second and overtly spiritual period of Stockhausen's music.

Family and Background

Questioned about the influence of war and its aftermath on his music Stockhausen asserted: 'I was not traumatised after the war.'[12] This beggars belief.

He was born 22 August 1928 in Mödrach, a small village in the Ville. He was to be curiously loyal to the landscape of his childhood, the hill country to the east of Cologne, much blighted by the lignite industry. His father, Simon Stockhausen, was something of an itinerant primary school teacher, till his promotion to a secondary in 1935 in Altenberg. To his dismay he discovered that he could no longer practise his Catholic faith and that the Cross in the school had to be taken down. He was leant on to join the party. We learn that he was a keen hunter and a lover of the theatre. His son described him as 'a fanatical front-line man.' In 1943 he was called up and fought as an officer on the Eastern front. He was killed in Hungary in 1945.

His mother, Gertrud Stupp, came from a prosperous farming family. Did she influence his future musical career through playing the piano and having a good singing voice? She was considered beautiful. She was, however, prone to depression and following the death of her son, Hermann-Joseph, shortly after birth, she had to be hospitalised. Later, in 1941, she fell victim to the Nazi programme of euthanasia. Here were to be terrible lasting memories for Stockhausen. When his mother was sectioned she cried out, Hell was below and Heaven above, and begged to taken to the attic. This scene was later incorporated into *Licht*. One of the reasons why Stockhausen became so taken up by radio was through his mother claiming to hear voices from the radio. By pressing his own ear to the transformer he developed an ear infection, poorly treated at the time, and this led to but 30% efficiency in his right ear for life. In 1938 his father remarried but Stockhausen never got on with his step-mother, Luzia. In a sense, by 1945 he was orphaned.

Inevitably he got caught up in the horrors of war. He was a fire-guard in Altenberg. There was his harrowing experience as a stretcher bearer in 1944 close to the western front. He witnessed terrible mutilation caused by phosphate bombs: 'I often tried to find a hole going into the mouth with straw to pour some liquid down it so that someone who was till moving could be nourished – but there was just this yellow spherical mess, with no sign of a face.': 'death became something completely relative to me.'[13] He recalled as a member of an ambulance crew seeing `trees cluttered with pieces of flesh after the strafing of planes.' And he added in a revealingly puritanical caveat, 'and it's hard to imagine the sexual behaviour in the midst of dying bodies in the hospital. I have no illusion about people who give up God.'[14]

After the war he moved to Cologne. In 1942 he had become a boarder at the Teacher Training College in Xanten, in part to escape his step-mother. From there he went in 1947 to the Music School in Cologne, though only formally passed its entrance examination the following year. In post-war Cologne he entered a Harry Lime world of urban devastation and corruption. He scrounged for cigarette ends, sold them on the black market or exchanged them for food. His was a background of real poverty.

For Stockhausen Nazism had been an experience of the dark forces. Hitler he saw as 'obsessed with the devil.' Disturbingly, he saw these forces as 'part of the divine realm: there's that real divine freedom when you can say no to God.'[15] This in part explains the role of the occult in his music. And how else could he exorcise these memories other than through his music?

The Personal and the Political

As Bohemian life-styles go Stockhausen's was not such an unusual life. But he had a talent for extrapolating extra-

ordinary melodrama from quite ordinary personal circumstances. The personal was to overlap with the political.

And here Stockhausen was part of a larger political aspect to
post-war music. In the immediate aftermath of war before the
onset of the Cold War, the new generation saw a connection
between rethinking music and rethinking society: serialism
and socialism went together. Aims differed, Boulez's 'if un-
disclosed, perhaps unknown,' though Griffiths points initially to 'an aesthetic of annihilation ... a need to demolish what
had gone before,'[16] Nono's socio-political. But Stockhaus-
en's were spiritual.[17] Despite all his rhetoric on revolution
Stockhausen was rarely overtly political. His was a romantic
vision of universalism. He delighted in New York as 'the
first model for a global society.'[18] In *Hymnen* he saw himself
as composing music for all races and nations and a fraternal
internationalism, though the left criticised the way he played
with national anthems to make his case. Then came 1968.

His music deeply focussed on his family life and its travails.
He met his future wife Doris Andreae in a circle of piano
players in Hamburg in 1948. They married 29 December
1951. There were to be four children. His love for her is
written into much of the music of the first phase. But then in
January 1961 in the Bohemian circles of Cologne he met the
American artist Mary Baumeister. Their relationship greatly
complicated his private life. Catholic Cologne was shocked. Her former lover threatened reprisals. He tried to keep
his family together and moved to Kurten. Yet he and Mary
went off together to work in Finland and Sicily. The tension between Doris and Mary is reflected in works such as
Momente. He and Mary were to marry in San Francisco 3
April 1967, one child born before, one after the marriage.
Erotic poetry inspired by Mary was written into *Stimmung*.
But the marriage unravelled and Mary threatened to leave
him. In May 1968 the personal and the political converged.

Stockhausen's rejoinder to Mary's threat was 6 May to go on
a hunger strike for seven days. It was a period of heightened

awareness. Just playing one note on the piano on day four was a revelation: 'how the note shocked me ... everything within me was so still, so empty – I was super-electric, super-sensitive – I heard notes of a length, a beauty, an inner life such as I had never heard before.' This fed into the political climate of 1968: 'once again we are making a revolution but this time across the whole globe. Let us now set ourselves the highest possible goal: a gaining of consciousness that puts the whole of humanity at stake.'[19] The blackmail worked and Mary returned but the marriage still broke down in 1971.

There were to be other friendships, one with the English art historian, Jill Purce, another with the American clarinettist Suzanne Stephen. He did not entirely withdraw from the world, for he still taught the composition class at the Hochshule für Musik in Cologne. In Kurten he was joined by his children, his son, Marcus, a trumpeter, Simon, a saxophonist, Christabel, a flautist, Majella, a pianist and a small circle of players. But he had withdrawn and he became ever more solipsistic.

His explanation as to why he fell out with Henze is revealing of his attitude to the political. Henze's music, with its reference to politics, is seen as banal: 'it just becomes *blang*, musically speaking. So everything becomes symbolic on a very primitive level.' There is an arrogance, he believed, in a music which excludes those who do not share its ideology: 'I'm not interested in this, neither in the producers, nor in the consumers. I can have a political opinion as a composer, but I shouldn't try to limit the music that comes about through me to what I think politically. That would be the worst thing in the world because it immediately cuts out all the people who have intellectually different opinions.' The meaning of music should always seep through to a larger audience.[20] For Stockhausen the spiritual was the conduit to this larger audience.

Religion and the Spiritual

Stockhausen's deep Catholic faith lay behind much of the music of his first phase. Both his parents were believers though his father had to give up worship on joining the Nazi party. Stockhausen dealt with the restriction by only praying at night. He took his first communion in Altenberg Cathedral Easter 1938. (Was this clandestine?) Interestingly, his Teacher Training College had been a former Carthusian monastery. When studying under Messiaen in Paris he went to a different church every Sunday for mass. As he explained in his conversations in 1971 with to Jonathan Cott, 'until 1960 I was related to the cosmos and God through Catholicism, a very particular religion that I chose for myself almost as a way of opposing the post-war Sartrean nihilistic attitudes of the established intellectuals.'[21] He was also intrigued by the connection between religion and the rational, an idea he acquired from Karl Goeyvaerts, a Belgian follower of Messiaen.[22] 'But then I began to float because I got in touch with other religions.'[23] No doubt the complexities of his private life took him away from Catholicism. Buddhism became all important. Stockhausen readily immersed himself in other cultures, ancient and present. Through these he retained a fascination with ritual: in ancient Aztec and Mayan culture, for example, 'I relived ceremonies which were sometime very cruel.'[24] He witnessed the extraordinary Muslim festival at Kataragama in Sri Lanka with its violence against the flesh, convincing him 'the spirit can completely dominate the body.'[25] This religious pluralism, supra-religion as he called it, naturally led him into his very idiosyncratic form of spirituality.

One source was in childhood. Here lay the origin of his fascination with flight. At the age of three and a half in Lent 1932 a small plane had made a forced landing at Mödrath and he was to witness its relaunch, 'the bird rolled downhill, took off and disappeared into the mist.'[26] As a child he watched over his grandfather's and uncle's cows and, as he recalled, 'I'd just lie on my back for an hour or more, watch the clouds and a small propeller plane would appear circling in a soft sound in the sky. This sound was drawing its lines in circles, it's been following me my whole life. And you find it again in *Hymnen* – these slowly wandering sounds in the sky.'[27] He was fascinated by birds in flight, by the experience of flying: 'I always say to my colleagues that musicians are the birds of the animals.'[28] Listening to the sound of planes whilst in flight over America in 1958 encouraged his idea of spatial music, of an audience in the centre surrounded by sound.

That Stockhausen was predisposed towards the spiritual is indicated by his early reading. Herman Hesse's *The Glass Bead Game,* read in 1948, was an essential text: 'it connects the musician with the spiritual servant. I found it prophetic, for I realised that the highest calling of mankind can only be to become a musician in the profoundest sense: to conceive and shape the world musically.'[29] Other influential texts were Thomas Mann's *Doctor Faustus* and Heidegger's collection of essays *Holwege*, published in 1950. At this stage he thought of becoming a writer and his short story on the Emperor Hamayun, Birth and Death, showed promise.

Mary Baumeister introduced him to Japanese Zen, Jill Purce to Sufism.

But the greatest influence was the Indian mystic, Aurobindo.[30] During the crisis in 1968 he read Satprem's book on Aurobindo, but a secondary source, and it is never clear how thoroughly he read Aurobindo's original writings. The evidence suggests he may have read his texts on Yoga, however improperly grasped, and his epic poem *Savitri.* He took on board Aurobindo's idea of the spiral: 'the circle which leads to ecstasy, the principle of the steady increase of consciousness-involution rather than evolution.'[31] 'There is a spiral once and forever in the cosmos everywhere, which means that you come back but never exactly to the same place.'[32] There is always a new point of departure. He absorbed Aurobindo's idea of supraconsciousness or supramentalism: 'only if you have gained supraconsciousness can you bring light into the caverns of our subconscious.'[33] But he always saw an expansion of consciousness in individualist rather than collective terms. Was this out of revulsion at Nazism? Whereas Aurobindo in his integral yoga saw the body as absorbing the divine, a quest taken over by the Mother, Mirra Alfassa, Aurobindo's partner, on his death in 1950, Stockhausen alternatively saw an escape from the body into the divine; 'eventually someone will be able to leave his body when he wants to take another form.'[34] 'Ultimately I think that a person who wants to get out of his body will just do it without pistols or poison: you'd choose a place to lie down and then you'd leave.'[35]

This connects with his ideas on Death and Apocalypse. Death was seen as 'necessary for washing out memory.' It is a way of forgetting the past and anticipating the future: 'I completely anticipate experience that comes sometimes hours, weeks, years later,' tapping into 'the layers of time that are coming – the superconscious or supramental.'[36] Here is his definition of Nirvana: 'Nirvana means to be in all the time and everywhere at once – and in an omnipresent state, *eternal* in reaching the timeless by incorporating everything.'[37] A teleological Christian sense of time is replaced by a Hindu cyclical. He foresaw catastrophe or apocalypse through over-population: 'the spirit cannot rise up if we continue to multiply bodies.'[38]

Yet he visualised a new spiritual community, its members with the appearance of 'the luminous and transparent angels'[39] portrayed in Grunewald's Issenheim altar-piece. Its members would be linked by a shared and heightened consciousness. 'It would look as if our earth were *shining*, there'd be an enormous light emanating from this thinking activity ... an enormous thinking brain. There would be such a community scattered across the globe.'[40]

There were other influences than Aurobindo. He drew on the Tibetan Book of the Dead. Then there was the Urania Book.

At a performance of *Hymnen* in New York 25 February 1971 a strangely dressed member of the Uranian Brotherhood of Chicago approached Stockhausen and sold him a copy of the Urania Book. In the short run this cultist book influenced *Inori,* though the Urania Society refused permission for the insertion of a section on prayer based on its principles. Stockhausen told his pupils in 1974 'if you want to go on being my pupils, you must read this,' slapping down in front of them a copy of the Urania book.[41] Its weird ideas greatly influenced *Licht.*

Urania is the Earth. The book itself had been copyrighted in 1955. It was translated into 6 languages. If Christian in inspiration it was unattached to any church. Through marriage to outsiders from other planets, the cult believed, a forgotten 5th revelation, one beyond the New Testament, would be brought back to memory and that modern knowledge be brought up to date. In Urania the human, and this may drag Stockhausen's music back to a this-worldly outlook, is not less than God.

All this highly personalised spirituality shaped his music. At a seminar he gave on *Stimmung*, 3 August 1972 he stated:

> The essential aspect in my music is always religious and spiritual; the technical aspect is mere explanation. I have often been accused of vague mysticism. These days, mysticism is easily misunderstood as something vague. But mysticism is something that cannot be expressed with words, that is: music! The purest musicality is also the purest mysticism in a modern sense. Mysticism is a very incisive capacity to see right through things.[42]

Bearing in mind Stockhausen's caveat on the technical aspect of his music, here it is its religio-spiritual aspects that will be explored. This will be selective and largely reliant on such of his music as I have heard. His music was the subject of two special Proms, 2 August 2008 and a Total Immersion day at the Barbican, 17 January 2009.

Music: First Phase

Stockhausen's was a formidably cerebral pursuit of new possibilities of sound, highly innovative in its exploration of electronic music. This will not looked at here. But we need to track the way religion and the spiritual appear in this first phase.

Following his encounter, indeed it induced a spiritual conversion, with Messiaen's *Mode de valeurs* at Darmstadt in 1951 came *Kruezspiel* (Crossplay), reflecting in its title both his Catholicism and a spiritual dimension, 'the possibility,' to quote Griffiths, 'of liberating more than creating sound structures that would have nothing human in their composition, that would be images of divine unity.' In the 'ruthlessly channelled disorder' of the piano Griffiths sees connections with non-European African and Asian ensembles.[43] In *Formel*, with its requirement of 'meditative listening,' and behind once again 'a seeming chaos of phenomena,' lay 'the purposes of God.'[44] Then came *Kontra-Punkte* (1952), Stockhausen's 'panache' conveying his belief that a new musical universe could evolve. On his return from Paris, and through the patronage of Herbert Eimert, he worked in the electronic studio of Cologne Radio. The later Stockhausen is foreshadowed: 'for Stockhausen as a composer, music even then was not the expression of human feelings and passions, but rather an attempt at re-creation, a reconstruction of the cosmic order and natural laws in sound.'[45] Looking back in 1984 Messiaen perceptively saw that Stockhausen had needed neither himself nor Eimert for inspiration but was always himself the innovator: 'ultimately remote from every teacher and every influence, he wrote the great works that the whole world knows today.'[46]

Gruppen

In August 1955, in Paspels, a small village in Graubunden, Switzerland, came the inspiration for *Gruppen*. He only wrote the score in 1957. At the time Stockhausen's flat in Cologne was the venue for the new generation of composers, Boulez, Ligeti, Nono. Artists were also close friends. Stockhausen had become fascinated by the ideas of Paul Klee. It was premiered 24 March 1958 on the site of Cologne's industrial fair. As Kurtz recalls, 'the premiere of *Gruppen* was one of the main musical events of the 50's: the movements of sound in space, the extraordinarily sophisticated and varied sound of the orchestra and the whole compositional conception of the work brought Stockhausen an outstanding success.'[47]

It is in one continuous movement lasting c 25 minutes. It is scored for three orchestras. As Robert Worby puts it: 'we hear solo instruments and great constellations of sound that swarm like musical insects.'[48] It was performed at the prom on 2 August 2008, one that had been specially planned to celebrate his 80th birthday. Anthony Holden felt its performance had not been a success: 'the work's special ambition remained stuck in mid-arena, between the two bands supposedly tossing chord-clusters back and forth to a third on stage.'[49] I experienced rather a magic moment when the three separate orchestras came into view: two had been obscured by the promenaders. The music seemed to pass over the Albert Hall like a summer storm. It echoed the paintings of Klee, with its pointilliste chords, these then filled out. Yet there seemed a reluctance to allow any continuous line of music, it was always rather helter-skelter, like a sky of shooting stars. There was one climax of angry brass and a piano's rumbling percussive sound, as if some St Catherine's wheel had skidded off its mount, only for the music to turn back to the fragmentary, oscillating between the ferocious and the quiet. Griffiths sees *Gruppen* bringing to an end Stockhausen's 'highly detailed and rapidly changing music.'[50]

From now on the music shifts towards slowness and more complex sounds, with a greater latitude in the execution of detail. It was a period of experimentation in sound. He saw in *Kontakte* 'the concentration on the Now – on every Now – as if it were a vertical slice dominating over any horizontal conception of time and reaching into timelessness which I call eternity: an eternity that does not begin at the end of time, but is attainable at every *moment*.'[51] He fell back on a close group of performers and between 1965 and the early 70's concentrated on ensemble playing.

Hymnen and Stimmung

Both pieces came out of that period of retreat.

In 1966 he had visited Japan at the invitation of Japanese Radio: 'my arrival in Japan made such an enormous change to my life that I felt like someone coming out of the provinces into the big wide world.'[52] He immersed himself in Japanese traditional culture. Out of this visit came *Telemusik* and a different sense of time.

Hymnen was his response to New York and its variety of people. It was premiered in Cologne 30 November 1967. Extravagant claims at the time were made for it, comparisons with Beethoven's *Missa solemnis*, Mahler's 8th, Schoenberg's *Moses und Aron*. Its political content has already been mentioned: along with Berio's *Sinfonia* Griffiths sees the music as reflecting 1968 and the emancipation of blacks, women and homosexuals. For a while 'their work seemed to be part of a global upsurge and to embody the new pluralism as it was coming into being.'[53] Yet it was equally personal, Stockhausen incorporating childhood memories, that plane in the sky, as well as a visit to the Yoshemite falls in California. Anticipating Apocalypse as he did, Stockhausen intended the music as 'purifying shock, this was music for the post-Apocalypse.'[54]

Stimmung (it can be translated variously as 'tuning' or 'mood, frame of mind') was composed in New York during the winter: 'there were unbelievably strong winds, and I just watched the white snow and the water in front of my two windows.'[55] It was scored for the Cologne Collegium Vocale and premiered in Paris 9 December 1968.

Stockhausen refuted any indebtedness to American minimalism and to La Monte, whose loft he had visited in New York, for had not La Monte been his pupil at Darmstadt? It is divided into 51 sections, 29 of which entail the recitation of magic names, those of tribal deities and gods. Here was his response to Aztec and Mayan sites in Mexico. Worby insists this is not mood music: 'we need to tune in, with the singers, as Stockhausen presents us with the quantum mechanics of his musical cosmos.'[56]

It was performed at the late night Prom 2 August 2008. Stockhausen wants us to let our minds wander into a kind of mystical space. In silence and barefoot the singers entered, bowed to one another, sat down in the manner of Plato's Symposium. This had the feel of the Hindu evening ceremony of Aarti. Theirs was a very basic language, incantatory, increasingly Buddhist in feel. But the words also incorporate Stockhausen's erotic poetry and it can feel as much sexual as spiritual. It was punctured by odd cat-like sounds and indeed all the singers miaowed. One of the sopranos went through an extraordinary range of octaves in the manner of Yma Sumac. There was whistling, raucous laughter, gargling sounds. Voices replicated the sound of an accordion, the vibrating sound of a rubber band, the hum of rubbing the rim of a glass of water. At one stage it became highly vocal and a considerable number of promenaders lay flat out, as if under a gas attack.

This is how Stockhausen envisages our response:

> Experience within yourselves times and spaces you
> have never known, never even dreamed of / let

> yourself be transported across the boundaries of
> your accustomed domain / learn that man has
> scarcely begun to be aware of his capacity for
> flight, his capacity to soar above his own head ...
> the new law of harmony is the freedom of the I to
> vibrate along with any sound it encounters, even
> the most alien: to soar with it, to unite with it, and
> to leave it behind so that then I may be joined ever
> more with the numberless sounds of the world.[57]

The most extraordinary performances of the piece were to
be deep in the caves of Jeita near Beirut. A Catholic priest
said of a performance: 'it was the longest prayer I have ever
known, and the happiest.'[58]

In contrast, Anthony Holden was unimpressed: 'it reminded
me of the more pretentious "happenings" of that era, of
which Stockhausen was very much a part.' If a one-off piece,
Holden sees it as 'at the point at which Stockhausen is drift-
ing off into his more experimental world, as remote from
reality as his belief in his planetary origins.'[59]

Music: Second Phase

He called his new music 'intuitive.' Both composer and performer became a conduit for music from without. This came
from Sirius, the brightest of stars, where 'music is the highest
form of all vibrations.' Stockhausen had always 'seen his
role more as an initiator than as a maker of works,' music
had to be found outside the self, it was more prayer than autobiography.[60] That of course is massively disingenuous for
there were few more autobiographical composers. He expected the same of his players: through 'a certain meditative concentration,' they become 'a wonderful instrument' and start
'resonating': 'the more open you are, the more you open
yourself to the new music by throwing out all the images, all
the automatic brain processes – it always wants to manifest
itself.'[61] In *Kurtzwellen* (1968) he invited his players to go on

a voyage 'to the edge of the world which offers us the limits of the accessible.'[62] Music's role was to advance spiritual aims.

It was music that needed a new physical setting for its audience. He found this in his metallic blue spherical auditorium in the German pavilion at the Osaka World Fair 1970. It was 28 metres in diameter, seating 550, speakers all around them, 'so I could make complete circles around the people, not only horizontal circles but vertical ones, below-above. Or spiral movements and all different loops.'[63]

In the text for *Litanei* (1997) a reworking of the 1968 *Aus den siebenTagen* (From the Seven Days) and part of *Mitterwoch* (Wednesday) from *Licht,* Stockhausen set out his intentions. Here is his theme of being a conduit: 'I do not make MY music, but only relay the vibrations I receive; that I function like a translator, that I am a Radio.' The players must follow suit: 'I will tune you like a receiver, but whether or not you sound clear depends on you'; he will transmit 'vibrations which come from a higher, directly effective sphere ... higher IN US AND OUTSIDE.'[64]

Inori

Another concept for music of the second phase was 'formula composition,' music based on very simple melodic structures, rather like DNA. It was first evident in the hour long *Mantra* (1969-70) for two pianos, highly dramatically in *Inori* (1973-4), premiered at the Autumn Donaueschingen Festival.

Inori, a Japanese word, translates as prayer. Having reconstituted the auditorium Stockhausen now recast the layout of the orchestra, lower instruments to the left, higher to the right. Two mime dancers perform on a platform above the orchestra, moving and swaying in perfect harmony with the music. Griffiths insists that 'while they command our attention, they direct that attention always to the divinity that *Inori* addresses, the divinity of sound.' Griffiths writes of 'a return to some basic "mother of all sound"'; 'through its shuddering into rhythmic and dynamic life, the work grows like some gigantic creature.'[65]

I responded somewhat differently to their performance at the Barbican. Yes, their gestures of prayer take up the music. But what are they doing? Libation to the Gods? Cupping their ears and tuning into the divine? Were the two dancers, bathed in light, in rapture? The piece was always full of suspense. I heard the sound of xylophone as a desperate cry from those in limbo. Alternatively, was this some Satanic ritual? At one point the male dancer descends and thrice smashes a kind of pillow, accompanied by a great crash and groan in the music. Was this a surrender to a higher power? At the end the dancers walked off to the side of the stage, only to return and exit centre stage, but high up at the back, and into a whiff of smoke. Heaven or Hell? Here is a worrying way in which Stockhausen's music connects with the occult.

Licht

From 1977 Stockhausen turned ever more in on himself and set aside the next 25 years for the writing of *Licht*. He drew on all his life's experience to compose a kind of personal mythology. He drew on the Book of Urania, Aurobindo and New Age Spirituality. How, the Book of Urania asked, could evil exist in a world created by God? Its answer was that we had to grow out of evil and move towards the light. A musician would come from outside and transform the world: Stockhausen, a prophet from Sirius, saw himself as fulfilling that role. There was no need for any institutionalised or monotheistic church. By opening ourselves to the vibrations of music we would open ourselves to spiritual communication – the ideas of Aurobindo here paramount – and so evolve into a higher spiritual consciousness. We had to draw on esoteric and occult insights as a way of drawing East and

West together. The music of other cultures were but dialects
of a universal music. All this was, of course, steeped in New
Age Spirituality. In ways reminiscent of C S Lewis's science
fiction novel, *Out of This Silent Planet* an electronic global
brain has to be created to save Mother Earth from extinction.[66] Stockhausen made a crucial admission: 'I am often
exposed to lively mixtures of other people's tendencies – interpreters, technicians and many people I work with. So it is
absolutely possible that I may receive satanic transmissions,
and let them into my work.'[67] But his was a quest for Nirvana, Stockhausen himself the herald of the Age of Aquarius.

The opera is cast in terms of the seven days of the week.
There are three main characters and in turn or in various
combinations dominate each of the seven operas. There is
Michael, the musician, an angel, one of the 634 sons of
God, a character from the Book of Urania, and Stockhausen's alter-ego. There is his opponent, Lucifer, the principle of lucidity. There is Eve, symbolising fertility and the
rebirth of a more musical mankind. Monday was Eve's day,
Tuesday the confrontation between Michael and Lucifer,
Wednesday the cooperation of all three, Thursday, Michael's
day, Friday the day of Eve's temptation by Lucifer, Saturday Lucifer's day, Sunday the mystical union of Michael
and Eve. *Donnerstag* was premiered at La Scala, Milan, 15
March 1981. Michael wanders the world, 'part-angel, part
Christ, part cosmic messenger, self-image on the part of the
composer,'[68] represented by the trumpet, a tenor and a male
dancer. He gets to know the world through just the same
childhood experiences as those of Stockhausen. He returns to
heaven to be greeted by Eve. In *Samstag*, premiered 25 May
1984 but this time in the Palazo della Sport, Lucifer's day
and all about death, Stockhausen making good use of *The
Tibetan Book of the Dead,* Lucifer seemingly dies, with an
embattled Michael trying to turn him towards the light. But it
is a pseudo-death, he returns, and in a ceremony inspired by
the Kataragama festival, sings a text of St Francis of Assisi,
so maybe the honours are even. *Montag,* Eve's day, was
premiered at La Scala 7 May 1988. Eve, the eternal female,

both Michael's mother, guardian and consort, is 'devoted to the mythology of femininity, to fertility, creativity, giving birth and eroticism.' It is 'a musical celebration of the rebirth of mankind.'[69] She is represented by a basset horn, soprano and female dancer. For Stockhausen the performers were not theatricals but figures from beyond and had, in the manner of performances of Kathakali or the Ramayana, to meditate beforehand. The outlandishness of the plots is described more fully by Kurtz.

In a fatal press conference, 16 September 2001, following the destruction of the Twin Towers, Stockhausen stated: 'I pray daily to Michael but not to Lucifer. I have renounced him. But he is very much present,' and went on to describe the events of 9/11 as 'the greatest work of art that exists in the whole cosmos, five thousand people are driven to Resurrection,' this the work of Lucifer, 'the cosmic spirit of anarchy.'[70] Stockhausen had come to inhabit a very strange phantasmagoric world.

Griffiths forms a more critical judgement of the opera in his book than in the programme notes for the Barbican event. 'The grandeur of the project is inseparable from its bathos. By its absurdity and by its mess, the work testifies to the impossibility of a real drama of the world and time being achieved at the end of the twentieth century. Its destiny is to be at once magnificent and ridiculous.'[71]

Klang

On completion of *Licht* Stockhausen embarked on another grandiose project, *Klang* (Sound), a cycle of 24 works, one for each hour of the day, and to be unfinished at the time of his death, 5 December 2007. Here was his continuing quest to place music, in this case electronic music, in a different kind of space, with the Albert Hall ideal, as it happened, loud speakers all around the arena.

One piece played at the Prom was from the 5th hour, with solo trumpet accompaniment. As I heard its long blasts, they were a human cry against our uncertain fate: why am I here? It moved into a more lyrical mode and a dying fall, a genuine farewell.

Cosmic Pulses, the 13th hour, was far more intimidating: 'great swathes of sound swirl around the upper ether, as if in some fearsome sonic solar system.'[72] This is how I heard it. Darkness reigns. This is music from Sirius, from science fiction, from Bladerunner. Is this the music Scriabin sought in his *Mysterium?* Messiaen would have liked the chords. The music is piled on with a terrible murmuring. Are we in a post-nuclear world? We seemingly fall into a nightmarish limbo, a black hole, though Angels, Kundera-like, are flickering on the outside. Yet some orchestral sound is trying to surface, the terrifying demons may yet give way. Can an oracle yet speak? But the composer seems lost in his own nightmare. The organ plays. It all dies away, with high flute sounds, maybe Messiaen's birdsong. This is a journey and an ending but without a vision. Is Stockhausen saying space is neutral?

Listening to this music was alarming. A friend developed vertigo. I heard it as diabolical and a dangerous encounter with the occult.

The artistic director of the Barbican, Graham Sheffield, describes how going to interview Stockhausen for the Immersion event 'was like going to interview God. I think he did think he was God, although he was quite rational in conversation.' He continues: 'in a way his death marked the end of 20th century music.'[73]

Notes

[1] Michael Kurtz, *Stockhausen: A Biography*, translated by Richard Toop, London and Boston: Faber and Faber, 1992, p.5.

[2] Griffiths, *Modern Music*, p.1 .

[3] Griffiths, *Modern Music*, pp.165-7.

[4] Griffiths, *Modern Music*, p.251.

[5] Griffiths, *Modern Music*, p.255.

[6] Griffiths, *Modern Music*, p.424.

[7] How Griffiths puts it in, 'Introduction, Making the impossible possible,' in the programme notes for the Barbican Total Immersion day, 17 January 2009.

[8] This is Griffiths' summary for the programme for the Total Immersion day at the Barbican, 17 January 2009.

[9] Philip Hensher, 'Stockhausen for ever,' *The Guardian*, 30 October 2008.

[10] Quoted in the Stockhausen Proms 20 and 21 programme, 2 August 2008.

[11] See Hensher, 'Stockhausen for ever.'

[12] Quoted Robert Worby, 'Dreams Nightmares and Other Visions,' Stockhausen Proms programme.

[13] Quoted Kurtz, *Stockhausen*, p.19.

[14] See Jonathan Cott, *Stockhausen: Conversations with the Composer*, London: Robson Books, 1974, p.52.

[15] Cott, *Conversations with the Composer*, p.52.

[16] Griffiths, *Modern Music*, p.15.

[17] Griffiths, *Modern Music*, p.79.

[18] Kurtz, *Stockhausen*, p.130.

[19] Quoted Kurtz, *Stockhausen*, pp.162-3.

[20] See Cott, *Conversations with the Composer*, pp.119-20.

[21] Cott, *Conversations with the Composer*, p.26.

[22] See Kurtz, *Stockhausen*, pp.35-6.

[23] Cott, *Conversations with the Composer*, p.26.

[24] Cott, *Conversations with the Composer*, p.163.

[25] Cott, *Conversations with the Composer*, pp.176-81.

[26] Kurtz, *Stockhausen*, p.11.

[27] Cott, *Conversations with the Composer*, p.123.

[28] Cott, *Conversations with the Composer*, p.124.
[29] Quoted Kurtz, *Stockhausen*, p.24.
[30] For a recent very scholarly biography, already cited, see Heehs, *The Lives of Aurobindo*, and my review in the *Journal of the Royal Asiatic Society* (July 2011) Vol.21, Part 3, pp.383-6.
[31] Cott, *Conversations with the Composer*, p.132.
[32] Cott, *Conversations with the Composer*, p.122.
[33] Cott, *Conversations with the Composer*, p.26.
[34] Cott, *Conversations with the Composer*, p.125.
[35] Cott, *Conversations with the Composer*, p.126.
[36] Cott, *Conversations with the Composer*, pp.159-60.
[37] Cott, *Conversations with the Composer*, p.170.
[38] Cott, *Conversations with the Composer*, p.124.
[39] Cott, *Conversations with the Composer*, p.126.
[40] Cott, *Conversations with the Composer*, p.172.
[41] Kurtz, *Stockhausen*, p.199.
[42] Quoted Kurtz, *Stockhausen*, p.199.
[43] Griffiths, *Modern Music*, pp.38-41.
[44] Griffiths, *Modern Music*, p.43.
[45] Kurtz, *Stockhausen*, p.41.
[46] Quoted Kurtz, *Stockhausen*, p.49.
[47] Kurtz, *Stockhausen*, p.92.
[48] Stockhausen Proms programme.
[49] *The Observer*, 10 August 2008.
[50] Griffiths, *Modern Music*, p.157.
[51] Quoted Griffiths, *Modern Music*, p.162.
[52] Quoted Kurtz, *Stockhausen*, p.141.
[53] Griffiths, *Modern Music*, p.189.
[54] Cott, *Conversations with the Composer*, pp.23-4.
[55] Quoted Kurtz, *Stockhausen*, p.156.
[56] Stockhausen Proms programme.
[57] Quoted Stockhausen Proms programme.
[58] Quoted Kurtz, *Stockhausen*, p.176.
[59] *The Observer*, 10 August 2008.
[60] Griffiths, *Modern Music*, pp.226-7.
[61] Cott, *Conversations with the Composer*, p.43.
[62] Quoted Griffiths, *Modern Music*, p.224.
[63] Cott, *Conversations with the Composer*, p.46.

[64] Quoted in Total Immersion, translated by Suzanne Stephens.

[65] Paul Griffiths in notes for Total Immersion, pp.20-2.

[66] Here I am indebted to lectures given by Markus Bendur and Ivana Medic at the Total Immersion day at the Barbican.

[67] Quoted Kurtz, *Stockhausen*, p.228.

[68] Griffiths, *Modern Music*, p.326.

[69] Kurtz, *Stockhausen*, pp.222-3.

[70] Quoted in Wikipedia entry on Stockhausen.

[71] Griffiths, *Modern Music*, p.327.

[72] Anthony Holden, *The Observer*, 10 August 2010.

[73] The Stockhausen Proms programme, p.11.

12. *Hans Werner Henze*

I struggled to connect the frail, avuncular figure I saw at the Barbican Total Immersion day, 16 January 2010 and at the subsequent performances of *Phaedra* and *Elegy for Young Lovers* with the rebellious and highly charged younger Henze. Here was the outcast come in from the cold. And given his engagement with revolutionary politics he does not seem a natural for this project. We have already seen how Henze and Stockhausen diverged, though Paul Griffiths suggested at the Total Immersion event that they are interdependent: you could not have the one without the other. Even so, Henze is still seen as a traitor to modernism, 'someone who turned down the chance to effect a deep cultural cleansing in music in favour of more immediate political and allegorical gains.'[1] It is true Henze broke from Darmstadt – he always claimed he'd never joined the club – and reengaged with 19th century Austro-German romanticism: 'his decisive if still uneasy rapprochement,' as Griffiths sees it.[2] Ian Bostridge, who sang the role of the dog in his recent *Immolazione,* sees his music 'as deeply romantic. It swings between heavy textures and lighter chromatic complex lines (fiendishly difficult to sing) and passages of incredible transparency and simplicity.'[3] And certainly Henze seems a world apart from the surreal spirituality of Stockhausen. Should we, by way of contrast, see him as above all a lyricist and sensualist, Simon Rattle's viewpoint, or as 'an impassioned humanist,' Tom Service's?[4] But this would be seriously to misread Henze's vision. True, few composers in the 20th century have done so much to reach out to and express the plight of the oppressed. But equally, he inhabits the borderline between reality and myth: myths which 'show mortals partaking in divinity, with the capacity to change the world and to recalibrate its relationship with the heavens.'[5] Myths are a crucial means by which a secular culture communicates with the divine. Henze lived beside the mythical. His home was near to the shore of Lake Nemi, a volcanic crater where there was once a shrine to the goddess Diana and which was the inspiration for James Frazer's *The Golden Bough*. Henze's this-worldly spirituality is a foil to Stockhausen's would be other-worldly.

Family and Background

Henze has written the richest of all autobiographies of 20[6]th century composers and there seems no reason not to use it as a biographical source. How did he become an outcast?

Henze's relationship with his father was evidently Oedipal. Franz Henze, born 1898, 'a thin bespectacled man,' was a fearsome patriarch. Wounded at Verdun, here was another itinerant primary school teacher, in time employed at a progressive school in Bielfeld: its Headmaster was to be imprisoned by the Nazis 1933-45 for Marxist sympathies. His father saw fit to join the Nazi party, his being exposed in the local press as 'this man buys from Jews' – he had bought nappies from a Jewish haberdashery – another good reason to rehabilitate himself. His son conceded this change of heart 'was undoubtedly due as much for fear of livelihood as it was to intimidation.'[7] But he became thoroughly Nazified. Interestingly, though, his own mother was a supporter of the anti-Nazi Protestant pastor, Martin Niemoller. In 1943 he volunteered for the Army: Henze saw this as an unforgivable dereliction of his duty to stay behind and defend the family. The fact that his father was an accordionist and once played the viola in the Bielefeld Chamber Orchestra did nothing to improve their relationship. Suspecting him of homosexual tendencies his father had threatened to send him to a music school run by the Waffen SS, to make a man of him. The last time they met he poured scorn on some of his son's early compositions as philo-semitic: three months later he met his death in 1945 on the Eastern front. Subsequently Henze dreamt of his father's return but as a broken man.

His mother, Greta Geldmacher, born 1907, came from a mining family in the Ruhr; she herself was a short-hand typist before her marriage. Clearly she had loved her husband and never gave up hope he would return from the war. Henze's was to be a loving and lasting relationship with his mother. She accommodated his homosexuality, though always struggled to understand his music. She visited him in Italy, took to his life-time partner, Fausto: there was to be none of that tension between mother and son as with Christopher Isherwood and his mother and her snobbish attitude to his working class boyfriend, Heinz. Henze believed his mother to be proud of his being a composer: listening to his music on the radio she would say: 'listen, it is my boy's music.'[8] She died of cancer on New Year's Day 1976: 'the sight of my poor dead mother is etched on my memory for ever.' 'It is an archetypal feeling of loss and irretrievability, mixed with remorse and regret, that opens up the individual consciousness like a vast gaping wound, a volcanic crater like the end of the world.'[9] His mother's love was one mitigating factor in his intense sense of revulsion from his German background.

He was born 1 July 1926 in Gütersloh, Westphalia, eldest child of six. One leg was shorter than the other, he had a squint, he was forced to be right-handed: 'it may well be that the reason for life-long attempts to achieve perfection as an artist lies in those physical defects and personal accidents and illnesses.'[10] He had a foul temper.

His was a direct exposure to the evil of Nazism. Possibly his first sense of what it was to be growing up under Nazism was through his joining the Hitler Youth and no longer being taught religion: he had to give up his confirmation classes. 'With the passing of years,' Henze reflected, 'we children came to regard these developments, including our own parents estrangement, like a daily dose of poison. In the end we forgot what it was to laugh.'[11] Then living in the town of Bunde, he witnessed Kristalnacht: 'we all pretended nothing had happened.'[12] He saw emaciated Russian POW's. By 1943 he knew about the death camps. In January 1944 he was called up to do three month pre-military service and dispatched to Poland; subjection to endless square-bashing by sergeant-majors would never be forgiven. There followed a proper call-up to the Seeckt barracks at Magdeburg. He was trained as a radio operator in a Panzer division and, indeed, became a skilful cryptographer. Might his unit have been transferred to Berlin to back up the July bomb plot? Weirdly he became part of a film unit making propaganda documentaries on the Eastern front. He witnessed an officer being blown apart during a fake exercise. He helped in clear-up operations after bombing raids, sorting out dead bodies: he was in Dresden the day after the raid. One memory was of a major raid on Berlin: 'I shall never forget the impression left of that night of bombing when the city's zoo was hit, and reptiles, elephants and beasts of prey broke out and roamed through the burning metropolis. It was just like Sodom and Gomorrah.'[13] At the end, to escape capture by the Americans, he went on a long retreat into North Germany and Denmark, before ending up himself a POW in Jutland. He was only released in August 1945.

In all, it was an experience of Nazi Germany that left him desperately ashamed of his country and its culture: 'for me German art – especially the middle-class nationalistic art of the nineteenth and early twentieth centuries – became insufferable and suspect.' 'Ever since I have felt ashamed of our country and of my fellow Germans and of our people.'[14]

Even then he was the rebel. A school friend and he had gained access to the so-called Poison Cabinet in the Bielefeld Public Library: 'we lived completely bound up in the world of forbidden pleasure.'[15] There they found all that literature banned by the Nazis, Stefan Zweig, Thomas and Heinrich Mann, Bertolt Brecht. In Magdeburg barracks he was part of a secret anti-military club. How far was his rebelliousness informed by his sexuality?

Sexuality

Henze grew up under a Nazi regime that drastically increased legal persecution of homosexuality under Paragraph 175 of the 1871 Penal Code. Magnus Hirschfeld's campaign to reform the law had foundered in the dying days of Weimar. A kiss, even an embrace, between men was now criminalised. A 1935 decree introduced compulsory sterilisation for homosexuals as one group amongst other 'degenerates.' How many homosexuals died in concentration camps? 50,000 were convicted of homosexual offences under the regime. It is estimated 'tens of thousands' ended up in the camps. Paragraph 175 was not abolished in West Germany till 1969, in East Germany – in fact a more tolerant state – in 1968.[16] Henze's father believed 'people like that' should be sent to concentration camps.

It took time for Henze to recognize his homosexuality. He felt insecure, knew he was not heterosexual, with women only attractive as 'people not as objects of desire,' and felt he was one of a minority. Looking back at the post-war years, 'there wasn't a man in sight who might have engaged my interest.[17] In fact he had felt a strong homo-erotic attraction for French POW's he saw in Dunne: 'I had never seen such beauty in a fellow human being.'[18] Did his music from the outset seek 'to recapture the unattainable ideals of beauty that existed in classical Greece'?[19] But then it all fell into place with his first date, 25 August 1948 with the ballet dancer Heinz Poll: 'I suddenly knew which my true home was, knew where I belonged, in whose society I would feel at ease and in whose I would not. I had become a human being, become a man. For the first time in my life I was truly happy.' But the affair was not to last: it gave way to 'a kind of cold-hearted promiscuity that I had started to feel more and more.'[20] 'I felt an insane thirst for life, yet for all my sociability, still felt a sense of desolation that nothing could console.'[21] His next affair was with the actor, Bohnet Folker, whom he met in Berlin in 1959, though they did not live together. At one stage his private fed directly into his music.

In searching how to give expression to Dionysiac passion for his opera *The Bassarids*, via a chance encounter in a bar on the Via Veneto in Rome, he was to discover the tempestuous love, that jealousy – 'from tender veneration to a very real longing for death' – feelings, in short, that had to be depicted in every bar of the opera.[22]

And then he met the 21 year old Fausto Moroni, his lifetime partner. They were to become 'two utterly inseparable friends.' He 'looked like the son of a Byzantine prince as depicted in a Ravenna mosaic or a maritime adventurer.' In fact, he was the son of a viticulturist and olive-growing peasant: there is a moving account of his death in the arms of his son. Henze cleverly drew Fausto into his life as overseer of building his new house, La Leprara, in Marino. He had to give up a career as an art dealer to wrap himself around all Henze's domestic and business needs.[23] They travelled everywhere together. Theirs was an exceptional mutual empathy: 'we try to ward off evil and hold it at bay through general attentiveness.'[24] But this did not prevent their both suffering from depression and Henze, who drove himself exceptionally hard, from frequent breakdowns.

Nor did it pre-empt other affairs. In 1977 there was an encounter in Amsterdam which 'overwhelmed Henze like some terrible disaster or natural catastrophe'[25] and, by April 1978, drove him into the arms of the Rome based psychiatrist, Michele Rossi: 'it needed a surgeon's knife to achieve the end.'[26] It was a professional relationship that lasted till Rossi's death in June 1981.

There was at least one very close female friendship, with the Slovene poet, (though from Austrian Carinthia), Ingeborg Bachmann. They met in Gottingen on October 1952. The impact of her reading her poetry in 'a hesitant, extraordinary bashful way as though whispering to herself' was lasting. At first, to endear himself he played the fool, but soon 'an elective affinity' took over. She joined him on Ischia, and they lived together in Naples. She attended all his first nights,

invariably exotically garbed. At the premiere of *Ondine* at
Covent Garden 27 October 1958 'she seemed to me the most
beautiful person in the world.'[27] She left him in 1959 to live
with Max Frisch. In September 1973 she was horrifically
burnt in her flat in Rome, failed to recover, and died in
hospital 17 October. Henze, who saw her at the last, realised
the scale of the disaster, and felt 'indescribable despair.'[28]

In the same way as Francis Poulenc, his homosexuality defined Henze. But convergence between his private life and
his music, as in Poulenc's opera, *Dialogue with the Carmelites,* with one exception already mentioned, is hard to
find. For all his identification with the gay liberation movement, we have to look elsewhere in his radical politics to
discover how politics came to shape so much of his music.

Politics and Music

Exorcising the experience of Nazi Germany initially usurped
the role of the political. Only in 1954 did an Italian communist introduce him to the ideas of Gramsci. Not until 1965,
when Ingeborg got him to read Herbert Marcuse's *Eros and
Civilisation* and Frantz Fanon's *The Wretched of the Earth,*
did he recognize how 'thoughtlessly and egocentrically' he
had lived his life': 'there were things in the world I now
realized which were more important than myself.'[29] In 1967
in America he engaged with the anti- Vietnam war protest:
'for the first time I saw and understood some of the links
between imperialist policies and the unregulated nature of
capital.' He visited Harlem and wholly identified with the
blacks: 'I prefer to be where there are no whites.'[30] He first
read the Communist manifesto in Baalbek in April 1968: 'I
was deeply shocked and thrown into a state of turmoil.'[31]

So he became an active presence in the revolutionary politics
of 1968. Through Hans Magnus Enzenberger he had met the
New Left leader, Rudi Dutschke. He had 'something of a
Protestant monk about him,' another Alyosha Karamazov,

and became a special friend. 'Seized not to say overwhelmed by joy in solidarity,' [32] he played a part in the Vietnam Conference in Berlin. Following the attempted assassination of Dutschke he joined the deputation to German Radio, insisting on the right of the extra-parliamentary opposition to broadcast: 'was I really awake or dreaming?'[33] Dutschke was to recuperate in Henze's house in Marino, inevitably attracting unwelcome press attention. Even so, Henze had to face the charge that he was no more than 'a champagne socialist.' Was it to refute this accusation that he turned to Cuba?

Henze's engagement with Castro's Cuba was poorly timed. So much had been invested by the European Left in the Cuban revolution. It had coincided with the anti-war protest, civil rights movement, decolonisation: if revolution could not succeed here, where else? And it had all seemed so promising, especially in the mass literacy campaign of 1962. But Castro had increasingly gravitated into the Soviet sphere, partly for economic reasons – Soviet Russia bought up most of Cuba's sugar – partly for geo-political Cold War reasons, partly because Castro had in fact no clear ideological agenda and found one in the Soviet Union: as Richard Gott puts it, 'Cuba was to subject itself to a make-over in the Soviet image.'[34] On 21 August 1968 Castro denounced the Dubcek reform programme and endorsed the Soviet occupation of Prague. Through an invitation engineered by Enzenberger, Henze arrived in Havana 21 March 1969.

Henze sensed the danger from the outset. He was of course too much the romantic individualist not to recognise the threat to the arts from collectivism: 'there could be nothing more terrible,' he saw, 'than a life or a world without the deviant element.'[35] He was appalled by the harassment and eventual imprisonment of the dissident poet, Heberto Pedilla. Cuba, he sensed, was falling foul of a Stasi regime. Even so, Cuba had seized his imagination and on his return in 1970 he threw himself as an agricultural worker into Castro's mad scheme to raise sugar production between November 1969 and July 1970 to an unprecedented 10 million tons. 'The

battle for sugar' was Castro's way of reincarnating 'revolutionary spontaneity.' In his 6th Symphony Henze reluctantly
recognised that for all his immersion in Cuba he was no
revolutionary and that his 'spiritual homeland' was western,
indeed 'bourgeois' music.[36]

But Henze had sought an answer the question, what is
revolutionary music? One reply was his oratorio *The Raft of
the Medusa*, subject of a scandalous première in Hamburg
April 1968. It was inspired by Gericault's painting and by
Che Guevara's *Socialism and the New Man*. Henze identified
Guevara, seen as an untarnished hero, with the mulatto Jean-
Charles, central figure in the painting and mythic symbol of
oppressed black people. Guevara lost his life in Bolivia 10
October 1967 and the piece became a Requiem. At the prem-
ière, with Dietrich Fischer-Dieskau cast as Jean-Charles, a
red flag had been attached to the conductor's podium, the
orchestra refused to play and pandemonium broke out: the
performance had to be abandoned. Tapes were later played in
Cuba. Henze was held in disgrace in Germany for ten years.
Another work even more directly inspired by Cuba was *El
Cimarron*, based on the legendary former slave and rebel
Esteban Montejo. Benjamin Britten had offered Aldeburgh
as a venue and there it was premiered 22 June 1970. Its
message was 'when and in what circumstances will we be
able to live in harmony with the world?'[37]

Then came his most overtly political work, *Voices,* a setting
of 22 protest poems, premiered at the Queen Elizabeth Hall,
4 January 1974. It was sung at the Barbican event. It begins
with a poem by Heberto Pedilla, one reflecting Henze's own
position, of poets being on the sidelines:

> *They go and shut the door to write alone*
> *When suddenly the wood cracks*
> *The wind sends them to perdition*

Here is a body of poems expressing the dissent of the 60's
and 70's and Guy Dammann wondered if the Barbican

audience, given 'the more general irony of leftist sensibilities today,' would share their anger. I was struck by the way the music fitted the words and the unobtrusive nature of the 15-strong orchestra. But Henze now recognized his political detachment as an intellectual and the need to seek inspiration from elsewhere.

Henze and Stockhausen

How, Henze puzzled, could a composer who saw himself as 'a messenger of a higher spirituality' be so hostile? Always the rebel, Henze was bound to reject the dogmas of Darmstadt. Listening to *Kontakte* and *Momente* at the International Society for New Music in Cologne in June 1959 he began to have doubts: here was new music 'fit as a fiddle and with all systems firing.' He admired Stockhausen's radical new departures, as well as 'an organistic hypnosis ... a mood of almost religious devotion.'[38]

Kontakte was played at the Stockhausen prom. Here is electronic music played on quite crude equipment, together with a piano and percussion. I can see why Henze experienced it as religious. One hears a Tibetan Tantric music, summoning up images of those carvings of demons outside Tibetan temples. I also heard wolves from the steppes, Joseph Beuys's territory. Pianist and percussionist clung to one another to survive. But can one hope to survive against such hostile forces? It was a sort of anti-Messiaen. Then came a human voice, but on whose side? In the end the presence of evil withdrew but this was a frightening experience.

So how different a trajectory was Henze's music to take? Bach and Mozart had made a huge early impression. He usually plays Bach at the beginning of the day to put himself in the right frame of mind for composition: in Mozart he heard 'a new form of truth – a truth that pays no heed to the Zeitgeist and that triumphs over death itself.'[39] At the Heidelberg Institute of Evangelical Music in 1946 he knew it was all up to him to fashion his own music. Once he'd put serialism and Darmstadt behind him, he knew he was still a novice. His had to be a music 'to do with the truth – inner truth – one's own private truth.'[40] 'My main concern was a spiritual examination of the different forms of German, English and Italian Romanticism.'[41] He justified dissonance: 'dissonance is not an empirical fact of life but an expression of pain, of the absence of beauty.' Looking back at his music in 1991 he reflected: 'my music has an emotional dimension, an emotional timelessness.' But he also admits to its artificiality, 'its dealing with illusion and utopias.'[42] Quite how this incorporated the spiritual will now have to be explored.

Myth

Henze had got to know Auden and Chester Kallman on Ischia in 1950 and they became good friends. In 1959 he asked Auden to write a libretto, 'a psychological drama, a chamber drama that could deal in the most general way with questions of guilt and atonement.'[43] Initially Auden proposed a reworking of the myth of Daphnis and Chloe but eventually came up with a story along the lines of his earlier play *The Ascent of F6*. It tells of a poet who each year seeks inspiration from a visionary old woman, Hilda Meck, whose fiancée had died on the Hammerhorn forty years ago, and, like a modern Penelope, awaits his return. So in part it is a reworking of myth. The poet, Gregor Mittenhofer, conspires to send two young lovers to their death on the mountain. Auden had Yeats in mind as the poet.[44] Henze insisted that these were all ordinary mortals, in no way superhuman. It was premiered at the Schwetzingen Festival, 18 May 1961.

It was Auden who proposed an opera based on Euripides's *The Bacchae,* if to take its name from Aeschylus's missing *Bassarids* (those who wear fox skins). It is the story of the way the god Dionysus 'slowly, insinuatingly, insidiously and finally with the most terrible brutality'[45] murders Pentheus. This is a reworking of myth *in extremis*. Henze drew on a personal love affair to express the Dionysiac. The shape of the Mahlerian Symphony influenced its form. It was premiered at the Salzburg Festival 6 August 1966. Griffiths sees it as 'the culmination of the sensuous unashamedly nostalgic style Henze had pursued since moving to Italy a decade ago.'[46]

In his 14th opera *Phaedra*, Henze reworks the story of Theseus, Phaedra and Hippolytus. Theseus has just slain the Minotaur. Phaedra falls guiltily in love with her step-son, Hipploytus. In the manner of Greek myth the gods participate; Aphrodite, herself in love with Hippolytus, tries to protect Phaedra from her suicidal tendencies, Artemis, goddess of the hunt, siding with Hippolytus, and he only has eyes for her. Artemis is sung by a counter-tenor and this can suggest a gay relationship and certainly in the production I saw they winked at one another.[47] Hippolytus only feels physical revulsion for his step-mother and, out of revenge, she accuses him of rape and Theseus orders his death. Poseidon allows the Minotoaur to rise up from the sea and Hippolytus and his horses are dragged onto the rocks and to his death.

Artemis restores him to life only to lock him up in a cage on the shore of Lake Nemi. Phaedra and Aphrodite claim him for the Underworld and Phaedra tries once again to seduce him. Meanwhile Artemis, for his safe keeping, has placed him in a cave. Hippolytus no longer knows who he is, staring at his reflection in the lake. In the end Artemis wins out and he becomes Lord of the Forest. Is there a hidden agenda in Henze's version of the story, of a gay man's rejection of female sexuality?

Twice over the opera is highly personal. It is set in his immediate environment, 'an ethereal landscape, that seems poised between myth and reality.' And, uncannily, between composing the first and second acts, between Hippolytus's death and resurrection, Henze had fallen into a two month coma in 2005: 'I stopped eating and I stopped speaking.' Friends assumed he had died and came for his funeral. 'And then one morning I just stood up.' Does the opera convey that near-death experience, Henze's own visit to the Underworld?[48]

Not all were won over. Michael Tanner saw the libretto as 'wordy, abstract, pretentious, it seemed hardly to relate to the complicated tale of illicit passion between Phaedra and Hippolytus: everyone seemed interested only in making world-historical pronouncements.' It all reminded him of Michael Tippett at his garrulous and vacuous worst.[49]

Requiems

Henze was not religious. Both his parents were and he had been brought up Protestant – 'Protestant sermons somehow always seem more like a warning or a reprimand'[50] – but, once the Nazi regime had banned religious instruction, he never returned to the faith. He was highly introspective – 'I wanted to build a citadel within myself'[51] – and seemed always to suffer from some form of existential anxiety. If he did not share Stockhausen's obsessive interest in New Age Spirituality, the experience of visiting Japan in late 1966 for a performance of *Elegy for Young Lovers* left a lasting impression. Noh theatre conveyed a different sense of time. His was 'an almost religious desire' to return to such an alternative culture, 'to disappear prematurely and fade away in a kind of earthly paradise.'[52] This ambivalence about religion and spirituality is conveyed in his two requiems, one to mourn the loss of a friend, the other his life-time partner.

Michael Vyner, Director of the London Sinfonietta, had always worked closely with Henze. Henze saw the requiem as 'a secular, multi-cultural piece,' one that mourned not only a particular premature and very painful death, but 'also speaks of other pains, of abandonment, of the death of friendship, of breaches of faith and trust, of loneliness and also of (the vain) hope of peace, peace of mind, calm and mental equilibrium.' It expressed a wish to follow friends to a beyond 'which in all likelihood does not exist, at least not for the eyes of us poor mortals,' 'the speechless fear of eternal darkness, of nothingness and of the end to all existence.'[53] He saw it as nine 'sacred concertos' and his own 'highly personal approach to the Catholic liturgy.'[54] The Dies Irae might also be the worst day in a person's life, the Ave Verum a medieval German or Baconesque *Pieta.* More controversially, the Tuba Mirum drew on the Leni Riefenstahl Nuremberg marches, 'the trumpeters exude crass stupidity in the moronic tonality of conformists and fellow-travellers.' The language of these monsters, he fears, is still with us. In the Sanctus 'the attendant mood is that of a Protestant Whitsun Festival or Catholic Epiphany or some other manifestation of divine or artistic comfort that involves the transcendent presence of archangels and cherubim.'[55]

The Requiem was first performed in its entirety by the Ensemble Modern in the Philharmonic Hall, Cologne, 24 February 1993, and a film of that performance was shown at the Barbican event. Häken Hardenberger was the trumpet soloist. Listening to it I reflected that it goes to show how a non-believer can write sacred music. The music circles around the divine in an often aggressive way and is highly adventurous. All kinds of liberties are taken with the Catholic mass and at times it teeters on the brink of a Black mass. Yet Henze steers it towards an ending which brings both life and death into its grasp.

Shortly after Henze's miraculous recovery from his coma Fausto died. Henze wrote a twenty minute Eulogy, to give it its full name, *Elogiuim mecum amatissimi amici nunc remoti* (Musical Eulogy for a Most Beloved Friend Now Departed). It is a setting of contemporary Latin poetry by Franco Serpa, Latin being seen as a sacred language: 'at once monumental and poignantly immediate in honouring his departed companion.' The singing of the chorus moves between lamentation and rage, the charm of memory, a string quartet leading into an 'in paradisum.' Here was Henze's attempt to imitate the way the gods gave their former lovers immortality.[56] It was 'a sacred cantata, a restrained Stravinsky-like work, allowing the audience to conjure their own private images of loss.'[57] As Henze put it: 'the loss that I've suffered is very strong, and it makes my whole life, the whole world, seem quite different from what I thought it was.'[58]

Whether Henze's politically inspired music matches the humanist spirituality claimed in this project for the late Symphonies of Prokofiev and Shostakovich is open to question. In all his music he is asking metaphysical questions and this is an aspect of transcendence. In his later work, through his reworking of myth, he more obviously crosses into the spiritual, though he never loses an abrasive secular tone. Maybe of all the composers studied, and he comes across as one of the most engaging, his is the most ambiguous approach to the divine.

Notes

[1] Guy Dammann , 'We're not out of the woods yet,' *TLS*, 29 January 2010.

[2] Griffiths, *Modern Music*, 2010, p.195.

[3] *The Guardian*, 15 December 2009.

[4] Tom Service, 'A Matter of Life and Death,' *The Guardian*, 15 December 2009.

[5] Dammann.

[6] Hans Werner Henze, *Bohemian Fifths: An Autobiography*, translated by Stewart Spencer, London: Faber and Faber, 1998.

[7] Henze, *Bohemian Fifths*, p.8.

[8] Henze, *Bohemian Fifths*, p.216.

[9] Henze, *Bohemian Fifths*, p.345.

[10] Henze, *Bohemian Fifths*, p.4.

[11] Henze, *Bohemian Fifths*, p.11.

[12] Henze, *Bohemian Fifths*, p.20.

[13] Henze, *Bohemian Fifths*, p.44.

[14] Henze, *Bohemian Fifths*, p.53.

[15] Henze, *Bohemian Fifths*, p.26.

[16] Heinz Heger, *The Men with the Pink Triangle*, London: Gay Men's Press, 1980.

[17] Henze, *Bohemian Fifths*, p.64.

[18] Henze, *Bohemian Fifths*, p.12.

[19] Henze, *Bohemian Fifths*, p .5.

[20] Henze, *Bohemian Fifths*, p.87.

[21] Henze, *Bohemian Fifths*, p.169.

[22] Henze, *Bohemian Fifths*, p.204.

[23] See Henze, *Bohemian Fifths*, p.211.

[24] Henze, *Bohemian Fifths*, p.461.

[25] Henze, *Bohemian Fifths*, p.368.

[26] Henze, *Bohemian Fifths*, p.375.

[27] Henze, *Bohemian Fifths*, p.154.

[28] Henze, *Bohemian Fifths*, p.326.

[29] Henze, *Bohemian Fifths*, p.203.

[30] Henze, *Bohemian Fifths*, p.228.

[31] Henze, *Bohemian Fifths*, p.238.

[32] Henze, *Bohemian Fifths*, p.237.

[33] Henze, *Bohemian Fifths*, p.238.

[34] Richard Gott, *Cuba: A New History*, New Haven and London: Yale University Press, 2004, p.235. I am following his analysis here.

[35] Henze, *Bohemian Fifths*, p.257.

[36] Henze, *Bohemian Fifths*, p.264.

[37] Henze, *Bohemian Fifths*, p.259.

[38] Henze, *Bohemian Fifths*, p.161.

[39] Henze, *Bohemian Fifths*, p.23.

[40] Henze, *Bohemian Fifths*, p.121.

[41] Henze, *Bohemian Fifths*, p.148.

[42] Henze, *Bohemian Fifths*, pp.55-7.

[43] Henze, *Bohemian Fifths*, p.164.

[44] See Adrian Mourby, 'The Monster Within.' Programme notes for *Elegy for Young Lovers*, Young Vic, April 2010.

[45] Henze, *Bohemian Fifths*, p.207.

[46] Griffiths, *Modern Music*, p.192.

[47] The Barbican, 17 January 2010.

312

[48] See Tom Service, 'A Matter of Life and Death,' *The Guardian*, 15 December 2009.
[49] Michael Tanner, Distorted account, *The Spectator*, 6 February 2010.
[50] Henze, *Bohemian Fifths*, p.27.
[51] Henze, *Bohemian Fifths*, p.20.
[52] Henze, *Bohemian Fifths*, p.236.
[53] Henze, *Bohemian Fifths*, p.471.
[54] Henze, *Bohemian Fifths*, p.57.
[55] Henze, *Bohemian Fifths*, pp.469-71.
[56] See Paul Griffiths's notes in the programme for the Total Immersion event.
[57] Guy Dammann.
[58] Quoted Tom Service.

Epilogue

Karlheinz Stockhausen

Epilogue

Does this exploration of music, politics and the spiritual in 20th century continental Europe lead to any generalisation or conclusion? Or, more persuasively, should we see each composer as unique and with their own very personal expression of the spiritual?

An American Comparison

Robert Wuthnow interviewed a number of creative artists, poets, painters, dancers, sculptors, many of whom emerged from the New Age spirituality of the 1960's, and all of whom saw the spiritual as the source of their art. The tension between religion and spirituality is addressed: 'to a striking degree contemporary artists speak more comfortably about spirituality than about organized religion.'[1] For many, experiencing religion in childhood and personal trauma proved the catalyst for a spiritual quest. Some alternatively valued religion as a way of focussing 'the diffuse power inherent in spirituality.' One Presbyterian musician believed that music 'reinforced the sense of being created by a creative God.'[2] Indeed, insistence by many on the need for some kind of meditative practice, even if this may take up no more than a few minutes a day, points to a continuing link between religion and spirituality: 'practice means cultivating one's relationships with God.'[3] Wuthnow discovered 'for some the sheer rhythm of their daily routine brings them closer to the essence of their being.'[4] And Wuthnow reflects, 'if theology is the practice of drawing connections between religious truth and contemporary cultural concerns, then artists may indeed be functioning as theologians.'[5]

But these are artists who are usually breaking away from organized religion. Wuthnow recognises a risk, however, in their indebtedness to New Age spirituality. 'A society rooted in market transactions encourages its members,' he reflects, 'to shop for spirituality, even if the result is a pastiche of beliefs and practises purchased from a variety of spiritual vendors.' But he exonerates the artists he has met 'from such casual spiritual shopping.'[6] Can one situate their spiritual quest within the spectrum of this-worldly and other-world-ly? Certainly a preoccupation with a this-worldly concerns many. As one artist put it: 'it's impossible to return to some Edenic state of bliss. There's no going back. We're in the position of being nature's caretaker whether we like it or not.'[7] Spirituality directs people 'to the times in which they live and not just what is happening inside themselves or at the edge of the universe.'[8] Some see their work as about Mystery. Others focus on Myth.: 'Myth for me is a psycho-logical, poetic way of perceiving and articulating reality. But it's not a lie – it's a way of speaking about the truth.'[9] Maybe the balance tilts slightly towards the other-worldly: 'in the final analysis,' Wuthnow summarises, 'these artists, musi-cians, sculptors and painters are less concerned with identi-fying aspects of the social world about which to be optimistic or pessimistic than they are in providing small experiences of transcendence that in themselves become reasons for hope.'[10]

Equally germane to this project is Wuthnow's observations on how American audiences respond to concerts. Some 32% felt they were exposed to something sacred. Was theirs a search for wholeness? 'The common element is that some-thing powerful emerges – an experience or insight that defies ready interpretation.'[11]

Usurping God

In claiming to express the divine, did composers take a fur-ther fatal step and usurp the role of God as creator? The inordinate claims made for the artist by the Romantic movement for the artist, Wagner to the fore, have much to answer for. Peter Conrad, in an awesome tome, has inter-preted western culture in terms of rival paradigms of the creator God of Genesis and the Promethean legend of stealing fire from the Gods, source of human creativity. Conrad favours Prometheus, but then, as a committed Darwinist and secular humanist, he is *parti pris*: 'I find it easier to believe in human creators than in their divine prototype; my lack of religious faith is contradicted by a faith in art.'[12] Schopenhauer had seen music as the conduit for the Divine, in his language, the Will. But what if, as Nietzsche pronounced, God was dead? As Conrad graphically puts it, 'artists clustered round God's sick-bed like impatient heirs. As soon as the announcement of his death was made, the legatees assumed power.'[13]

One such legatee in Conrad's book was Gustav Mahler. In his 5th Symphony he wrote music to reflect cosmic creation, wondering what his audience would make 'at the chaos, perpetually giving birth to a new world, which is destroyed at the next moment.'[14] Conrad has an extraordinary account of how Mahler used the 9th century pentecostal hymn *Veni Creator Spiritus* in his 8th Symphony: 'the "spiritus creator" took hold of me and shook me and drove me on.' But Mahler had taken on Nietzsche's interpretation of the hymn, its wrongfully attributing creativity to God, a creativity man is seen as already possessing. Mahler linked this version to the Faust of Goethe's imagination, the heavenwards striving human will. When Alma Mahler heard the symphony, she could well see why Mahler identified himself with the demiurge.[15]

Another legatee was Arnold Schoenberg. He was convinced his 12 note scale contained the revealed truth: 'the arrays of chosen tones often seem to be written on the air in letters of flame,' 'he had reconfigured the universe.' In a lecture given in 1943 he saw the composer 'as an absolute originator, who demonstrates what the process of genesis really means.'[16] Admittedly, he had the humility to leave *Moses und Aron* unfinished, as he did not believe he could find the music to express the words Moses used to draw water from the rock: 'its curtailment marks a tragic break between God and man, or between divine creation and its human mimicry.'[17] In

1915 Schoenberg had planned a vocal symphony in which, following God's funeral, art would take on God's work. It was inspired by Ernest Dowson's poem, based on Balzac's *Seraphita*, in which the poet contrives to adjust to Seraphita's visionary outlook. Balzac's mystical novel had exercised a profound influence on the Romantic imagination. Schoenberg himself shared Kandinsky's belief that art was born of catastrophe and that his own art was dredged from his unconscious: To quote Conrad, 'God was Schoenberg's surrogate, even his obliging deputy: in Freudian terms a buried and not censorious superego.' Was he, indeed, as he saw himself, the Supreme Commander? Alternatively, he identified with Christ, 'crippled by a burden of expiatory guilt that nevertheless he shouldered.'[18] In one of his last but unfinished pieces *Die Jacobsleiter*, intended as a contribution to a collective work by émigré composers in Los Angeles, entitled *The Genesis Suite,* the Archangel Gabriel encounters the artist as Prophet and Martyr, all this a reflection of Schoenberg's paranoia at being driven out of Berlin by the Nazis and ignored in California.[19]

There was of course no inherent connection between composers who sought to express the divine and such delusions of grandeur. Admittedly in this project both Scriabin and Stockhausen do seem to have succumbed to this syndrome. Stravinsky was wholly opposed. He attacked the atheist tendency as he saw it in modernism. He opposed its claims for the artist, seeing himself as 'a humble copyist,' an artisan at best. In submitting his own piece on Babel to *The Genesis Suite* he insisted 'the Divine should be illustrated in no way whatsoever. He is too great. Music should illustrate nothing whatsoever. Such is not its function.'[20] 'Creation,' he told Robert Craft in an interview in 1959, meant 'nothing' to him: 'Only God can create.' He looked on Chaos as sin. The final bars of his short musical play *The Flood* 'briefly eavesdrop on the origins of art: music has returned to the sky from whence it came.'[21] And surely Messiaen, not mentioned in Conrad's book, would rightly have been horrified at any suggestion that he usurped the role of the divine in his sacred music.

Painting and Liminality

Can works of art access the divine in the same way as is claimed for music?

Certainly the iconic founders of Modernism believed this to be so. Both Piet Mondrian and Wassily Kandinsky read deeply into the writings of Theosophy and Anthroposophy and convinced themselves painting could directly express the divine. Mondrian joined a Theosophical Lodge 25 May 1909 and was in close touch with this occultist movement during his transition from naturalism to abstraction. In his monumental triptych *Evolution* (1909-11) three female figures represent the Theosophical idea of man's evolution from a low or materialistic stage to one of spirituality and higher insight. An interest in esoteric mathematics going the round of Dutch Theosophical circles rubbed off on Mondrian's emergent geometrical style. On moving to Paris in late 1911 he first rented a room from the French Theosophical Society. Influenced by Cubism, and a fascination with the skyline of Parisian buildings, Mondrian progressed to what he christened Neo-Plasticism. If too independent a spirit to tolerate the constraints Rudolph Steiner put on painting – he insisted on the discovery of the spiritual world through the natural – even as late as 1919 Mondrian told fellow abstractionist Theo van Doesberg: 'I got everything from Madame Blavatsky's *The Secret Doctrine*.'

Kandinsky was even closer to both Theosophy and Anthroposophy, closely read Annie Besant's and Charles Leadbeater's *Thought Forms* (1904) – proposing that thoughts through their astral vibrations acquired forms – attended Steiner's lecture in Berlin 28 October 1909 and went on to annotate closely his journal *Lucifer-Gnosis*. He shared Steiner's belief in the symbiosis of music and painting. (And

of course this lay behind his engagement with Schoenberg.)
Steiner's Christian writings – and he broke away from the
parent body of Theosophy in part through his privileging
Christianity as against eastern religions – had a special impact. Kandinsky favoured Russian Orthodoxy and its divine
service. He shared Steiner's sense of impending catastrophe
and believed that only in struggle lay any prospect of redemption, the triumph of spirit over matter. Here again he was at
one with Schoenberg. In this pre-war phase came those extraordinary Expressionist works, *Deluge, Last Judgement,
Horsemen of the Apocalypse.*

But it could be argued that up to this stage both painters were
at a point of transition between a this-worldly or phenomenal outlook and an other-worldly or noumenal, still on the
threshold, in a liminal position. Is their belief that they moved beyond the liminal to a direct expression of the divine
justified? Alternatively, does this attempt in fact weaken the
intensity of their art?

In Neo-Plasticism Mondrian believed he had escaped the
phenomenological world into one of abstraction, entirely
shaped by the imagination. But are we staring divinity in
the face in these cold geometrical paintings, and how do they
compare with his earlier paintings on the threshold? When
Kandinsky returned to Germany and the Bauhaus in 1923,
having been in Russia since 1914, his expressionist painting
had been profoundly modified by exposure to Malevich and
Constructivism. He now saw his 'concrete' painting – a
concept he preferred to abstract – as wholly conceived in the
mind and owing nothing to nature or the sentiments. He
sought to dematerialize the picture plane and create a sensation of indefinable space. So again, how do these cold and
aloof paintings compare with the extraordinary energy of his
pre-war? Even Kandinsky had his doubts and, out of a
lingering loyalty to Steiner, in the 1930's began to paint
zoological and biomorphic forms.

All this is to raise doubts as to whether the claims of Mondrian and Kandinsky to reach beyond the liminal are delusional. But is there an alternative and figurative route to expressing the spiritual? Compare Marc Chagall and Wassily Kandinsky. Both drew heavily on their Russian background, Chagall more in personal terms, on his childhood in Jewish Vitebsk and its Hasidic Judaism, Kandinsky more in terms of Russia's past and its mythology. Both Chagall and Kandinsky produced their best work in response to the threatening Apocalypse of the Great War and Revolution. Chagall had been equally exposed to Constructivism and Cubism but chose not to go along the path to abstraction and to remain loyal to his figurative style. His painting always possessed a universal archetypal quality, apparent in his painting on the plight of European Jewry and the Holocaust. Through his transformative genius he gave a new vitality to the iconography of the Crucifixion, Christ rearticulated as both wandering Jew and Chagall himself. A like exploration of the painting of Matisse could be made. Does this suggest that painting in its portraying the spiritual is at its strongest on the threshold of the divine?

In the end all this can but be a subjective judgement but it does raise a tantalising debate as to the respective claims of painting and music to gain direct access to the divine.[22]

Family Background and Sexuality

Family conflict seems little to have affected this cluster of composers. Scriabin's over protective upbringing accounts for his narcissism. Probably Messiaen's relationship with his depressed mother does something to explain the conflicted nature of his Tristan music. Certainly Henze's negative one with his father does much to explain his protest music.

Is the libido the source of creativity? Is its sublimation the source of spirituality? Claims for the libido as a dominant drive in creativity seem negated by the music of composers under the Soviet system. It is as if the libido is itself crippled by the intrusion of the totalitarian state and composers had to search elsewhere for inspiration. This lay in an intense humanism. The early music of Prokofiev is frankly erotic, but this was music composed in exile. And rather than the libido being sublimated by non-Soviet composers it seems rather to have played into a conflicted sexuality, as is demonstrated in Messiaen's Tristan music, the spiritual anguish to be found in Scriabin and above all in Poulenc.

Is homosexuality a special case? Scriabin showed homo-erotic tendencies and was probably bi-sexual, both Poulenc and Henze were gay. So varied are the needs and preferences of homosexuality it seems improbable that any generalisation can be made and certainly this project questions any essentialist link between it and music. Yet, as a phenomenon, it was widely persecuted in all regimes in the 20th century. France an exception though it was still frowned on and any expression in public harassed, and the Soviet Union went through a brief spell of legal toleration till this was swept away by Stalinism – and its repression can but add to the spiritual anguish expressed in the music of homosexual composers.

Politics and a this-Worldly Spirituality

Certainly in the so-called short 20th century, but really throughout, this was a century dominated by politics. And it is very hard to concur with recent statistical findings that this was not the most violent century ever. The intrusiveness of the totalitarian state, be it the Soviet model, or the Nazi that spread through Occupied Europe, drove composers ever more inward. The most common denominator of the spiritual is a search for meaningfulness and significance. Blocking off the expression of the religious, as was blatantly the case in Soviet Russia, intentional within the Nazi, narrowed the field of expression and necessitated a more secular expression of the spiritual. One exception within the Soviet system was

Poland, where the Catholic Church never lost its role in the public sphere and Polish composers of the Polish renaissance were able to draw on their faith. In time the dissident movement challenged the Soviet system.

Through the pressure of the political composers had to grapple with contemporary conflicts and this led to a kind of this-worldly spirituality. This is nor an easy concept to grasp. Possibly a comparison with another expression of this spirituality, in the life and philosophy of Gandhi, will be illustrative. Earlier interpretations of Gandhi saw his engagement with politics as a search for *moksha*, his personal way through to spiritual salvation and *nirvana*. But Anthony Parel has argued that Gandhi's was a re-evaluation of the Indian value system and that he saw in *artha,* politics and wealth, a set of values not to be eschewed but itself the means of salvation. It is an interpretation that very considerably raises the profile of a this-worldly spirituality.[23]

An Other-Worldly Spirituality

For the secular-minded this is an impossible concept. It seems so intangible. And I doubt if any amount of argument will alter the mind of the disbeliever.

But the question has been addressed: can music reach beyond the liminal and express the divine?

In Russia Scriabin set a benchmark for Maximalism, Taruskin's word for the other-worldly in music. A second generation of Soviet composers also sought to express the other-worldly, in Pärt's case, in a serene meditative way, in Schnittke's in something far more fractured and dissonant, in Gubaidulina's music almost frighteningly transcendental.

When freedom of expression was possible composers either fell back on a conventional expression of their faith, as was the case with Messiaen and Poulenc, or else broke away into new expressions of the spiritual, often inspired by New Age spirituality, as was the case with Stockhausen.

But there are controversial issues here. All along it has been argued that there is a tension between religion and spirituality. Of course there will be those who claim that the best forms of Theology embrace all expressions of the spiritual and the mystical. A number of doubts have here been raised about this claim. It has been argued that the claims of religion can be restrictive and act as a barrier to a more creative and freer expression of the spiritual. Organised religion has always distrusted its mystics. And there are several composers, such as Shostakovich, who have no truck with religion and yet we see them as expressing the spiritual. But there is also the risk that spirituality, unchecked by religion, will fall, as Jung warned, into the occult, and this is exemplified in the music of Scriabin and Stockhausen.

So does music express the transcendental? Barenboim has pointed to its essential ephemerality, its tragic nature.[24] Can we really sustain a case for its reaching beyond the liminal? Does the spiritual anyway lie beyond the music in the silence, as Sarah Maitland has claimed?[25] Or should we go for George Steiner's claim that all great art is informed by a Real Presence?

The true role of the spiritual in music, be it the humanist and this-worldly or transcendental and other-worldly, is to raise our awareness of the mystery of Being and strengthen our sense of ultimate purpose.

Notes

[1] Robert Wuthnow, *Creative Spirituality: The Way of the Artist*, Berkeley and Los Angeles: University of California

325

Press, 2001, p.77. I thank Ursula King for directing me towards this text.

[2] Wuthnow, *Creative Spirituality*, p.62.

[3] Wuthnow, *Creative Spirituality*, p.272.

[4] Wuthnow, *Creative Spirituality*, p.10.

[5] Wuthnow, *Creative Spirituality*, p.139.

[6] Wuthnow, *Creative Spirituality*, p.42.

[7] Quoted Wuthnow, *Creative Spirituality*, p.231.

[8] Wuthnow, *Creative Spirituality*, p.233.

[9] Quoted Wuthnow, *Creative Spirituality*, p.100.

[10] Wuthnow, *Creative Spirituality*, p.262.

[11] Wuthnow, *Creative Spirituality*, p.40.

[12] Conrad, *Creation*, p.7. See my review, 'Oversimplifying the Paradigms,' in *Blunter Edge 1*, June 2008, pp.11-14.

[13] Conrad, p.473.

[14] Quoted Conrad, p.265.

[15] See Conrad, pp.115-17.

[16] Conrad, p.493.

[17] Conrad, p.98.

[18] Conrad, p.497.

[19] See Conrad, pp.493-502.

[20] Quoted Conrad, p.502.

[21] Conrad, pp.502-7.

[22] This commentary on painting has been rehearsed in Roy Oxlade's journal: 'See Liminality: Art and the Spiritual,' *Blunt Edge 4*, April 2004, pp.7-9; 'Theosophy, Anthroposophy and the Birth of Modernism,' *Blunt Edge 7*, April 2007, pp.15-21; 'Figurative Art and the Spiritual: Marc Chagall and Cecil Collins,' *Blunter Edge 3*, May 2009, pp.27-8.

[23] See Anthony J Parel, *Gandhi's Philosophy and the Quest for Harmony*, Cambridge: Cambridge University Press, 2006.

[24] A point he made in his Reith lectures but see also Daniel Barenboim and Edward Said, *Parallels and Paradoxes: Explorations in Music and Society*, London: Bloomsbury, 2003.

[25] Sara Maitland, *A Book of Silence: A Journey in Search of the Pleasures and Powers of Silence*, London: Granta, 2008.

Photo Credits

In sequence:
Sergei Prokofiev / no author credit found
Dmitri Shostakovich / no author credits found
Kzrystof Penderecki / no author credit found
Henryk Górecki / Source, Wikimedia Commons, no author credit given
Sofia Gubaidulina / Source, BIS Records AB, no author credit given
Arvo Pärt / Source, La Revue Inactuelle, no author credit given
Alfred Schnittke / Fant Gubaev
Alexander Scriabin / no author credit found
Olivier Messiaen / Source, Naxos, no author credit given
Hans Werner Henze / Source, Wikimedia Commons, no author credit given
Francis Poulenc / Source, Last.fm, no author credit given
Karlheinz Stockhausen / Werner Scholz; Source, Stockhausen-Stiftung für Musik

Resources

Festival and Concert programmes

Alexander Scriabin

BBC Proms, The Poem of Ecstasy, Philharmonia Orchestra, under Esa-Pekka Salonen. 20 August 2008.
BBC Proms, Piano Concerto in F sharp minor Op 20 (1896-7), Nelson Goerner, piano, BBC Philharmonic, under Vassily Sinaisky. 23 July 2010.
BBC Proms, Symphony No 1 in E major Op 26, London Symphony Chorus, London Symphony Orchestra, under Valery Gergiev. 16 August 2010.
BBC Proms, Symphony No 3 in C major, 'The Divine Poem,' Sydney Symphony, under Vladimir Ashkenazy. 24 August 2010.

Sergei Prokofiev

Edinburgh International Festival:
Symphony No 1 'Classical,' Symphony M No 2,Violin Concerto, Leonidas Kavakos, Symphony No 3, London Symphony Orchestra under Valery Gergiev. 15 August 2008.
Symphony No 4, Symphony-Concerto for cello and orchestra ,Tatyana Vassiljeva, cello, Symphony No 5 London Symphony Orchestra, under Valery Gergiev. 16 August 2008.
Symphony No 6 Violin Concerto (Leonidas Kavakos), Symphony No 7, London Symphony Orchestra, under Valery Gergiev. 17 August 2008.
Semyon Kotko Act 111, Mariinsky Opera and Orchestra, under Valery Gergiev. 24 August 2008.

Royal Opera House, The Gambler, Royal Opera Chorus, Orchestra of the Royal Opera House, under Antonio Pappano. 25 February 2010.

Dmitri Shostakovich

Barbican, Chronicle, Symphony No 13 in B flat minor Op 113, 'Babi Yar,' Sergei Leifurkus, Gentlemen of the London Symphony Orchestra, London Symphony Orchestra, under Yuri Temirkanov. 24 February 2008.

Barbican, Chronicle, Symphony No 14 for soprano, bass, strings and percussion Op 135, Olga Sergeeva, Sergei Leifercus, London Symphony Orchestra, under Daniel Harding. 30 March 2008.

BBC Proms, Symphony No 8 in C minor Op 65, London Symphony Orchestra, under Valery Gergiev. 24 August 2009.

BBC Proms, Symphony No 9 in E flat Op 70, BBC Symphony Orchestra, under David Robinson. 2 September 2009.

BBC Proms, Symphony No 5 in D minor, BBC Symphony Orchestra, under Edward Gardner. 17 August 2010.

BBC Proms, Cello Concerto No 1 in E flat major Op 107, Alisa Weilerstein, cello, Minnesota Orchestra, under Osmo Vänskä. 27 August 2010.

Polish Renaissance

Sounds New Contemporary Music Festival: Polish Connections. 23 April-3 May 2009.

Canterbury Cathedral, Kzrystof Penderecki, St Luke Passion, National Polish Radio Symphony Orchestra, under the Composer. 2 May 2009.

Conference programme, Polish Music since 1945, Canterbury Christ Church University. 30 April-2 May 2009.

BBC Proms, Witold Lutoslawski, Concerto for Orchestra National Youth Orchestra of Great Britain, under Vasily Petrenko. 8 August 2009.

Royal Festival Hall, Henryk Górecki, Symphony of Sorrowful Songs, London Philharmonic, under Marin Alsop. April 2010.

Arvo Pärt

BBC Proms, Symphony No 4 'Los Angeles,' Philharmonia
Orchestra, under Esa-Pekka Salonen. 20 August 2008.
Canterbury Festival, Shirley Hall, The King's School, Fratres
for cello and piano, Robert Cohen and Julius Drake. 19
October 2009.
BBC Proms, Cantus in memoriam Benjamin Britten, BBC
Symphony Orchestra, under Edward Gardner. 17 August
2010.
BBC Proms, St John Passion, Endymion, BBC Singers,
under David Hill. 17 August 2010.

Alfred Schnittke

Edinburgh Festival, Queen's Hall, Suite in the Old Style,
Leonidas Kavakos. Violin. 18 August 2008.
BBC Proms, Nagasaki, London Symphony Chorus, London
Symphony Orchestra, under Valery Gergiev. 24 August
2009.
South Bank Centre, Programme Between Two Worlds,
London Philharmonic Orchestra, under Vladimir Juroswi. 15
November-1 December 2009.

Sofia Gubaidulina

BBC Proms, St John Passion, St John Easter. 25 August
2002.
Barbican, A Journey of the Soul, BBC Symphony
Orchestra,under Martyn Brabbins. 12-14 January 2007.

Olivier Messiaen

Southbank Centre, From the Canyons to the Stars,
Philharmonia Orchestra. 7-23 October 2008.
Southbank Centre, Queen Elizabeth Hall, Quartet for the End
of Time, Nash Ensemble. 3 February 2008.

Southbank Centre, Queen Elizabeth Hall, Vingt Regards sur L'Enfant –Jesus, Pierre-Laurent Aimard, piano. 13 February 2008.
Westminster Abbey, Apparition de L'Église Éternelle, La Nativité du Seigneur, Olivier Latry, organ. 22 February 2008.

Canterbury, Programme Sounds New Festival, Messiaen and his Legacy, 11-19 April 2008. Including:

> Canterbury Cathedral Quire, La Nativité du Seigneur, BBC Singers, under Nicholas Cleobury. 11 April 2008.
> Canterbury Cathedral Nave, L'Ascension , Kent County Youth Orchestra, under Peter Stark. 12 April 2008.
> St Gregory's Music Centre, Le Merle Noir, Karen Jones, flute. 13 April 2008.
> St Gregory's Music Centre, Visions de l'Amen, Peter Hill and Benjamin Frith. 14 April 2008.
> Canterbury Cathedral Crypt, Quartet for the End of Time, Ensemble Intercontemporain. 16 April 2008.
> Canterbury Cathedral Quire, Et Expecto Resurrectionem Mortuorum, Thallein Ensemble, Birmingham Conservatoire, under Nicholas Cleobury. 19 April 2008.

Westminster Abbey, Meditations sur le mystère de la Sainte Trinité, Gillian Weir, organ, Lay Vicars from the Choir of Westminster Abbey. 15 July 2008.
BBC Proms, La Transfiguration de Notre Seigneur Jésus-Christ Philharmonia, Voices BBC Symphony Orchestra, under Thierry Fischer. 27 July 2008.
BBC Proms, Turangalila Symphony, Berliner Philarmoniker, under Sir Simon Rattle. 2 September 2008.
BBC Proms, Saint Francis of Assisi, The Netherlands Opera Chorus of the Netherlands Opera, The Hague Philharmonic, under Ingo Metzmacher. 7 September 2008.
St Paul's Cathedral, Les Corps Glorieux, Thomas Trotter, organ. 30 October 2008.

Southbank Centre, Music and Spirituality Conference, 1-2
February 2008, Jonathan Harvey and James MacMillan
present.

Francis Poulenc

Guildhall School of Music, Dialogue des Carmèlites. March
2011.
Linbury Studio, Covent Garden Opera, La Voix Humaine,
Nuccia Focile, Southbank Sinfonia, under Garry Walker.
June 2011.

Karlheinz Stockhausen

BBC Proms, Stockhausen Day, Gruppen, Cosmic Pulses
(Klang), Harmonien (Klang) Kontakte, BBC Symphony
Orchestra, under David Robinson.
Stimmung, Theatre of Voices, Paul Hillier. 2 August 2008.
Barbican Total Immersion Day, including Litanei 97, Inori,
Hymnen. 17 January 2009.

Hans Werner Henze

Barbican, Total Immersion Day, including Voices,
Symphony No 4, Requiem, Elogium musicum, BBC
Symphony Chorus, BBC Symphony Orchestra, under Oliver
Knussen, Ryan Wigglesworth. 16 January 2010.
Young Vic, Elegy for Young Lovers, Orchestra of English
National Opera/Young Vic, under Stefan Blunier. 24 April
2010.

General

Abrahams, Gerald, *Eight Soviet Composers from 1800 to the
Present*, Westport Connecticut: Greenwood Press, 1943.
Applebaum, Anne, *Gulag: A History*, London: Penguin
Books, 2003.
Armstrong, Karen, *The Case for God: What Religion Really
Means*, London: Vintage, 2010.

Armstrong, Karen, *A Short History of Myth*, London: Canongate, 2005.

Barenboim, David and Said, Edward, *Parallels and Paradoxes: Explorations, Music and Society*, London: Bloomsbury, 2003.

Bartlett, Rosamund and Fay, Laurel (eds.), *Shostakovich in Context*, Oxford: OUP, 2000.

Bernac, Pierre, *Francis Poulenc: The Man and his Songs*, London: Gollancz, 1977.

Bowers, Faubion, *Scriabin: A Biography*, Mineola, New York: Dover Publications, Inc Second revised edition, 1996.

Bowlt, John, *Moscow and St Petersburg 1900-1920: Art, Life and Culture in the Russian Silver Age*, New York: The Vendome Press, 2008.

Brooks, David, *Bobos in Paradise: The New Upper Class and How They Got There*, New York: Simon and Shuster, paperback, 2000.

Buckland, Sidney (editor and translator), *Francis Poulenc: Echo and Source. Selected Correspondence 1915-1963*. London: Victor Gollancz, 1991.

Buckland, Sidney and Myriam Chimènes (eds.), *Francis Poulenc: Music, Art and Literature,* Aldershot: Ashgate, 1999.

Burleigh, Michael, *Earthly Powers*, London: Harper Collins, 2005.

Burleigh, Michael, *Sacred Causes*, London: Harper Collins, 2006.

Cahill, Carmen, *Bad Faith: A Forgotten History of Family and Fatherland*, London: Jonathan Cape, 2006.

Chamberlain, Lesley, *The Philosophy Steamer: Lenin and the Exile of the Intelligentsia*, London: Atlantic Books, 2006.

Cone, Michèle, C *Artists under Vichy: A Case of Prejudice and Persecution*, Princeton: Princeton University Press, 1992.

Conrad, Peter, *Creation, Artists, Gods and Origins*, London: Thames and Hudson, 2007.

Copley, Antony, *Sexual Moralities in France 1780-1980*, London and New York: Routledge, 1989.

Copley, Antony, *A Spiritual Bloomsbury: Hinduism and Homosexuality in the Lives and Writing of Edward Carpenter, E M Forster and Christopher Isherwood*, Lanham etc: Lexington Books, 2006.

Cott, Jonathan, *Stockhausen: Conversations with the Composer*, London: Robson Books, 1974.

Dawkins, Richard, *The God Delusion*, London: Transworld Publications, 2006.

Dillenger, John, *Paul Tillich on Art and Architecture*, New York: Crossroads, 1987.

Dingle, Christopher, *The Life of Messiaen*, Cambridge: CUP, 2007.

Ehrlich, Dimitri, *Inside the Music: Conversations with Contemporary Musicians about Spirituality, Creativity and Conscience*, Boston and London: Shembala, 1997.

Figes, Orlando, *A People's Tragedy: The Russian Revolution 1891-1924*, London: Pimlico, 1997.

Figes, Orlando, *The Whisperers: Private Life in Stalin's Russia,* London: Penguin edition, 2008.

Gay, Peter, *Modernism: The Lure of Heresy from Baudelaire to Beckett and Beyond*, London: Vintage books, 2009.

Glover, Jonathan, *Humanity: A Moral History of the Twentieth Century*, London: Jonathan Cape, 1999.

Gott, Richard, *Cuba: A New History*, New Haven and London: Yale University Press, 2004.

Griffiths, Paul, *Modern Music and After*, 3rd edition, Oxford: OUP, 2010.

Grossman, Vasily, *Life and Fate*, London: Vintage, 2006.

Heehs, Peter, *The Lives of Aurobindo*, New York: Columbia University Press, 2008.

Heelas, Paul and Woodhead, Linda, *The Spiritual Revolution: Why Religion is Giving Way to Spirituality*, Oxford: Blackwell, 2005.

Heger, Heinz, *The Men with the Pink Triangle*, London: Gay Men's Press, 1980.

Henze, Hans Werner, *Bohemian Fifths: An Autobiography*, translated by Stewart Spencer, London: Faber and Faber, 1998.

Hesse, Hermann, *The Glass Bead Game*, translated Richard and Clara Winston, London: Vintage, 2000.

Hill, Peter and Nigel Simeone, *Messiaen*, New Haven and London: Yale University Press, 2005.

Hillier, Paul, *Arvo Pärt*, Oxford: OUP, 1997.

Ivashkin, Alexander, *Alfred Schnittke*, London: Phaidon, 1996.

Ivry, Benjamin, *Francis Poulenc*, London: Phaidon, 1996.

Jackson, Julian, *Living in Arcadia: Homosexuality, Politics and Morality from the Liberation to Aids*, Chicago: University of Chicago Press, 2010.

Jacobson, Bernard, *A Polish Renaissance*, London: Phaidon, 1996.

Judt, Tony, *Postwar: A History of Europe since 1945*, London: Pimlico, 2007.

Jung, C G, *Psychology and the Occult*, London and New York: Routledge, 1982.

Jung, C G, *The Spirit in Man, Art and Literature*, London and New York: Routledge, 2001.

Kirch, Arthur, *Auden and Christianity*, New Haven and London: Yale University Press, 2005.

Kripal, Jeffrey J *Kali's Child: The Mystical and the Erotic in the Life and Teachings of Ramakrishna*, Chicago: Chicago University Press, 1995.

Kurtz, Michael, *Stockhausen: A Biography*, translated by Richard Toop, London and Boston: Faber and Faber, 1992.

Kurtz, Michael, *Sofia Gubaidulina: A Biography*, Bloomington: Indiana University Press, 2001.

Lesser, Wendy, *Music for Silenced Voices: Shostakovich and His Fifteen Quartets*, New York: Yale University Press, 2011.

Littell, Jonathan, *The Kindly Ones*, London: Chatto and Windus, 2006.

Luukanen, Arto, *The Party of Unbelief: The Religious Policy of the Bolshevik Party 1917-1929*, Helsinki: Studia Historica, 1994.

McManners, John, *The Oxford Illustrated History of Christianity*, Oxford, New York: OUP, 1992.

Macdonald, Hugh, *Skryabin*, London: OUP, 1978.

Maitland, Sarah, *A Book of Silence: A Journey in search of the Pleasures and Powers of Silence*, London: Granta, 2008.

Mandlestam, Nadezhda, *Hope Against Hope*, London: Harvill Press, 1971.

Mellors, Wilfrid, *Francis Poulenc*, Oxford: OUP, 1993, reprinted 2003.

Morris, Mark (ed.), *The Pimlico Dictionary of Twentieth Century Composers*, London: Pimlico, 1996.

Morrison, Simon, *The People's Artist: Prokofiev's Soviet Years*, Oxford: OUP, 2009.

Nice, David, *Prokofiev: From Russia to the West 1891-1935*, New Haven and London: Yale University Press, 2003.

Nouwen, Henri J M, *The Return of the Prodigal Son: A Story of Homecoming*, New York etc: Image Books Doubleday, 1994.

Oppenheim, Janet, *The Other World: Spiritualism and Psychical Research in England 1850-1914*, Cambridge: CUP, 1985.

Parel, Anthony, *Gandhi's Philosophy and the Quest for Harmony*, Cambridge: CUP, 2006.

Pasternak, Boris, *I Remember: Sketch for an Autobiography*, translated David Magershack, New York: Pantheon, 1959.

Peris, Daniel, *Storming the Heavens: The Soviet League of the Militant Godless*, New York: Cornell University Press, 1998.

Prokofiev, Sergei, *Autobiography* and *Soviet Diary 1927 and Other Writings*, translated Oleg Prokofiev, London: Faber and Faber, 1991.

Reichert, Marcus (ed.), *Art and Death*, London: Ziggurat, 2008/9.

Ross, Alex, *The Rest is Noise: Listening to the Twentieth Century*, London: Fourth Estate, 2008.

Sanders, Frances Stonor, *The Cultural Cold War: The CIA and the World of Arts and Letters*, New York: The New Press, 2000.

Sassoon, Donald, *The Culture of the Europeans: From 1800 to the Present*, London: Harper Collins, 2006.

Schama, Simon, *Rembrandt's Eyes*, London: Penguin Books, 1999.

Schloezer Boris de, *Scriabin: Artist and Mystic*, translated by Nicholas Slonimisky, Berkeley and Los Angeles: University of California Press, 1987.

Scruton, Roger, *The Aesthetics of Music*, Oxford: OUP, 1997.

Sereny, Gitta, *Albert Speer: His Battle with Truth*, London and Basingstoke: Macmillan, 1995.

Sereny, Gitta, *Into That Darkness*, London: André Deutch, 1991.

Shenton, Andrew (ed.), *Messiaen The Theologian*, Farnham and Burlington: Ashgate, 2010.

Spotts, Frederic, *The Shameful Peace: How French Artists and Intellectuals Survived the Nazi Occupation*, New Haven and London: Yale University Press, 2008.

Stedall, Jonathan *Where on Earth is Heaven?* Stroud: Hawthorn Press 2009.

Steiner, George, *Real Presences: Is there anything in what we say?*, London: Faber and Faber, 1989.

Storr, Anthony, *Music and the Mind*, London: Harper Collins, 1999.

Swan, Alfred J, *Scriabin*, London: John Lane, Bodley head, 1923.

Tacey, David, *The Spirituality Revolution: The Emergence of Contemporary Spirituality*, London and New York: Routledge, 2004.

Tacey, David, *How to Read Jung*, London: Granta Books, 2006.

Taruskin, Richard, *Defining Russia Musically: Historical and Hermeneutical Essays*, Princeton: Princeton University Press, 1997.

Taruskin, Richard, *The Oxford History of Music Volume 4*, Oxford: OUP, 2004, and *Volume 5*, Oxford: OUP, 2005.

Thielemann, Serena, *The Spirituality of Music*, New Delhi: APH Publishing Corporation, 2001.

Thomas, Adrian, *Górecki*, Oxford: Clarendon Press, 1997.

Vernon, Mark, *After Atheism: Science, Religion, and the Meaning of Life*, Basingstoke: Palgrave MacMillan, 2007.

Volkov, Solomon, *Testimony: The Memoirs of Dmitri Shostakovich*, London: Faber and Faber, 1989.

Wilson, Elizabeth, *Shostakovich: A Life Remembered* (New edition), London: Faber and Faber, 2006.

Wuthnow, Robert, *Creative Spirituality: The Way of the Artist*, Berkeley and Los Angeles: University of California Press, 2001.

Zweig, Stefan, *Chess*, translated Anthea Bell, London: Penguin Books, 2006.

Zweig, Stefan, *The World of Yesterday*, translated by Anthea Bell, London: Pushkin Press, 2009.

Journals

Ascherson, Neal, 'When hope faded in the streets of the East,' *The Observer*, 20 January 2008.

Ascherson, Neal, 'A time when hope replaced repression.' *The Observer*, 2 October 2009.

Ascherson, Neal, 'An accident of history,' *The Guardian*, 17 April 2010.

Ash, Timothy Garton, '1989!,' *The New York Review of Books*, 24 October 2009.

Ash, Timothy Garton, 'The path of the fallen wall,' *The Guardian*, 8 November 2007.

Ash, Timothy Garton, 'It was Europe's finest hour,' *The Guardian*, 5 November 2009.

Bibby, Bob, addition to the Górecki obituary, *The Guardian*, 26 November 2010.

Conrad, Peter, 'Listen to that siren solo,' *The Observer*, 9 March 2008.

Copley, Antony, 'Music in the Himalayas: Alexander Scriabin and the spiritual,' *Studies in History Volume 26 Number 2*, August 2010, pp.211-26.

Copley, Antony, 'Liminality: Art and the spiritual,' *Blunt Edge 4*, April 2004, pp.7-9.

Copley, Antony, 'Theosophy, anthroposophy and the birth of modernism' *Blunt Edge 7*, April 2007, pp.15-21.

Copley, Antony, 'Figurative art and the spiritual: Marc Chagall and Cecil Collins,' *Blunter Edge 3*, May 2009, pp.27-8.

Copley, Antony, 'Oversimplifying the paradigms,' *Blunter Edge 1*, June 2008.

Dammann, Guy, 'We're not out of the woods yet,' *Times Literary Supplement*, 29 January 2010.

Fitzpatrick, Sheila, 'Many promises,' *London Review of Books*, 14 May 2009.

Gray, John, 'Tyrannies of Old,' *New Statesman*, 31 August 2009.

Hensher, Philip, 'Stockhausen for ever,' *The Guardian*, 30 October 2008.

Humphrey, Nicholas, 'The Human Factor,' *The Guardian*, 29 July 2006.

Jaggi, Maya, 'History repeating,' *The Guardian*, 21 August 2010.

Jones, Rick, 'Settling old scores,' *New Statesman*, 9 November 2009.

Kleinzahler, August, 'Diary,' *London Review of Books*, 2 December 2010.

McBurney, Gerard, 'In from the cold,' *Saturday Guardian*, 14 January 2006.

McBurney, Gerard, 'Obituary Tikhon Khrennikov,' *The Guardian*, 19 September 2007.

Maddocks, Fiona, 'Two masters, two centenaries,' *The Observer*, 21 December 2008.

Milne, Seamus, 'The real lesson of Berlin is that nothing is ever settled,' *The Guardian*, 12 November 2009.

Morrall, Clare, 'Hitting the right note,' *Saturday Guardian*, 12 April 2008.

Nichols, Roger, 'Obituary Yvonne Loriod,' *The Guardian*, 10 May 2010.

Poole, Steven, 'Sound of the Century,' *The Guardian*, 15 March 2008.

Potter, Keith, 'Obituary Henryk Górecki,' *The Guardian*, 13 November 2010.

Rose, Steve, 'Delusions and grandeur,' *The Guardian*, 15 November 2011.

Ross, Alex, 'Revelations: Messiaen's quartet for the end of time,' *The New Yorker,* 22 March 2004.

339

Rusbridger, Alan, 'Sound and vision,' *The Guardian*, 19 March 2008.

Sabaneev, Leonid, 'Scriabin and the idea of religious art,' *The Musical Times*, 1 September 1931.

Sandbrook, Dominic, 'The year that changed the world,' *The Observer*, 22 October 2006.

Scammell, Michael, 'Obituary Solzhenitsyn,' *The Guardian*, 8 August 2008.

Schiff, David, 'Fruit of the poison tree' *Times Literary Supplement*, 6 May 2005.

Scruton, Roger, 'Resounding reason,' *Times Literary Supplement*, 15 July 2005.

Service, Tom, 'A matter of life and death,' *The Guardian*, 15 December 2009.

Snyder, Timothy, 'Bloodlands,' *New York Review of Books*, 18 July 2009.

Solchany, Jean, 'Les Bienveillantes ou l'histoire à l'épreuve de la fiction,' *Revue d'Histoire Moderne et Contemporaine*, Vol.3, 2007.

Tanner, Michael, 'Distorted account,' *The Spectator*, 6 February 2010.

Tavener, John, 'The holy fool of music,' *The Guardian*, 19 January 2007.

Index